New Labour

New Labour

Politics after Thatcherism

STEPHEN DRIVER
AND
LUKE MARTELL

Polity Press

First published in 1998 by Polity Press in association with Blackwell Publishers Ltd.

Reprinted 1999, 2002

Editorial office:
Polity Press
65 Bridge Street
Cambridge CB2 1UR, UK

Marketing and production:
Blackwell Publishers Ltd
108 Cowley Road
Oxford OX4 1JF, UK

Published in the USA by
Blackwell Publishers Inc.
350 Main Street
Malden MA 02148, USA

A catalogue record for this book is available from the British Library.

Library of Congress Cataloging-in-Publication Data
Driver, Stephen.
  New Labour : politics after Thatcherism / Stephen Driver and Luke Martell.
    p.   cm.
  Includes bibliographical references (p.   ) and index.
  ISBN 0–7456–2050–7 (alk. paper).—ISBN 0–7456–2051–5 (pbk. : alk. paper)
  1. Labour Party (Great Britain)   2. Great Britain—Politics and government—
  1997-   I. Martell, Luke.   II. Title.
JN1129.L32D75   1998
324.24107'09'049—dc21   98-16531
                                                                             CIP

Typeset in 11 on 13pt Adobe Caslon
By Ace Filmsetting Ltd, Frome, Somerset
Printed in Great Britain by Athenæum Press Ltd, Gateshead, Tyne & Wear

This book is printed on acid-free paper.

Contents

Introduction

Tony Blair became leader of the Labour Party on 21 July 1994 following the death of John Smith. The 'modernization' of Labour, begun under Neil Kinnock after the party's defeat in the 1987 general election, entered a remarkable and decisive phase. Under Blair, Labour has been remodelled and redefined. Old ideas and policies have been discarded and new ones embraced. Throughout this, the party membership remained loyal to Blair and their numbers even swelled. Indeed, Labour's new leader mobilized an unprecedented breadth of support from the members of a party for whom disloyalty to the leader had been almost a condition of membership. When Blair routed the Conservatives in the 1997 election, most of his new cabinet had no experience of government at all. When Blair became an MP in 1983 his party had already been in opposition for four years of Thatcherism, the significance of which Labour was then only just waking up to.

This book is about the radical redefinition of the Labour Party in the 1990s and about what's new about Blair's *New* Labour in terms of ideology and policy. The central argument of the book is that New Labour represents an exercise in *post-Thatcherite* politics. To some this may be an unwelcome intrusion of academic jargon on to the real world. As social scientists we inevitably bring to the subject of British politics some of the baggage of our disciplines – although we hope not too much. But the term 'post-Thatcherism' is not one we have plucked out of the air in a desperate attempt to add an academic gloss to reality. Blair himself has used 'post-Thatcherism' to describe New Labour.[1]

Taken too literally, post-Thatcherism is just one of those meaningless terms. 'Post', of course, simply means anything 'after'. So anything Blair cares to put on Labour's agenda will by definition be post-Thatcher: she has gone to another place. But the idea of post-Thatcherism means more than this, not just for Labour but for British politics as a whole (and not least for the Conservative Party – although that is another story!). For a start, post-Thatcherism means that New Labour, as well as merely coming after Thatcher, is also defined by her. Umberto Eco, writing on postmodernism, said that the past, 'since it cannot really be destroyed . . . must be revisited'.[2] In a similar manner, post-Thatcherism involves, in politics, building on what was left by Mrs Thatcher. The ground broken and reset by her and John Major provides the framework for subsequent political debate. Such debate does not just come after Thatcher but is in large part defined by her. Blair has his own way of expressing this: 'How do we give our own people security and opportunity in this new age? Our answer is not to turn the clock back . . . But we do have to move on from the 1980s. There were good things as well as bad. We seek not to dismantle but to build.'[3]

New Labour accepts the Thatcherite ground in part by saying that there is no turning back to the pre-Thatcher days of Old Labour. Blair rejects what he perceives as the rights-claiming culture of social democracy, as well as most of the policies of the postwar Labour Party such as Keynesian economics, nationalization and planning, and egalitarian tax-and-spend social policies. Blair and the modernizers also believe that much of what Mrs Thatcher did was of merit. It is, we believe, evident that New Labour has become more Thatcherite, if that is taken to mean the party is more committed to free trade, flexible labour markets, sound money and the spirit of entrepreneurial capitalism, not to mention greater individual self-help and private initiative in welfare. Such ideas are characteristic of Thatcherism; and they provide just some of the policy positions to which, as we shall show, New Labour is committed.

Shifts in this direction have led commentators on both sides of the political spectrum to read post-Thatcherism as Thatcherism. For the Left, Blair has sold Labour's soul to the neo-liberal devil. Writing just before the 1997 general election, Stuart Hall and Martin Jacques expressed doubts that 'a New Labour government will amount to anything more than a crypto-Conservative administration'.[4] For some on the Right, Blair has at last made Labour see the sense of eighteen years of radical Tory government. On the morning after the 1997 poll William Rees-

Mogg wrote: 'Thatcherism is safe with New Labour: that is the core message.'[5]

But there is another side to Blair's modernization of the Labour Party which is as much a reaction to, rather than a reflection of, Thatcherism. In a speech in 1995, Blair said: 'we do not live by economics alone . . . a society which is fragmented and divided, where people feel no sense of shared purpose, is unlikely to produce well-adjusted and responsible citizens.' Blair went on to attack both the 'do your own thing' social individualism of old social democracy and the 'get what you can' message of Conservative neo-liberal economic individualism.[6] While fully embracing the market, New Labour is repelled by the individualistic message of Thatcherism and by 1990s Conservative politicians' loss of touch with people – especially, but not only, the excluded sections of the population. New Labour has attempted to strike a balance between economic success and 'social inclusion', the market and the community. New Labour offered a greater popular sensitivity in politics, and a concern 'for the many and not just the few'. Labour, in short, is both attracted and repulsed by Thatcherism. There is no going back to the pre-Thatcher era, and much that she has left is now part of a landscape that Labour accepts. But on this ground changes have to be made, often guided by sentiments which are far from Thatcherite. What New Labour has become is defined by Thatcherism. But the new Labour government is post-Thatcherite.

This book is not intended to cast a *particular* judgement on New Labour, although inevitably we shall make many judgements along the way. It is intended, rather, to describe and, we hope, to some extent explain what New Labour, in ideology and policy, means. Our restraint from pressing a specific evaluation is partly a practical matter. While, as co-authors, we share a common view of what New Labour *is*, we are not always so united on its merits or what we think it *should be*! But this limitation has, in fact, become a virtue because it allows us to set out a relatively neutral picture, suggesting many evaluative judgements without being swayed by partial commitments in the direction of one particular political viewpoint or another. Furthermore, our focus on just telling it how it is does not make this book any less political. By setting out in detail what we believe New Labour to be, we hope it will provide readers with the equipment to make judgements for themselves on what they feel are the merits or limits of New Labour or, where appropriate, where the alternatives may lie.

Much of this book attempts to compare New Labour not just to Thatcherism but also to 'Old Labour'. By 'New' and 'Old' Labour we do not intend to suggest that the party in either guise was a monolithic bloc or under the rule of factional hegemony. Rather we are referring to *dominant* stated ideas and policies, particularly as proposed by official party publications and speeches and statements by leading party figures. Which brings us to our sources: to pin down and define what we believe New Labour to be we have referred to party publications, policy documents and manifestos. We have referred to the speeches and statements of leading Labour modernizers – Tony Blair most prominently but also figures such as Gordon Brown. These party documents and statements by leading modernizers are the crux of what we have taken to be the public face of New Labour ideology and policy. We have also examined the reports and pamphlets of independent think-tanks and commissions where they have explicitly fed into Labour thinking or been relevant to it. And we have referred to the contributions of academics such as John Gray and Anthony Giddens who are known to be taken seriously by Labour leaders or whose ideas are relevant to the party's rethinking. We have, of course, also taken into account those commentators' analyses of New Labour that there have been so far, although, as will be seen, we often depart from the conclusions they have come to. Where party documents or leading modernizers seem to differ between themselves or over time we have tried to make that part of our analysis, as we have differences between modernizers and others on the Centre Left. But we believe there is a clearly identifiable group of modernizers – Tony Blair, Gordon Brown, Jack Straw, Peter Mandelson and others – widely recognized publicly and by commentators as such. There are certainly differences between them and their ideas have changed over time. But they also share key commitments, most notably the desire to update Labour's ideas on economics and social policy in particular directions and in tune with specified economic and social developments perceived to define modern times.

We have made a special effort to write the book so that it will be accessible and stimulating for students and non-academic readers as well as providing a new contribution for those with special expertise in this area. The book breaks down into three main parts. Chapter 1 outlines the background to Blair's modernization of the Labour Party. We chart the course of modernization before Blair and introduce some of the key elements in Labour's rethinking under his leadership – some of the 'big ideas'. This chapter is basically about Labour before it was, and as it was becoming, 'New'. Throughout the book we have tried to link Labour's new policies to influences from abroad and to ideas such as globalization, post-Fordism, stakeholding and communitarianism. Chapters 2, 3 and 4 are the substantive core of the book. They lay out what New Labour's ideas and policies have become, respectively, in the areas of economics, welfare and social policy, and constitutional and political reform. In these chapters we compare New Labour's ideas with those of Old Labour and show the thinking that has gone on behind the development of new policies. Chapters 5 and 6 tie it all together and bring out our overall interpretation about what New Labour has become. In Chapter 5 we set out different interpretations of New Labour and explain more fully what we mean when we say that Labour has become more neo-liberal and conservative and is 'post-Thatcherite'. Finally in Chapter 6 we draw out the implications of Labour's new politics for the redrawing of boundaries – in politics and political thought – from Left to Right.

We are extremely grateful to the many people, too numerous to mention, who have offered us advice and help with our work. This book is dedicated to our children, Alice and James Driver and Katie and Jake Martell.

1

From Old Labour to New Labour

Labour landslide

The 1997 British general election was a landslide for the Labour Party. The numbers make a compelling case: of the votes cast, Labour took just over 13.5 million against the Conservative's 9.6 million; 43.2 per cent for Labour against 30.7 per cent for the Tories. By contrast, in the previous election in 1992, over 14 million people voted Conservative and 11.5 million for Labour (42.3 per cent against 35.2 per cent). Labour's advantage at the ballot box – very roughly, for every four Labour voters, three voted Tory – was turned into a landslide in parliamentary seats by the first-past-the-post electoral system. In 1992 the Tories took 336 seats, Labour 271. In 1997 Labour overturned this deficit, winning 418 seats against 165 for the Conservatives. In British electoral history, Labour had never secured so many votes or won so many seats.[1] And as the new electoral maps of Britain were drawn, it became clear that Labour had successfully won over large sections of that Tory beast, Middle England. The 'southern comfort' for which the party had thirsted in the early 1990s now flowed as Labour won Conservative strongholds in the south of England.[2]

If the result was an electoral landslide, it was also a triumph for Tony Blair's bold and skilful leadership of the party. To be sure, Labour's 1997 election was marked by caution. Blair repeated throughout the campaign that Labour would promise only what it could deliver. To Blair, the manifesto was a 'covenant' with the people to which he and a Labour administration could be held. Labour said that they wanted to restore the public's trust in politicians and government. But Labour's strategy was also designed to deflect accusations from the Conservatives that it was the devil in disguise; that behind the smiles and soundbites of New Labour lay the slumbering Old Labour monster. When the newly swelled ranks of Labour MPs met at Church House in Westminster (the only place big enough to seat them all) days after the election, Blair cautioned discipline on his troops. But the caution of the campaign followed nearly three years of permanent revolution in which the Labour modernizers led by Blair thought the unthinkable – and the party followed.

Blair's victory followed the re-election in 1996 to the US presidency of the man who has been a key inspiration behind both the politics and the policies of New Labour, Democrat Bill Clinton. And within weeks of Labour's victory in Britain, the French Socialist Party led by Lionel Jospin won control of the National Assembly in an election called by the Gaullist President Jacques Chirac. Jospin was appointed prime minister. The Left were now in power, either alone or as coalition leaders, in ten out of the fifteen European Union member states. Only in Germany and Spain were they in opposition. From the dark days of the 1980s, when the Western world seemed under the New Right spell of Margaret Thatcher and Ronald Reagan, this was quite a turnaround of political fortunes – and political climate.

Speaking just a month after Labour's landslide victory at the polls, Blair addressed a meeting of the European Socialists' Congress in Malmö, Sweden. He said: 'Our task today is not to fight old battles but to show that there is a third way, a way of marrying together an open, competitive and successful economy with a just, decent and humane society.' The Left, Blair said, had to 'modernize or die'.[3]

But how in Britain did Tony Blair and the modernizers drag the Labour Party out from eighteen years in the political wilderness? In this chapter we shall briefly examine the rise and fall of postwar social democracy. We shall then look at the background to the Blair reforms in the Labour Party in the late 1980s, assess competing explanations for this early phase of modernization, and look abroad to Europe, North America and Australasia for other signs of reform on the Left. Finally, we shall introduce key ideological features of the Blair revolution which will be expanded on in the subsequent chapters.

Social democracy, old and new

By 1995 Tony Blair was happy in public with the label 'social democrat'. Blair also affected a rapprochement with the old Labour social democrats who had left the party in 1981 to set up the Social Democratic Party (SDP). He even brought some, such as Roger Liddle and Derek Scott, into his inner circle of policy advisors and speech writers. Here was new social democrat making peace with old.

In the twentieth century social democracy promised if not a heaven on earth then at least an end to the hell on earth. Economic management and collective welfare provision by the state would stabilize market capitalism, bring greater equality and social justice, and forge a sense of common citizenship transcending individual and class interest. In the postwar democracies of Northern and Western Europe, social democracy set the political agenda. The mixed economy and the welfare state provided an alternative to free market capitalism and the nightwatchmen state. In Britain, Norway, Sweden, France, Austria and the Benelux countries, and later in West Germany and Italy, social democratic governments enjoyed significant periods in office, although the detail of policies often had marked national variations.[4]

In Britain, Tony Crosland set out the revisionist social democratic view. Widespread ownership of property, political democracy and Lord Keynes had, for Crosland, consigned Marx to the museum of political ideas. New times demanded new ideas from the Left about the means to achieve the old socialist value of equality. To this end, Crosland argued that Keynesian demand management and state investment would maintain full employment. Economic growth would pay for the state social welfare programmes which would bring greater equality to society, not just in terms of opportunities but in egalitarian outcomes too. For Crosland, the future of socialism – and capitalism for that matter – lay in this brand of social democracy in which private property remained largely intact, but the state took a significant and sometimes dominant role as owner, planner, investor and provider.

But in the turmoil of the past twenty-five years social democracy has been in retreat, politically and intellectually. The prosperous economic conditions which had sustained social democracy had by the late 1960s melted away. The combined effect of monetary instability, multinational production, competition from the newly developing countries and liberalization of world trade served only to unmask the underlying structural weaknesses of the British economy and, some argued, of national policymaking itself. Crosland's social democracy hit the brick wall of stagflation – low growth and high inflation. Guarantees of full employment, economic growth and low inflation were not worth the paper they were printed on. And, as economic growth deteriorated, public expenditure continued to grow, requiring higher taxes and raising widespread fears about the sustainability of the public sector and welfare state.

To some, the record of postwar social democracy, even in the 1960s and 1970s, is nowhere near as bleak as it is made out to be – and what followed was even worse.[5] But, villain or victim, disillusionment with the postwar social democratic consensus was widespread by the mid-1970s. The New Right argued that the state was doing too much: high public expenditure, especially on welfare, and high taxes were undermining incentives, crowding out private investment and creating a dependency culture. Social democracy, whether practised by the Tories or by Labour, was the villain leading Britain if not down the road to serfdom then at least down the drain. The strength of the New Right lay not just in its attack on the practice of postwar social democracy but perhaps more importantly on social democracy's intellectual principles.

Disillusionment with social democracy came too from the Left, who argued that the state should do more. The task for Labour, to the Left, was not the amelioration of capitalism but its transformation to socialism. Labour's 1974 election manifestos even promised a 'fundamental and irreversible shift in the balance of power and wealth in favour of working people and their families'. Stuart Holland developed the influential thesis that the growth of multinational companies in an international economy meant that a Labour government should further nationalize strategic businesses to allow national priorities to be set and for the British economy to be able to compete head to head with the rest of the world.[6] Holland's ideas foreshadowed Labour's left-wing Alternative Economic Strategy, which formed the basis for its 1983 general election manifesto.

But, in government, Labour under Prime Minister James Callaghan moved to the right. In 1975, against Crosland's Keynesian logic, Labour cut public spending mid-recession. A year later, under pressure from the US government and the International Monetary Fund, Callaghan announced that the era of tax-and-spend Keynesianism was over. Public expenditure was cut and the commitment to full employment, which had underpinned the postwar welfare state, was gone. The party, as Crosland put it, was over.

Breakaway social democrats

By the early 1980s, social democrats in the Labour Party found themselves caught between two ideologies for which they cared little: free market liberalism and state socialism. But they were also trapped by their own political commitments, which they feared had had their day, without any clear idea of the way forward. This was the dilemma faced by Roy Jenkins, Shirley Williams, David Owen and Bill Rodgers when they broke with Labour in 1981. Labour's social democratic remedies were clearly failing to deal with the manifold problems facing the British economy and society. Or at least it was believed that they were. The perceived failure of Labour's brand of corporatist social democracy in the 1970s was later to provide New Labour modernizers with one of their central arguments for a post-Thatcherite politics: that there could be no going back to the policy remedies of the 1960s or 1970s. New times demanded a new Labour Party.

Back in the 1970s, the reaction from the Right to social and economic paralysis was a mix of liberal free market economics and conservative social policies in the name of enterprise and national pride. The Left, on the other hand, looked to the state and economic planning to create socialism in one country. The founders of the SDP were left struggling to find a new brand of social democracy. They shared with the Right an unease with bureaucratic collectivism and the central state.[7] But their instincts took them less to *laissez-faire* and more to the continental European model of the social market, constitutional reform and decentralized forms of decision making. Under the early leadership of Roy Jenkins, they advocated support for small businesses, employee profit-sharing schemes, measures to encourage technological change, and education and training to help people back into work. And, while recognizing the limitations of national policy-making, SDP figures such as David Owen in the early 1980s still clung to prices and incomes policies and to the mixed economy.[8]

10

After 1983, under Owen's leadership, the SDP evolved a 'tough and tender' line on social democracy: pro-defence, pro-constitutional reform, pro-market and pro-social justice. 'Competitiveness', in Owen's words, was to be matched by 'compassion'. In this Owenite phase, which was to prove no more effective at breaking the mould of British politics, the SDP clearly distanced itself from the old social democracy of corporatism, Keynesianism and state welfarism. To Dr Owen, Mrs Thatcher had a point. For social democracy, this was the great leap forward. And because of this, according to Peter Riddell, 'the SDP in its Owenite phase was a forerunner to new Labour.'[9]

With the death of the SDP – finally in May 1990 – social democrats went their many ways. Some left party politics. The majority remained with the Liberal Democrats, which had been formed in 1988 when the SDP minus Owen had merged with the Liberal Party. Some younger Owenites, such as Danny Finkelstein, joined the Conservatives.[10] And, after Blair became leader, a number of prominent ex-SDPers, such as David Marquand, rejoined Labour.

Marquand himself provided one of the most influential Centre-Left political tracts of the late 1980s – certainly one which pointed the way from Old to nascent New Labour. In *The Unprincipled Society*, Marquand, drawing on contemporary communitarian political philosophy, attacked what C. B. Macpherson had called 'possessive individualism'.[11] The ills facing British society, Marquand argued, have their origins in a possessive individualistic view of man and society which has deep roots in the history of British society and, in particular, its governing institutions. 'How', Marquand asked, 'can a fragmented society make itself whole? How can a culture permeated by possessive individualism restore the bonds of community?'[12] In Marquand's view, society had to re-educate itself. In themes which have became familiar New Labour ones in the 1990s, Marquand insisted that a communitarian view of society provided a vocabulary for describing the individual's place in the community, for the common purposes which cross society, and for the duties and obligations that membership of a community entails. And, for Marquand, such a communitarian re-education required political and constitutional change – something which he believes postwar social democrats such as Crosland ignored in their error.[13]

By the early 1990s, Marquand, who went on to be a critical supporter of New Labour, was writing of the Centre Left as 'intellectually becalmed, unable to make sense of a world which has suddenly become alien, and still less able to devise plausible projects for changing it.'[14] A decade of Thatcherism and the collapse of communism in Eastern Europe and the Soviet Union led some even to talk of the death of socialism.[15] The 1980s were Labour's wilderness years: banished from power, facing an implacable and seemingly all-conquering Tory government and condemned to a permanent internal struggle for the soul of the party. But if Labour found no Mount Sinai nor any ten commandments, it did start on the long march to the promised land. Thatcherism had got to it. After defeat in the 1987 general election, the modernization of the Labour Party began in earnest.

Old Labour, New Labour

In the July 1994 leadership election following the death of John Smith, Tony Blair won convincingly. His victory, the first under an electoral system based on individual party members, was a clear mandate for the modernizers in the Labour Party. Because of one member one vote (OMOV), Blair could claim the support of all card-carrying members, not just Labour MPs, trade union leaders and constituency activists. Blair and the modernizers have used the tactic of appealing directly to individual party members to great effect: in particular, over the rewriting of Clause 4 of Labour's constitution, which had committed the party to the common ownership of property, and the endorsement of its interim pre-election *Road to the Manifesto*. The modernizers, as Andy McSmith writes, have a leader in Tony Blair 'who is elevated above the swirling morass of factions and interest groups which make up the party, who can exert his authority in his own way, free from the risk that he can be effectively challenged. For good or ill, that must permanently change the nature of the Labour Party.'[16]

At the autumn party conference following Blair's election, the slogan 'New Labour, New Britain' was unveiled. The adjective stuck. The Labour Party acquired a new name by constant repetition. Blair and the modernizers have shown little respect for Old Labour's sacred cows: state ownership, economic planning, Keynesian demand management, full employment, tax-and-spend welfarism and close links with the trade unions. To the outside world, New Labour took on Old Labour and won. And, apart from John Prescott and Margaret Beckett, no prisoners were taken.

Blair took most of the plaudits following the rapid turnaround in Labour's political fortunes after 1994. Certainly opinion polls during the 1997 campaign suggested that Blair, unlike Neil Kinnock in 1992, was a man whom the voters could trust to be prime minister. Blair had fought in 1994 on an explicitly modernizer's ticket. Accepting the leadership of the party, he said: 'It is the confident who can change and the doubters who hesitate. A changed Labour Party, with the vision and confidence to lead Britain in a changing world – that is our pledge to the people of this country.'[17] But was 1994 really New Labour's year zero? Did the modernization of the party, if that is what it is, start with Tony Blair?

'We've stopped all that nonsense'

When Blair beat John Prescott and Margaret Beckett – both then Old rather than New Labour – to the leadership of the party, he was the recipient of a favourable political legacy.[18] First, Neil Kinnock and John Smith as Labour leaders in the 1980s and early 1990s had introduced significant party rule changes which weakened the power and influence of the Left and gave the leadership a power base in the party membership at large. New rules to expel party members and OMOV effectively killed off the Far Left, and seriously weakened the influence of the trade unions, within the party. Old Labour – Right or Left – had lost their grip on the Labour Party machine. Moreover, with the appointment of Peter Mandelson as the party's communications director in 1985, Labour became an increasingly effective and professional campaigning and communications machine using techniques drawn from the worlds of advertising, marketing and the media. This further strengthened the hand of the party leadership.

Secondly, by the late 1980s Labour had already started on the long road back from the state socialist policies of the early 1980s when the Left was at its high point of influence. Labour's 1983 general election manifesto, *A New Hope for Britain*, included policies to renationalize the privatized industries, partial state control of major British companies, economic planning agreements with the private sector and trade unions, exchange and import controls, withdrawal from the European Commu-

nity, a public-sector-led reflation to create full employment, and unilateral nuclear disarmament. While Neil Kinnock as the new Labour
leader had done much to attack the Far Left inside the Labour Party –
for example in his 'impossible promises' speech attacking the left-wing
dominated Liverpool council at the 1985 party conference – the 1987
manifesto was essentially a watered-down version of the 1983 document. But the search for votes had begun. As Eric Shaw writes: 'Policy
was increasingly subordinated to strategic considerations, as the leadership sought to winnow out those commitments – most notably the
Party's stances on the sale of council houses, membership of the European Community, repeal of Tory industrial relations legislation, the reversal of privatization and unilateralism – which opinion polls indicated
lacked public support.'[19] Labour still fought the 1987 general election
with commitments to bring into the public sector the privatized industries – albeit now using a rather more complicated formula; the repeal of
most of the Conservative trade union legislation (mandatory strike ballots would be kept); and unilateral nuclear disarmament. These policies
remained despite the efforts of the party leadership in private to drop
them. Neil Kinnock even made public his doubts about old-style nationalization against the benefits of the market economy. As Tudor Jones
argues: 'the compromises and ambiguity inherent in the 1987 manifesto
reflected the fact that between 1983 and 1987 Labour's policy changes
had been tentative and piecemeal. In 1987, therefore, it was still uncertain to what extent those limited changes signified a corresponding ideological shift from traditional state socialism to some variant of European
social democracy.'[20]

Labour's third election defeat in 1987, massive in terms of seats in the
House of Commons and only marginally better on the share of the vote,[21]
marked a turning point in the party's search for the centre ground in
politics and for the votes of middle class Middle England. Kinnock's
insistence that Labour had to rethink their ideas – 'we've stopped all that
nonsense' – in the light of three election defeats and rapidly changing
economic and social conditions was helped by the fact that the Labour
Left itself was in a state of change. The 'hard' Left Campaign Group of
MPs, led in large part by Tony Benn, was becoming increasingly isolated. The Tribune Group of MPs, once the centre for the socialist politics of Bevan and Foot, increasingly came to represent a 'soft' Left, willing
both to work with a reforming leadership and to countenance policy

changes. Tribune was also the chosen group of newer MPs such as Tony Blair, Gordon Brown and Jack Straw who had little in common with the old Left. The realignment of the Left under Kinnock was central to the emergence of the modernizers as a significant political movement inside the party, certainly one which eventually went beyond traditional social democratic revisionists on the Right such as Roy Hattersley.

The Policy Review, 1987–1992

In the aftermath of Labour's 1987 defeat at the polls, a Policy Review was established, starting with the ill-attended 'Labour Listens' initiative. Shadow ministers were dispatched around the country to listen to the views of local community members on what Labour's policies should be. Policy Review groups were established to study proposals for reform. These groups published a series of reports, endorsed at the party conference, leading up to the 1992 general election manifesto. The Policy Review did significantly shift Labour policy.[22] On the economy, the party became increasingly pro-market, limiting the role of government to the enforcement of competition and to market failures such as training, research and development and regional development. Labour's commitment to the renationalization of the privatized utilities – or, for that matter, public ownership at all – slowly disappeared. The party flirted with ideas of non-state 'social ownership' such as worker cooperatives and employee share-ownership schemes. The Policy Review also saw the disappearance of Keynesian demand management and the withdrawal from the European Community. In their place the Labour leadership, in particular the shadow chancellor John Smith, advocated stable macro-economic management, including a commitment to low inflation, and membership of the European Community's Exchange Rate Mechanism. Increased spending on welfare was to be financed from economic growth – except pensions and child benefits, where top tax rates would be increased. Trade union legislation would remain largely in place. And what was perceived as the party's albatross during the 1987 election, unilateral disarmament, was buried.

The Policy Review, then, led to significant shifts in Labour's position on the economy, industrial relations, Europe and defence. These policy shifts were paralleled by a bout of revisionist thinking in the party. Deputy

Labour Leader Roy Hattersley's *Choose Freedom* equated socialism with freedom and the social conditions which might maximize individual liberty.[23] Equality, for Hattersley, went hand in hand with increasing the opportunities for individuals to pursue their own goals in life. It was a means to freedom rather than an end in itself. Socialism was liberalism that really meant it.

Hattersley drew inspiration from the past to counter what he and Kinnock saw as the increasing influence of Marxist ideas in the party. Hattersley looked to the early twentieth century New Liberals such as Leonard Hobhouse and T. H. Green and to the ethical socialists such as R. H. Tawney to provide a moral basis for Labour politics. The New Liberals had abandoned the nineteenth-century liberal commitment to liberty as defined exclusively by property rights and to its political equivalent *laissez-faire*. Instead, they argued that the state should work to create the material conditions whereby everyone might be able to find the freedom to develop their abilities and to take control of their lives. Herein lies the twentieth-century conjoining of liberalism and social democracy which Hattersley wished to prolong. Ethical socialists have always seen socialism as a moral crusade, not the product of an impersonal class struggle or the materialistic forces of history. The case against capitalism was that it was immoral, not that it would collapse under the weight of its own contradictions. The case for socialism was a normative one – what society ought to be – rather than a scientific or materialistic one gleaned from a study of history. Socialism would involve, in Tawney's terms, a 'remoralization' of society. Socialist values such as community and equality were superior to capitalist ones such as individualism and freedom. Indeed, ethical socialists maintained that meaningful individual development and real (positive) freedom could only be achieved through the application of socialist values such as community and equality.

New liberalism and ethical socialism are central to the story of the Labour and trade union movement in the twentieth century. But in the 1970s and early 1980s they went out of fashion as Labour shifted to the Left and British Marxism saw a revival, especially in academia. Just as Kinnock stemmed the tide of political influence of the Left inside the Labour Party, so the 1980s also saw the ebb and flow of ideas turn in favour of a more ethically grounded politics.[24] There was, to be sure, some debate over the substantive character of socialist values such as equality and community and how these related to notions of rights and responsibilities, duty and obligation, pluralism, citizenship and freedom. There was also no clear agreement about the means by which such values might be realized: on the balance between the state and the market; the extent to which government should be decentralized; and the role of constitutional reform, including Britain's place in Europe. During the late 1980s and early 1990s, the modernization of the Labour Party was led by those who were more interested in the social conditions which might maximize individual freedom than with what people did with their liberty. The argument for a more dutiful socialism would have to wait for Blair. On the question of means, Labour modernizers during the Policy Review did what Crosland had done in the 1950s, and what Blair would do in the mid-1990s: change them because, they argued, times had changed. Kinnock and Hattersley, as well as Giles Radice and Bryan Gould, grasped the torch of Labour revisionism by insisting that public ownership and the abolition of private property were only means and not the ends of socialism – and could therefore be dropped. Socialist means needed to be updated in order to deliver socialist ends.

In hard policy terms, this meant a reappraisal of the role of the market economy. In Hattersley's *Choose Freedom*, the party's 1988 *Statement of Democratic Socialist Aims and Values* (largely written by the deputy Labour leader), its 1989 document *Meet the Challenge, Make the Change*, and in books by Gould and Radice,[25] the market was endorsed and large-scale state intervention in the economy rejected. Some modernizers, such as Gould and Hattersley, remained committed to an essentially Keynesian social democratic view of the world. Gould was in particular critical of Labour's increasingly orthodox macro-economic policies, especially its support for membership of the European Exchange Rate Mechanism, and in favour of a more active role for government in promoting investment in British industry – investment which Gould felt the City of London had failed to deliver. For others, such as John Smith, the modernization of the Labour Party meant, economically, the slaying of Keynesianism, not just state socialism.

The logic of Labour's Policy Review in the late 1980s would have been to rewrite Clause 4. Some modernizers, such as Radice and Jack Straw, made no secret of their wish to see a change to Labour's constitution.[26] But the prevailing view at the time of the Policy Review was that the party could be modernized while retaining many of the outward symbols of its past. At the time of his death in 1994, John Smith was preparing a supplement to Clause 4 based on an earlier statement of his Christian socialist beliefs – an approach, Jones writes, 'consistent with the gradualist and conciliatory style of Smith's leadership'.[27]

The Policy Review: Thatcherism, modernization or social democracy?

These tensions *within* the modernizers' ranks raise important questions of interpretation of the Policy Review – which throw light too on the subsequent development of New Labour. In embracing the market, all modernizers remained critical of Mrs Thatcher's market liberalism which they saw as little more than crude nineteenth-century *laissez-faire* – a charge she herself denied. And, despite rejecting public ownership, the modernizers still saw a positive role for the state in regulating, selectively intervening in, and making up for the deficiencies of the market. Some Keynesians, such as Bryan Gould, saw far more deficiencies in the market than those, such as John Smith, who were sceptical of the power of governments to create employment by managing demand and spending money. Labour remained united in its hostility to the market reforms of the welfare state in the late 1980s and early 1990s. But Gould's later defeat by Smith for the leadership of the party after the 1992 general election represented the growing ascendency within the party of arguments which saw the defeat of inflation and the creation of stable economic conditions as the central goal of macro-economic policy.

So, to Eric Shaw, Labour's Policy Review marks the steady *abandonment* of Keynesian social democracy – finally completed by Blair's New Labour. This has led, according to Shaw, to a new macro-economic consensus which confines government 'largely to maintaining the monetary and fiscal conditions required to enable the market to maximize investment, output and employment.'[28] Colin Hay makes a similar claim when he suggests that the Policy Review amounts to an *accommodation with Thatcherism*, contributing to a new political consensus around the central reforms of the Conservative governments in the 1980s: privatization, low taxation, trade union reform and nuclear deterrence.[29] Responding to Hay, Martin Smith suggests that the accommodation with Thatcherism thesis is too simplistic. Smith is in doubt that Labour shifted to the Right from 1987; 'but it shifted policy within its own tradition and returned to the sorts of policies followed by the Labour

Government in the past (whether social democratic or not).' Smith believes that Labour under Kinnock began a process of *modernization* in the face of changing economic, social and political conditions: 'The acceptance of the market, the desire to reform the trade unions, and the abandonment of nationalization are not new to the Labour Party. Labour remains committed, rhetorically at least, to state intervention in order to achieve equality and social justice. These principles are firmly within Labour's ideological tradition and a long way from Thatcherism.'[30] Commenting on both Hay and Smith, Mark Wickham-Jones suggests that, rather than seeing Labour after 1987 as either Thatcherite or modernized, it should instead be seen as an attempt to *recast social democracy* in the light of changes brought about by Thatcherism. He writes:

> The result has been a renewed commitment to reformist objectives including social justice as well as more general goals of economic efficiency. Labour has paid attention to the preferences of both the electorate and the City. The result has been a curious mix: Labour has developed a distinct social democratic perspective and attempted to persuade both voters and the financial institutions of its desirability.[31]

This exchange of views raises important points about the nature of the Labour beast, not just under Kinnock and Smith, but also under Blair. In particular, it raises questions about what might be regarded as the ends of socialism and the means necessary to achieve them. Does the loss of public ownership as a means of socialist policy – one of the central planks of the Policy Review – constitute a corresponding loss of socialist goals? Tudor Jones, writing in 1989, thought that it did: 'For what is at stake is not merely the rejection of an outmoded instrument of policy. Public ownership has meant more to Labour than that. Since 1918 it has played a central role in the party's thinking, programmes and strategy.'[32] Even to those on the Left, such as David Miller, who embrace the market as a tool of socialism, the nature of property ownership remains a significant part of the socialist equation.[33] Jones also casts doubt on what would become one of Blair's central arguments: that socialism is an ethical rather than an economic doctrine. Jones wrote:

> For the fact is that the ethical and economic aspects of British socialism have been inextricably linked. The ideology's driving force – a moral critique of capitalism – has been continually strengthened by a radical

economic analysis of that system. Labour's overriding aim has consequently been both moral and economic – the gradual replacement of capitalism by an economically, socially and morally superior alternative.

To Raymond Plant, the real point of the Policy Review was that it brought the official aims of the party into line with what it had previously done in government and what it might wish to do in the future in the context of a more affluent and individualistic society.[34]

Plant may be right that the Policy Review brought together the theory and practice of the Labour Party in a changing world – and recent studies of Labour by Jones and others reinforce certain features of this argument. But, whatever the virtues of pragmatism, the view that the Policy Review left, for good or ill, the traditions of British socialism intact is difficult to sustain. In particular, the Policy Review marked a clear shift away from the political economy of socialism, ethical or otherwise.

Whatever interpretation is given to the Policy Review, it is quite clear that it prepared the ground for New Labour. Old Labour was beaten before Blair became leader in 1994: the modernizers were already directing the course of Labour policy-making. So what is the nature of New Labour? Is it simply Thatcherism Mark II? Or is it a revived form of social democracy – perhaps with much in common with Western European Centre-Left politics? To Eric Shaw: 'the real ideological significance of New Labour is the abandonment of Keynesian social democracy in favour of pre-Keynesian orthodoxy.' New Labour is thus a shift towards Thatcherite neo-liberalism, certainly in terms of its macroeconomic policies. To Tudor Jones, writing in the mid-1990s: 'Blair's achievement may be seen . . . as the symbolic fulfilment of the desire of Labour's revisionists and their successors clearly to establish the Party's identity in the mainstream of European social democracy.' New Labour is not so much a shift to the Right, but 'a more realistic view of the limits imposed on national governments by global economic forces and by the pressure of electoral politics'.[35] Donald Sassoon agrees that Labour was rejoining the European mainstream but not on the old terms: 'Between 1987 and 1992, Labour did not simply refurbish its image, as it had done before 1987, but accepted much of the agenda propounded by the Conservatives. In so doing, it joined the other parties of the West European Left on the road towards a new revisionist synthesis preparing, or so they hoped, a socialism for the twenty-first century.'[36]

European social democracy: retreat and reform

The British Labour Party was not alone in facing adverse conditions in the 1980s. Socialists and social democrats on the continent also found that the political tide was moving to the Right. The sense of crisis was not, writes Sassoon, a rumour put about by the Right: 'It was the object of agonizing discussions and analysis by socialism's most fervent supporters.'[37] In France, the election of François Mitterrand as president in 1981 with a majority in the National Assembly saw one of the last attempts by the European Left to embark on a radical programme of nationalization, economic planning and Keynesian reflation. Within two years the policies lay in ruins; and the French Socialist Party moved pragmatically to the Right. As Stephen Padgett has shown, by the early 1980s the collapse of the postwar Keynesian consensus was sending shock waves right through European social democracy: not just in Britain and France, but in Germany, Austria, Italy, Denmark, Norway and the Low Countries. In many cases, Centre Right governments were formed after long periods in which the Centre Left had been in power. For very different reasons, Sweden and the new Mediterranean democracies of Spain, Greece and Portugal stood firm against this rightward tide – although not for long. As Padgett suggests:

> The new liberal era was an almost impossibly difficult one for social democracy, characterised as it was by the rolling back of the state, deregulation and the liberalisation of market forces. Bound by their interventionist traditions, social democrats found it hard to redefine the relationship between the market and the state, Moreover, it was hard to reconcile the individualism of the market with the traditional social democratic ethos of social solidarity. Attempts to solve these dilemmas lacked coherence, relevance and political force, leding many to the conclusion that social democracy has lost its historical role.

To be sure, the main Left parties across Europe during the 1970s and 1980s did not all decline uniformly. Some, such as the Dutch Labour Party and the French, Italian and Spanish socialists, showed significant electoral gains; while some, such as the German and Austrian social democrats, and the French and Italian communists, showed significant falls; others, such as the social democrats in Finland and Sweden, were marked by no significant change.[38]

By the second half of the 1980s European social democracy was in a bout of revisionism. Many on the Left were coming round to the idea that the decline of the male industrial worker, the globalization of the economy and the collapse of communism challenged some of the basic tenets of socialist and social democratic politics: its class and male bias; the reliance on national policy levers; and the commitment to central planning and a large public sector. The Left, it was argued, must look, politically, to building coalitions across society and, economically and socially, to the European Community and the market.

The continental Left led the way along the revisionist path not just in terms of speed but of direction too. By contrast, the British Labour Party appeared rooted in outdated class politics, unwilling to reach out to the new social movements and clinging to anachronistic commitments to public ownership, anti-Europeanism and unilateral nuclear disarmament, all of which lacked credibility with the electorate. On the continent, the Left was drawn to the extension of democratic rights; to the co-option of feminist and green concerns; to greater European integration; and to reform of the welfare state.

The French socialists, after a period in opposition and with only a slender majority in the National Assembly, were in the late 1980s in the forefront of the new revisionism. Like the socialists in power in Italy and Spain, the French socialists 'rediscovered' the market and were willing to trade low inflation for rising unemployment. The French socialists were also in the forefront of European integration, arguing that the European Community was more than a free trade zone and that social and regional policies were an essential component of the European project. The Europeanism of the French socialists was in large part a reflection of their belief that globalization had undermined national means of pursuing economic growth and employment; and that greater integration was necessary if European capitalism was to compete with North American and Japanese capitalism. In Sweden, social democrats began to experiment with welfare and labour market strategies to create a skilled mobile workforce to beat unemployment.

By the early 1990s virtually all Centre-Left parties in Europe were in the grip of what Sassoon calls 'neo-revisionism'. This, he says,

> implies that markets should be regulated by legislation and not through state ownership. It means accepting that the object of socialism is not the

abolition of capitalism, but its co-existence with social justice; that regulation of the market will increasingly be a goal achieved by supra-national means; that national – and hence parliamentary – sovereignty is a limited concept; that the concept of national roads to socialism should be abandoned. It means that the historic link with the working class, however defined, is no longer of primary importance, and that the trade unions are to be regarded as representing workers' interests with no a priori claim to have a greater say in politics than other interest groups. It means giving a far greater priority than in the past to the concern of consumers. Neo-revisionism entails accepting important aspects of the conservative critique of socialism – including the association between collective provision and bureaucratic inertia.[39]

The Left down under and across the pond

European social democracy has had an undoubted influence on sections of the British Left. Reformist social democrats such as David Marquand have long been drawn to the continental model of the market economy, believing it to combine efficiency with social justice.[40] Before the 1997 election the Conservative MP David Willetts tried to paint New Labour as a political project in the traditional mould of European social democracy – and so to damn it for not being new at all.[41] But, for Blair and the British 'neo-revisionists', events in Australia and New Zealand, and in the United States, have been of greater significance.

Down under, economic and social reform in the 1980s was led by parties of the Left not the Right – parties intent on building broad electoral support for pragmatic, market-led policies. In Australia, the Labor government, first under Bob Hawke and then under the former economics minister Paul Keating, pursued policies to deregulate and restructure the economy. There was an emphasis on consumers rather than producers; on greater selectivity in welfare; and on supply-side reforms to retrain workers. Labor, Keating argued, had to demonstrate their ability to be sound managers of the economy – and this required tight control of taxation and public spending. Fiscal and monetary responsibility was also at the heart of the New Zealand Labour government first elected in 1984. Indeed, the government's decision to grant independence to the New Zealand central bank in 1989, and requiring it to keep inflation under 3 per cent, has been widely cited as an important model for Gordon

Brown's decision to give the Bank of England control over monetary policy soon after Labour's 1997 election victory. Between 1984 and 1990 the New Zealand economy under Labour was opened to international trade, the tax regime was made less progressive, income differentials were allowed to rise and the labour market was deregulated. In social policy the goal was to 'do more with less': tight control of public expenditure was matched with greater selectivity in welfare benefits.[42]

Perhaps the most important influence on Labour modernizers has come from the USA. Bill Clinton's victory in the presidential elections in 1992 – the year of Labour's demoralizing defeat by John Major – demonstrated that a party of the Left could win power after a long period of conservative hegemony – but only if it moved onto the political centre ground. The impact of Clinton's victory was immediate – partly because a close associate of Blair's, Philip Gould, went on the campaign trail with the Clinton Democrats.[43] Clinton had campaigned as a *New* Democrat in an attempt to distance himself from the progressive Democratic tradition associated with Roosevelt's New Deal in the 1930s and Truman's Great Society in the 1960s. This tradition had close associations with the unions and the welfare state; with high taxes, protectionism and government intervention in the economy. Clinton nailed his colours to free trade in the Americas and around the globe; to tax cuts, deficit reduction and supply-side economics; and, above all, to value-for-money welfare reform. He projected a populist communitarianism of rights and responsibilities, civic duties and family values. And he also promised to be tough on crime.

The triumph of New Labour

Despite Labour's Policy Review, the party went down to the Conservatives under John Major in the 1992 general election. The Right's forward march appeared unstoppable. There was even debate among political scientists whether Labour could ever win again.[44] This fourth consecutive election defeat at the hands of the Tories saw leading modernizers urge further radical reform of the party. Giles Radice, in a series of Fabian pamphlets, argued that Labour's only chance of forming a government was if it won more seats in the south of England. And to do that, he suggested, it had to win over the new Middle England: the

24

white collar and skilled workers – the C1s and C2s – who had provided the Conservatives with such loyal support since 1979. Middle Englanders were Thatcherites in the 1980s precisely because Thatcherism spoke their language – of ownership, opportunity and choice, not equality and state control. The people of Middle England, as the advertising world put it, were 'aspirational': they wanted to 'get on'. But Radice suggested that Middle England also hankered after decent public hospitals, good state schools and streets which were safe to walk on at night. Labour, argued Radice, must reach out to Middle England and to its values. The message, not just the messenger, had to change.

In the last of the series, published in September 1994 after Tony Blair had become leader, Radice wrote with Stephen Pollard that:

> To be credible, the basic core of Labour's ideas – community, fairness and opportunity – has to be clearly linked to a few key policies such as crime, education, employment and health. Labour has also to demonstrate its economic competence by continuing to emphasise the need to control public spending and to ensure value for money. The new Labour leadership needs to show that it is building on the reforms introduced by Neil Kinnock and John Smith. A revision of Clause Four would provide a symbol that the Labour Party has really changed and is self confident enough to put forward a vision of the future.[45]

'Let us say what we mean and mean what we say'

When Blair stood up on 4 October 1994 at the Labour Party conference in Blackpool to make his leader's speech, only a handful of close supporters knew what he was going to say. Although not mentioned by name, Clause 4 of Labour's constitution, which committed the party to the traditional socialist goal of common ownership, was Blair's target. 'Let us say what we mean and mean what we say', said the Labour leader:

> We should stop saying what we don't mean and start saying what we do mean, what we stand by, what we stand for. It is time we had a clear, up-to-date statement of the objects and objectives of our party . . . This is a modern party living in an age of change. It requires a modern constitution that says what we are in terms the public cannot misunderstand and the Tories cannot misrepresent.[46]

For Blair, the old Clause 4 was a noose for the party. It committed Labour to something it neither believed in nor had any intention of putting into practice. As Radice had urged on the new leader, the world outside the Labour Party, the people who voted governments into power, needed a symbolic gesture that Labour really had changed. The rewriting of Clause 4 was thus a *public* break with Old Labour and the past. It was the moment of confession when Labour renounced the old socialist idea that the capitalist market economy was immoral, exploitative and inefficient. In the new Clause 4, agreed by the party at a special conference in April 1995, Labour abandoned the idea that the role of the Left was to replace the market with state ownership and government planning. In his 1995 *Spectator* Lecture, Blair argued that the new Clause 4 made Labour a party of 'aspiration and ambition'. In an interview the following year Blair said: 'I think one of the great changes that has happened in the whole Labour culture is to recognise that we need entrepreneurs and people who are going to go out and be wealth creators and who are going to become wealthy by their own efforts. I support that, I want that, a successful economy needs that.'[47]

For left-wingers inside the party and out, the new Clause 4 marked Labour's final break with socialism. Socialism challenged the capitalist market order or it was nothing. According to Tony Wright, this view is misguided: 'The real problem with the old Clause Four was not that it seemed to commit Labour to nationalize everything in sight, though it did; but that it represented a classic confusion of means and ends. Politics are for changing, as circumstances and problems change. Values are for keeping, as the enduring reference point by which policy compasses are set.'[48] So, new times demanded a new Labour Party with a new set of policies to deliver the old socialist values.

New times, New Labour, old values

'New times' had become a familiar slogan in the 1980s among revisionist thinkers on the Left associated with *Marxism Today* – a journal of the British Communist Party edited by Martin Jacques which, paradoxically, was streets ahead of the Labour Party in thinking the unthinkable. Writing at the end of the 1980s, Jacques and Stuart Hall suggested that: 'The world has changed, not just incrementally but qualitatively.' As we shall show in the following chapters, new times brought together ideas about how modern (and to some, *post*-modern) societies were being transformed by new economic and cultural forces such as 'post-Fordism' and 'globalization'; how the old class structures and political allegiances were disappearing; how society had become less bound by tradition, deference and patriarchal relationships; and how society was more differentiated, multicultural, pluralistic and individualistic (or 'reflexive', as the sociologist Anthony Giddens put it). For Jacques and Hall, the political consequences of 'new times' was that the Left must move with them and found a new politics 'beyond Thatcherism'.[49] There was, and there remains, much debate on the Left over the character of new times, how the Left should respond to them and what a politics 'beyond Thatcherism' might look like for the Left. There is in particular disagreement over whether social and cultural individualism or pluralism, especially when it relates to the family, is to be celebrated or not. And there are many on the Left who doubt whether times are new at all: to them the Left has no need to go 'beyond Thatcherism'; old socialist ideas are as relevant as ever.

For Labour modernizers, the idea of new times underpins the whole New Labour project. In a changing world, new means are required to deliver old ends. The values remain the same, but the policies needed to put them into practice have to be modernized. As Blair argued in his 'Faith in the City' speech: 'Our values do not change. Our commitment to a different vision of society stands intact. But the ways of achieving that vision must change.' Blair's own intellectual development gives us important clues to the first of these values: community. Blair was unattached in any party sense at university. But he was part of a group whose main intellectual interests were politics and religion. Through this group – and, in particular, his friendship with a mature Australian student, Peter Thomson – Blair read and discussed the communitarian philosophy of John Macmurray as well as Christian ethical socialists such as Tawney. Blair's attachment to community as a core value of socialism comes, according to one of his biographers, John Rentoul, 'directly from Macmurray'. Macmurray's idea of community is relatively straightforward. Individuals are created through their attachments to other people in families and communities. By seeking to forward the interests of the community, individuals can make society a better place. In the 1930s Macmurray's philosophy was a direct attack on liberalism and its individualistic world view. This, as Rentoul perceptively argues, provides the distinctive basis for Blair's politics: 'It is precisely the combination in Macmurray of Christian socialism and a 'conservative' critique of liberalism which underpins the apparent novelty of Blair's political philosophy.'[50]

So, in New Labour thinking, community is used sociologically as a retort to the neo-liberal 'no such thing as society' view: individuals are created by society. Community is also used ethically to suggest that the life of the individual has value and meaning only within the context of society. The 'good life' is not chosen independently by the individual but is formed in the context of the community. Here is one example of where Blair develops the sociological view of the person and tries to set out a normative argument for the good community:

> For myself, I start from a simple belief that people are not separate economic actors competing in the marketplace of life. They are citizens of a community. We are social beings, nurtured in families and communities and human only because we develop the moral power of personal responsibility for ourselves and each other. Britain is stronger as a team than as a collection of selfish players.[51]

The community is bound by a web of duties, obligations, rights and responsibilities which place demands on individuals as citizens, parents, neighbours, teachers – even members of the government. This web of mutual obligation – and the institutions such as the family which are founded on such ties – bind the community together, forming the basis for a settled and cohesive society. It is then the job of government to help to sustain the community in part by demanding that members of the community accept their responsibilities and fulfil their obligations. This communitarian view of the relationship between the individual and society has the added advantage for Labour modernizers that it does not rest on notions of class affiliation: we are all part of 'one nation, one community', as Blair puts it.[52] New Labour can thus avoid the exclusive politics of Old Labour, reaching beyond the boundaries of class to all groups in society. Communitarianism also offers Labour modernizers a political vocabulary which eschews market individualism, but not market capitalism; and which embraces collective action, but not the state.

Communitarianism is at the heart of New Labour's post-Thatcherite politics because it combines a critique of postwar social democracy with a critique of liberalism – both the North American rights-based liberalism associated with John Rawls and the neo-liberalism associated with F. A. Hayek.[53] Politically, communitarianism provides Labour modernizers with an alternative to Conservative neo-liberalism (Thatcherism) and allows them to distance New Labour from Old Labour's postwar social democratic record and from the liberal influence on this record. In his 1995 *Spectator* lecture, Blair argued: 'Individuals prosper best within a strong and cohesive society . . . a society which is fragmented and divided, where people feel no sense of shared purpose, is unlikely to produce well-adjusted and responsible citizens.' Blair went on to assert that the Left in the past had been guilty of two things: first, in equating a strong society with a strong state; secondly, by believing that it was the role of the state to grant rights without demanding corresponding responsibilities. This, Blair suggested, was linked to a social libertarianism on the Left which was alien to traditional Labour thinking. If these, for Blair, were the sins of the Left, then the Right was equally guilty of neglecting the community. The Right, Blair argued, came to power championing individual liberty and limited government. But, he suggested:

> In a mirror-image of the Left's confusion, the Right started to define personal responsibility as responsibility not just for yourself but to yourself. Outside of a duty not to break the law, it appeared to exclude the broader notion of duty to others. It became narrowly acquisitive and rather destructive. The economic message of enterprise – of the early 1980s – became a philosophy of 'get what you can'.

According to Blair: 'The only way to rebuild social order and stability is through strong values, socially shared, inculcated through individuals, family, government and the institutions of civil society.'[54] Communitarianism is New Labour's answer to Thatcherism; so too is it Blair's rebuff to Old Labour. Community will restore the moral balance to society by setting out duties and obligations as well as rights. And where Old Labour looked to the state for action, New Labour talks of 'reinventing government' through collective action in the community.

Social justice is a second value which figures prominently in New Labour thinking. Social justice to New Labour involves an important element of equality: that individual life chances are unequal and that it is the role of government, especially through the welfare state, to make individual opportunities more equal. New Labour also argues that the pursuit of equality – creating more job opportunities for more people – does not come at the price of reduced economic efficiency. Social justice is good for business; and a successful economy is good for social justice. However, New Labour's version of social justice does not involve any strong notion of egalitarianism, that life's outcomes should be made more equal. The redistribution of wealth and income is not on New Labour's post-Thatcherite agenda. In its place, New Labour argues the value of 'fairness' (taxes should be fair, reflecting hard work and the need for incentives, not just the demands of equality) and 'inclusiveness' (welfare to work to bring the socially excluded, the unemployed, back into society via the labour market). Whether fairness and inclusiveness involve any element of equality is a moot point, whatever their individual merits.

Taken together, community and social justice combine in New Labour thinking to provide the basis for what is hoped is a politics beyond Thatcherism. Three themes – ethics, economic efficiency and social cohesion – are interwoven. Economic success – particularly more jobs – will bring greater social justice and social cohesion; which is further strengthened by a more dutiful and responsible citizenry; and more social cohesion will in turn help create a more viable market economy. The idea of 'stakeholding', which Blair introduced into the New Labour lexicon in a speech in Singapore in January 1996, bridges community and social justice. For Labour modernizers, stakeholding gives a sense of being part of a community; of being included, of having a stake in society which throws up rights as well as responsibilities; of there being greater opportunities, more fairness and social justice; and of there being more democracy and accountability in government and politics.

These core New Labour values, community and social justice, *are* traditional values of the Left. New Labour claims that the modernization of the party, especially its policies, has left these values intact: New Labour believes the same things as Old Labour, only the means to achieve those values have changed because times have changed. As we shall examine in the rest of this book, Labour modernizers, for good or ill, are understating their own radicalism. Policy reviews under Blair have led to re-evaluations and reintepretations of Labour values. The Left's traditional sense of community involving notions of cooperation, fellowship and solidarity and a shared experience of life, especially in terms of membership of the working class, has little place in the market-orientated, 'one nation' politics of New Labour. And the Left's understanding of social justice, rooted in a sense that the inequalities of wealth, income and opportunity in society were based on the class ownership of property, has been explicitly rejected under Blair.

The post-Thatcherite agenda

In this chapter we have suggested that the Blair revolution in the Labour Party has its roots in an earlier phase of modernization under the leadership of Neil Kinnock. Further, Labour's revisionism is not an isolated phenomenon: the Centre Left worldwide has undergone a process of political modernization. There remains, as we have seen, some dispute about what label can be attached to this whole process of political transmutation. Has modernization taken Labour back into the mainstream of European social democracy? Or has it led Labour beyond social democracy into the arms of neo-liberal Thatcherism? Or has it even led Labour onto new political ground entirely?

In the rest of this book we shall suggest that New Labour has a 'post-Thatcherite' quality about it: a quality which marks it off from the reforms to the party introduced under the Policy Review; and which marks it off from other Centre-Left parties abroad. New Labour is post-Thatcherite because it resists a return to the politics of postwar social democracy; and because it is simultaneously attracted and repelled by the politics of Thatcherism.

2

The New Economics

In 1997 a Labour Party was elected to government that had rejected both nationalization and Keynesianism. Where Gaitskell had failed and John Smith shied away, Tony Blair had replaced Clause 4 of the party constitution which dedicated Labour to common ownership. In the late 1970s, under pressure from the International Monetary Fund, Prime Minister James Callaghan and his Chancellor Denis Healey, to uproar in the party, turned their backs on Keynesian reflation and accepted cuts in public expenditure. By 1997 the prudent economics of Gordon Brown had the official IMF seal of approval and were received acquiescently by his party and unperturbed by the City.[1] In a remarkable turnaround in political rhetoric, it was Labour who was accusing the Tories of too many tax rises, not the other way round. New Labour was promising not, in Healey's words, to 'squeeze the rich until the pips squeaked' but to keep income tax rates down and to run market capitalism more dynamically than the Conservatives.

To the New Labour modernizers, the economic debate has centred on what model of capitalism is best for Britain; any idea of counterbalancing, let alone overthrowing, capitalism has been decisively rejected. New Labour's economics have left behind an ideological commitment to public ownership for a pragmatic stance on the public and private sectors. And they have shifted the role for the active state from Keynesian demand management to supply-side interventions. The supply side here means not economic or industrial planning but the provision of education and training. Because of globalization, as Labour perceives it, national governments can no longer manage demand. Instead they must intervene on the supply side. Capital is mobile and cannot be controlled. But governments can enhance labour. Labour is committed to a flexible workforce but to flexibility plus education and training. These, it argues, will provide a well-trained, flexible workforce which can attract investment and provide the basis for skills-based growth. In a post-industrial economy it is human capital and skills which are at the basis of economic success. At the same time, supply-side measures give workers the skills they need to participate in the labour market and adapt to flexibility and change in the economy to ensure future employment. They provide, in short, for inclusion, security and an economy in which all individuals can have a 'stake'. At the macro-economic level, prudency and orthodoxy on fiscal and monetary matters have replaced tax and spend. Labour's policies are based on a commitment to low taxes, tight controls on public expenditure and tough inflation targets. Stability secured through these measures, rather than demand management or control of capital, are seen as the way to attract investment, stimulate growth and create employment.

But what *exactly* has occurred in Labour's economics since the dark days of the 1970s? How much significance should we attribute to the differences between Labour Chancellors pre- and post-Thatcher? Do Labour's new economics amount to a new form of social democracy – perhaps the eclipse of social democratic economics altogether? In this chapter we shall first outline what Labour's economics looked like before Blair. Then we shall outline perceived changes – such as globalization, post-industrialism and post-Fordism – which have led New Labour to rethink its economic policy. We shall turn then to debates over issues such as different models of capitalism and stakeholding which have played a part in Labour rethinking under Blair. Finally we shall discuss the way in which Labour's economics are intended to get beyond the economics of both Old Left and New Right and shall tie up what the main features of New Labour's new economics are.

Old Labour and the economy

There are some key instruments which characterized Labour's economics before Blair.[2] Until quite recently Labour advocated public ownership as a tool of economic policy. It did so to different degrees in different

33

periods, with diverse objectives in mind, and in practice often failed to live up to its stated intentions on this issue. But public ownership was part of Labour's approach to the economy. Forms of planning were also party policy through a number of phases of postwar politics. While the caveats are similar here as for public ownership, planning was, nevertheless, long advocated as a means for achieving Labour's aims in the economy. Keynesian demand management was intended as a tool for indirectly influencing the direction of the economy: public spending aimed at stimulating demand, boosting production, creating jobs and providing the revenue, through taxation, for a redistributive welfare state.

Directly or indirectly, public ownership, planning and demand management were means for the government to intervene in the direction of the economy. With them capitalism could be run more efficiently than if the market was left to itself. Furthermore they added a socialist element at the heart of capitalist society. Their presence was what made the economy mixed rather than a free market. They were intended as tools for pursuing greater equality in the distribution of wealth and income. And they were the means for pursuing public rather than just private priorities in the economy. For Tony Crosland, in fact, a moderate Labour minister writing in the 1950s, Keynesianism, combined with progressive taxation, the managerial revolution and liberal democracy, made capitalism socialist.[3]

Planning and public ownership

In 1945 Labour came to power committed to a full employment welfare state. The government was guided by a sense of social justice, the aim to be inclusive, to build common citizenship, to improve conditions for the less well off and to reduce differentials between them and the rich. Labour saw itself as a national government, pursuing social reform for the people through the state. The 1945 manifesto proposed extensions of public ownership, planning, a large-scale housing programme, the establishment of the NHS, full employment and social protection. The Attlee government made radical promises, many of which it delivered on, particularly in the fields of health and housing. It was a government motivated by socialist ideas, elected on a landslide, intent on real effective reforms in the interests of the people as it perceived them.

Back in the 1930s, Left and Right had been impressed by the Soviet Union's rapid and planned industrialization. Influenced too by the apparent success of planning in the wartime economy, the postwar Labour government advocated national planning, not a return to *laissez-faire*. It proposed that public ownership of the essential instruments of production was essential to deliver socialist objectives: greater efficiency under coordinated planning than the market could deliver; the redistribution of wealth (the profits of industry could be used for public need rather than appropriated privately); and better conditions for workers. Indeed, for many on the Left in the period, public ownership was itself the very definition of socialism: what made it different from capitalism, which was defined as private ownership of the means of production. It was the goal, not just a means for achieving other ends. Planning was the socialist alternative to markets. By the end of the Attlee government's term in office, coal, rail, cable and wireless, a great deal of road haulage, civil aviation, gas, electricity, iron and steel had been brought into public ownership.

Labour's plans for public ownership and planning were never completely fulfilled. Nationalizations of industries that were unprofitable hindered the redistributive aims of public ownership. Nationalization did not challenge internal structures. In the name of enterprise autonomy public corporations were not subjected to state planning. Insufficient thought was given to how ownership might be used for public ends, and economic and political pressures, including the conservatism of ministers and civil servants, restricted the radicalism of the government's economic ambitions. Indirect demand management came to be more of a favoured tool than direct ownership and planning. But, in terms of what defined it ideologically, the 1945 Labour government was committed to socialist goals of more egalitarian redistribution, intervention in pursuit of collective rather than private priorities, and the welfare of workers. And it intended to pursue such goals through instruments such as public ownership and planning. This was its public socialist ideology.

Keynes and the welfare state

In the 1950s Labour was out of power. Revisionism, exemplified by Crosland's *The Future of Socialism* and by the party leader Hugh Gaitskell, defined debates over its thinking. Crosland and others argued that old socialist emphases on public ownership and the evils of markets confused means with ends. Public ownership and planning were means to what were really the point – ends such as equality and social justice. Furthermore such means were no longer appropriate to the achievement of these ends. Instead Keynesianism could achieve efficiency and socialist goals such as equality. By managing demand, slumps could be averted and growth maintained. Growth could secure full employment, good standards of living and a revenue base for the welfare state. The welfare state, together with progressive income tax and tax on wealth and unearned income, could be the basis for economic redistribution. Indirect management of the economy supplanted direct control of companies through ownership. After the 1959 election Gaitskell tried to ditch Clause 4 but he failed to gather sufficient support from all sections of the party for what most still believed to be the symbol of the Labour Party.

But in the revisionist days of the 1950s, markets were not regarded as anathema to public needs. Because of the divorce between corporate ownership and control, managers now ran companies. And they were as likely to be interested in social as purely profit-orientated goals. Profit-seeking itself was seen as desirable, serving consumer demand and providing capital for investment and jobs. Crosland celebrated the mixed economy, the welfare state and full employment and argued that these were worthy achievements that government, through macro-economic management, could maintain. British society had reached a stage where socialist gains had been made and politics ruled the economy. Capitalism and the markets could co-exist with Keynesian, redistributive welfare socialism: in fact each could enhance the other. While different from the socialism of public ownership and planning this also departed from free market economics. It saw a role for collectivist institutions, redistribution and state intervention in the economy, something on which Labour and the Conservatives held similar views until Thatcherism.

There are themes later echoed by Blair here: the distinction between means and ends and the critique of public ownership; the emphasis on modernization to fit in with new social and economic circumstances; and the acceptance of the market economy and its functions for, rather than antagonism with, social justice. Yet in other areas, as we shall argue, New Labour is different. Labour modernizers espouse some thing more liberal than the mixed economy; and Keynesianism and the politics of taxation and redistribution no longer define New Labour's economics.

Planning revisited

After Gaitskell's death in the early 1960s, his successor as party leader, Harold Wilson, led Labour into the 'white heat of technology'. Wilson emphasized technological change and he criticized investment and management in the economy under the Tories and their 'stop-go' economic policies. Attitudes and hierarchies were, he argued, outdated. Modernization and technological revolution were needed. Labour came to power in 1964 with a programme for a National Plan, Keynesian macroeconomic management, a more progressive tax system and increased public spending financed by growth. In a climate of general interest in planning, Labour proposed projections for the economy intended as guidelines for business to aim at. Labour pledged to nationalize steel and expand existing public industries. But Labour's radicalism in opposition was not matched in power. Some proposals were vague or lacked enforceability. The government was knocked off course by the pressure to protect sterling. And there was perhaps a lack of political will to push through certain elements of Labour's programme.

Blair and New Labour have brought comparisons with Wilson and Labour in the 1960s with the emphasis on new technology, modernization and economic stability. New Labour's appeal to public–private partnerships also echoes the Wilson years. But there are differences as well as comparabilities between Wilson and Blair. Labour's 1964 manifesto included policies on economic planning and Keynesian demand management. These were to be the basis for a progressive and redistributional social programme. The party in 1964, unlike Labour in 1997, was still committed to moderately expanding public ownership. On these items, as with many others, Blair has severed the party's ties with 'Old Labour'.

Labour's defeat at the polls in 1970 began a period when the Left grew in influence inside the party, especially over economic and industrial policy. Stuart Holland, an economist and later MP, argued that Crosland's view of politics ruling economics was undermined by multinational corporations which controlled large sections of the economy and which were able to ignore attempts by national governments to regulate them.[4] To Holland, the interests of private capital were incompatible with national interests, rather than as Crosland had suggested. *Labour's Programme 1973* and Labour's 1974 manifesto suggested that indirect Keynesian intervention would not be enough to deal with the multinational economy. Direct intervention in company behaviour through planning agreements and a National Enterprise Board (NEB) with holdings in major firms were required. Big firms in different sectors would be nationalized to assist the government in influencing pricing, investment and exports. The revisionist shift to Keynesian social democracy seemed to be under attack from traditional state socialism. Multinational companies needed tackling. Public ownership was a key economic strategy.

The decline of social democratic economics

The 1974 Labour government witnessed a retreat both from this burst of state socialism and from Keynesian social democracy. The new government inherited an economy which was going from boom to bust. Nationalization was restricted to firms in trouble, such as British Leyland, British Aerospace and the shipyards. Profitable sectors were left alone in the name of securing business confidence. The powers of the NEB to buy into industry were limited. Planning agreements were voluntary and never got off the ground. The government's industrial strategy was reduced to a more modest attempt to persuade companies to follow examples of best practice. And the government decided in 1975 to rein back high levels of public expenditure on pay, pensions, benefits, food subsidies and housing. In 1976 Wilson resigned and was replaced by James Callaghan. Funds were borrowed from the IMF to prevent a decline in sterling, with further public spending cuts required as a condition of the loans. In this context Callaghan made his famous statement to the party conference breaking with Keynesianism. Both demand management and public spending, as economic policies designed to foster growth and employment, were dead, at least as far as the prime minister and chancellor of the Labour government were concerned.

A government which had started off nominally committed to state-engineered socialist strategies for the economy ended up denying both that left-wing alternative *and* Keynesian social democracy. Changing global circumstances were perceived, rightly or wrongly, to have made these alternatives impossible, a theme to be echoed in New Labour economics. In 1979 Labour lost the general election and Mrs Thatcher came to power, committed to firming up the break with socialism and social democracy and installing a neo-liberal monetarist alternative.

What was .the alternative for the Labour Party? The Left retained confidence in their view and fought for reforms to party organization in the early 1980s which gave them more influence in the party. Under its leader Michael Foot, Labour's 1983 manifesto showed the clear imprint of the Left. Growth and full employment was to be pursued through large-scale spending on public-sector projects. Exchange and import controls were to be established to prevent capital flight and deal with the balance of payments; and the party committed itself to withdrawal from the European Economic Community – all amounting to a sort of British socialism in one country. Privatized industries were to be renationalized with limited compensation and the government was to obtain substantial holdings in sectors of the economy deemed particularly significant. Partnership with the unions, economic planning, industrial democracy and a radical redistribution of power and wealth to the working class were promised. In all these commitments there is little to compare to Labour under Tony Blair. Labour lost the 1983 election very badly, reduced to 28 per cent of the vote and its traditional but declining industrial, urban, working-class core of support.

Embracing the market

As we saw in Chapter 1, the leadership of Neil Kinnock in the 1980s began a process of party reform. Kinnock started on the Left of the party – he was a protégé of Foot's. But, as leader, he set about marginalizing the Left through reforms to internal party organization and by attempting to make Labour's policies more popular with the voters. Labour lost the 1987 election having recovered little electoral ground. The poor performance was put down to a continuing perception of extremism and disunity in the party, Labour's unilateral disarmament policy and distrust of the party on taxation and issues such as home ownership. Labour responded by announcing a Policy Review, the aim of which was to rid the party of its remaining unpopular policies and to reach out beyond its traditional supporters to other groups in the electorate.

The Policy Review saw Labour embrace the market. The role of government was seen not in directing the economy but stepping in only where the market failed, in the provision of public goods and areas such as training and research and development. Gradually during Kinnock's leadership Labour dropped policies for extending public ownership and the renationalization of privatized companies. Modernizers in the party argued that national demand management was no longer possible in an interdependent global economy. Membership of the European Exchange Rate Mechanism (ERM) was seen as important in ensuring stability and retaining the confidence of the City. The relatively more interventionist and Keynesian Bryan Gould lost ground to more orthodox figures such as John Smith committed to a fixed exchange-rate policy and to fiscal and monetary stability based on membership of the ERM. Pledges of higher taxation to support social programmes were restricted to the top 10 per cent of earners. By the 1992 election, employment spokesperson Tony Blair had shifted party policy to retaining most of the Tory industrial relations legislation rather than repealing it.

Labour's 1992 election defeat was widely blamed on what was left of Labour's tax-and-spend policies – in particular, its proposals for higher taxes for top earners to finance child benefit and pensions. At this point in time, Labour was still advocating that higher earners pay more in tax to fund welfare benefits whose main beneficiaries were the less well off. In 1992 redistributional tax-and-spend policies remained part of Labour's policy hand. The death of John Smith, the chief architect of Labour's 1992 budget, after only two years as party leader, and the succession of Tony Blair marked the beginning of the end of Labour as a party committed to the politics of redistribution.

At first sight it appears that the break with the economics of social democracy and state socialism was made before Blair became leader – in the late 1980s and early 1990s under Neil Kinnock and John Smith. Certainly the Policy Review saw off the vestiges of public ownership, planning, Keynesianism and tax-and-spend welfarism, all central elements of the ideology and policy of Labour in the postwar period. But it was Blair who made the decisive, and public, break with Labour's past, in particular by ruling out increases in income tax and, most symbolically, writing out the party's commitment to common ownership in Clause 4 of its constitution. The market was accepted under Kinnock. Under Blair it has become positively celebrated. Some of the themes of

Labour's supply-side economics geared around stability were emerging under Kinnock and Smith. But under Blair these were developed into a coherent package linked to a radically new orientation to welfare and social policy. Prudency and orthodoxy in macro-economic policy were not properly sealed until Gordon Brown became Blair's shadow chancellor. Labour, we argue, was not truly *New* Labour until Blair. We shall turn shortly to the policies that have emerged from New Labour's economic rethink. But first, what were the circumstances and ideas that led to the formulation of Labour's new economic policy?

'New, new, new: everything is new'

New Labour's economic rethinking rests on perceptions that the world has changed dramatically.[5] In a speech to European socialists shortly after becoming prime minister, Blair argued:

> The critical challenge is to connect [our] goals to a world that has undergone a veritable revolution of change. Technology, trade and travel are transforming our lives. Our young people will work in different industries, often those of communications and design, not old mass production. Many will work in or own small businesses. Jobs for life are gone. Nine to five working is no longer universal. Women work, which brings new opportunities but new strains for family life. South East Asia can compete with us, in many parts on equal terms. Money is traded across international boundaries in vast amounts twenty-four hours a day. New, new, new: everything is new. There is an urgent task to renew the social democratic model to meet this change.[6]

Labour's old values, Blair argues, remain the same – community, inclusion, fairness and social justice. But the world has changed so much that the old policy instruments of the Left for achieving such ends – Keynesianism, public ownership, planning – are no longer relevant. New times require new means for pursuing the old values. These new times include changes such as globalization, the rise of the information society, post-Fordist flexibility and increased insecurity.

Globalization, information, insecurity

The perception that we live in a globalized world is the key to New Labour's loss of faith in Keynesian macro-economics. In the global economy, it is argued, capital is mobile and demand is affected by factors beyond national boundaries. Governments cannot, therefore, control capital but can intervene to improve the capacities of labour. They have limited control over demand but can be active on the supply side, through education and training. This can provide for a skilled and flexible labour force to attract investment and ensure competitiveness. Countries like Britain and the USA cannot compete with less developed countries on low wages so they must focus on providing a more skilled workforce. This direction of policy fits not only with globalization but also with the perception that we live in a hi-tech, rapidly changing post-industrial world in which skills and training are at a premium. Training forms the basis for economic success in the new skills-intensive industries and helps workers adapt to change in an insecure labour market. The perception of globalization has implications for macro- as well as micro-economic policy. Governments have to keep taxation, spending and inflation at levels which are comparable with those of competitor countries in order to attract capital, hence ruling out any looseness with inflation, tax rises or public spending. When capital can invest where it likes, it is at the level of labour skills and technology, stability and competitiveness that success is secured, and it is here that governments can intervene.[7]

Some of these ideas developed by New Labour modernizers echo earlier ideas about the information society, as well as post-Fordist theories which had been pushed in the pages of *Marxism Today* in the 1980s. The notion of an information society dates back to the post-industrial theories of Daniel Bell and Alain Touraine, among others, in the 1970s.[8] These argue that in the postwar period we have shifted from economies based on manufacturing production to a greater role for information industries in the service economy. Computers rather than machinery for the production of goods are the key technologies. Information, research and design rather than capital are the crucial resources. The most significant workers are professional information workers rather than male, manual manufacturing workers. Production is based less on producer interests: workers operate with more of a service ethic orientated to consumers. Post-Fordist themes have also played a part in Labour's rethinking.[9] Post-Fordist theories posit a shift away from the Fordist world of mass production and consumption, machinery dedicated to long runs producing standardized goods, and unskilled workers. With post-Fordism, diversified markets and flexible technology have, it is argued, allowed for a shift to short-run production of diverse goods. Workers have to be skilled and flexible. Consumption and the market are more determinant than production and the plan.

Fused onto ideas of the post-industrial information society and post-Fordist flexibility in Labour thinking are further notions about a shift to a globalized world of insecurity. Writers such as Anthony Giddens suggest that with greater globalization events distant from our own lives affect us. Our actions, in turn, can have long-distance effects.[10] The value of the currency in our pockets is affected by globally distant factors, for example; and our choice of consumer goods can have globally distant effects on producers or the environment. Globalization exposes us to greater diversity and change. We feel less secure and more affected by forces outside our control. We are forced to be more flexible and make more choices than we used to. For Giddens the task of Right and Left is to move with radical change yet balance it with a 'philosophic conservatism' which can provide security and social cohesion amid all the flux. Ironically, the Left, which used to be thought of as radical, seems to be more in touch with the need to do the latter; the Right, traditionally conservative in thinking, has become so much the party of radical individualist change that it is unable to provide the security, repair and conservation needed.[11] How have these ideas of globalization, the information society and insecurity been taken up by New Labour?

New times in New Labour

Tony Blair is not the first Centre-Left politician to be drawn to these post-industrial ideas. US Vice-President Al Gore, for example, has emphasized the importance of information technology in an information age. In Australia, an influential theorist of post-industrialism is the Labor politician Barry Jones. Both in the USA and Australia, the Centre-Left has supported rapid developments in information technology as being at the cutting edge of economic development. Both have also supported the view that globalization creates new and intensive patterns of competition which are disruptive of traditional socio-economic structures; and that workers must be skilled and flexible to cope with the insecurities thrown up by new times.[12]

The post-industrial, post-Fordist vision of a high-technology, globalized world characterized by flexibility, knowledge and insecurity is reflected in new thinking, especially that of Gordon Brown. The new Labour chancellor acknowledges that, in a globalized economy, capital is footloose; and that demand is affected by factors beyond national boundaries – and beyond the control of national governments. The only role for governments is to promote stability and incentives for capital investment and to influence the supply and quality of labour. Hence the shift from Keynesian demand management to an anti-inflationary macro-economics allied to a micro-economic strategy focused on the supply of labour.[13]

New Labour's supply-side economics is seen to reflect the insecurities of the global economy. Workers need to have the skills and flexibility to adapt to the rapidly changing demands of a labour market shaped by globalization. Moreover, Labour sees its education and training policies as being particularly appropriate to a post-industrial and post-Fordist economy where knowledge, information and creativity are crucial to business success. Blair has remarked that Britain, which led the first industrial revolution, is currently 'in the middle of a second revolution defined in part by new information technology but also by creativity', a revolution comparable in significance to the first. The 'key to survival in the modern world is access to knowledge and information', Blair argues; 'information is the currency of our economies.' In New Labour thinking the cutting edge of production is post-industrial, in design and information technology, for example. Brown argues that: 'Britain is increasingly leading the world in those industries which most obviously depend on the skills and talents of their workers – communications, design, architecture, fashion, music and film.' To Labour modernizers, Britain faces a world of rapid technological change dominated by the new computer-based information and communication technologies. And governments can play their part in fostering the post-industrial economy by acting in partnership with business to innovate in the new technologies. Blair, in fact, argues that post-Fordism is a revolution towards flexible diversity that happened to business in the

1970s and 1980s and needs now to be generalized into areas such as education.[14]

In addition to the micro- and macro-economic approach we have already touched on, this vision of a global, flexible information society has spawned a range of further specific proposals from Labour. As broadcasting, telecommunications and computing increasingly interpenetrate, Labour's policy is to negotiate public–private agreements to allow competition in the entertainment services industry and access for companies such as British Telecom. New entrants to these markets will, in return, wire up schools, hospitals, health centres, libraries and citizens' advice bureaux to the internet. Labour argues this can ensure information-literate generations in touch with the latest communications technologies, and make certain, in accordance with stakeholder ideas of inclusion and equal opportunity, that the information revolution is available to the many and not just the few. Labour proposes tax incentives for technological development and public–private investment to advance the information technology industries. Labour aims to promote the media industries through, for example, tax breaks for British films, changes in competition policy to encourage competition and prevent excessive mergers, and promotion of digital technology. Blair, meanwhile, has made it his mission to present New Labour as a government for the media, design and communications industries. He has engaged agencies such as the Design Council to assist in advice on promotion and best practice in media, design and communications and entertained figures from the cultural industries at 10 Downing Street.[15]

This idea of new times is not, of course, a vision shared by all. There have long been doubters as to whether we do actually live in a globalized, information or post-Fordist society. Many believe that new times display as many continuities with the past as they do breaks. Critics have questioned how fundamental these new features are to defining modern society today; and if such features are significant, do they mark a break from an industrial era of mass production and nation-state sovereignty that came before? If such processes are part of the (post)modern world, are they as desirable as Blair and his colleagues make them out to be?[16]

These counterblasts to post-industrialization, post-Fordism and globalization have given perspective to the debates. Where there are fewer dissenters, however, is over the post-communist character of New

Labour. In a world once torn between, and informed by, capitalism and communism, the post-communist world is one where capitalism rules supreme.

Capitalism versus capitalism

The eclipse of Keynesian social democracy in the West has been matched by the collapse of communism – and its command model of economic development – in the East. The impact of the fall of communism has been felt by the Left worldwide. Post-communism, the Left has debated the relative merits of different models of capitalism, not whether socialist political economy is superior to market capitalist. In Britain, the early days of New Labour saw many look to European, more particularly German, capitalism as offering an attractive model. Indeed, debates on stakeholding reflected this continental European influence. But as time has passed, New Labour has shifted away from Europe and has instead been drawn to North America and Australasia and the Anglo-Saxon model of capitalism. This shift to a more market-orientated and individualistic form of capitalism has been crucial to the emergence of a distinctively *new* Labour.

Old Labour, New Labour and capitalism

Old Labour's interest in public ownership, planning and Keynesianism was, in part, to do with running capitalism more efficiently than the free market. Yet such instruments were also intended to be counterbalances to capitalism. They were intended to further equality and working-class interests, redistributing wealth and income where disparities grew too wide and using capitalism's wealth to help the poor. They were concerned with the pursuit of collective as well as private interests within capitalism. They advocated non-market, universal, common provision of welfare, health and education, free at the point of delivery, based on need not ability to pay and financed by progressive taxation. These socialist principles provided an antidote to the economic individualist and competitive ethos of capitalism. It is this combination of the private and capitalist with the collective and socialist that social democracy held to and which made postwar Britain a *mixed* economy. Labour saw its distinctive role as furthering the socialist elements in this mix.

Under New Labour, however, the collapse of Eastern bloc state socialism and Keynesian social democracy has led to a more fulsome celebration of the liberal market economy. Socialist principles and instruments, even within capitalism, seem, to many, to have lost their viability. The debate is no longer about diluting capitalism with socialist concerns but about running capitalism in the most efficient way: antidotes to capitalism have given way to the form of capitalism which best provides the wealth and flexibility in a condition of globalization. Within this framework, the least well-off have not been given up on: but their well-being is now seen as better delivered by the success of capitalism than its dilution. There is, then, the basis for a new consensus between Left and Right on economics, although important differences in detail remain – for example, the windfall-tax-funded welfare-to-work scheme.

Three capitalisms

The Centre Left, then, is concerned less with capitalism versus socialism and more with what model of capitalism is best. The debate on this issue has been exemplified in books such as Michel Albert's *Capitalism against Capitalism* and Will Hutton's *The State We're In*.[17] Some social democrats advocate the Anglo-Saxon model (Tony Blair's New Labour and Bill Clinton's New Democrats), some the continental European model (the French socialists and German social democrats). All glance nervously at the rapid growth of the East Asian economies. Whose model to follow, what success stories to imitate, which institutions to copy? These are the questions on the lips of politicians and commentators on the Centre Left.

It is usually suggested that there are three versions of capitalism on offer: Japanese (or East Asian), the German (or Rheinland) model, and Anglo-American (or Anglo-Saxon). Japanese capitalism is seen to benefit from attempts to capture gains from cooperation in a competitive environment. Important values are those of trust, continuity, reputation and cooperation. The emphasis is on labour and human capital, and contracts are less market-based than in Europe or North America and based more on cooperative long-term relationships. The financial system involves greater commitment and lower returns. Employees and subcon-

47

tractors are said to be seen to be as important stakeholders in the firm as banks. Banks offer more generous credit and show a keener interest in their firms succeeding than elsewhere. Commitment within the firm is high, wage differentials are lower than in other capitalist economies and companies promise security and protection. Recruitment is tough, high skill levels are demanded and training and retraining are offered. Government plays a big role in building consensus, guidance and leadership. Similar features are said to characterize other East Asian economies – China, South Korea, Thailand, Taiwan, Indonesia, Singapore and Malaysia: community firms, state support, investment and education.[18]

This is a quite different story from Britain and America: too different, most on the Centre Left agree, for Anglo-Americans to be able to borrow very concretely from it. But North European capitalism, while different in many ways, gains from related emphases. In Germany and across the European Union, business and employees are partners and finance is less market-based and so more committed to its investments. In Germany capital–labour partnerships are embodied in co-decision-making at board and works council level. Industrial relations are said to be less adversarial and more geared to cooperation in pursuit of productivity gains and investment. Work is relatively secure and well paid. Banks forgo short-term returns in preference for long-term stable backing and involvement in companies. Government attempts to build consensus in a complex network of unions, employers, regional and national government, regional banks and the Bundesbank. A large medium-sized business sector benefits from long-term committed finance, skilled workers, long-term contracts and cooperation.[19] For Michel Albert and Will Hutton this is the model from which Europeans and North Americans could learn a lot. Albert, however, fears it is a model in decline, being supplanted by the competitive individualism and flexibility of the Anglo-American world.

Between Britain and the USA there are differences but also similarities. The financial system is market-based and requires high returns. Companies have to be flexible and able to shed workers to maintain profits for shareholders. Consequently it is important that unions are weak and employment regulation minimized. Partly because of firm flexibility, unemployment is lower than in the rest of Europe, but job insecurity is greater and inequality and poverty worse. Companies are owned by stockholders trading shares on the stock market, and short-term profits and dividend pay-outs have to be kept high to keep share prices up in case of merger or takeover. Relations with suppliers are heavily market-based. Values are based more on competition, individualism, flexibility and entrepreneurialism than cooperation or commitment. Relationships are more market-based and less committed. Capital–labour relations are adversarial. There is less emphasis on labour and skills and more on the interests of capital. Intra-firm organization is more hierarchical and less consensual.[20]

New Labour and models of capitalism

Of course there are variations within these different models, and not everyone shares this picture from the Centre Left. The Right often has a different account of, for example, the bases of East Asian success or the merits of the Anglo-American model. Furthermore there is some debate about the future of the Japanese and German models and the perception, in some quarters, of convergence around the Anglo-American model.[21] But it is Centre-Left perceptions we are concerned with here. Whatever the most accurate story about the real world, the key concern here is with how New Labour reacts to this debate over capitalisms, how it perceives reality, and how it responds in its economic policy. Within the mainstream of New Labour, the capitalism versus capitalism debate has permeated two major aspects of New Labour's economic rethinking.

First, the capitalisms literature intrudes into Labour's advocacy of a stakeholder approach across its economic, social and constitutional policies. This approach, to which we shall return shortly, suggests that society, and perhaps most specifically companies, should incorporate and include groups and individuals currently excluded from their structures. It is about inclusion, membership and involvement: giving people more of a stake. The unemployed or lone parents should not be left outside society. Companies should be responsive to more than just shareholders: to other stakeholders such as employees, consumers or suppliers. Shareholders themselves should be more committed in their involvement. This stakeholder model seems to owe something to Japan and Germany, where a wider range of groups are seen to have more committed relationships in firms and the economy than is found in Britain. Yet, as we shall discuss shortly, the company stakeholder model faded from New Labour thinking between 1995 and 1997, and Labour has opted for an Anglo-American approach rather than institutional change in a German direction.[22]

Accordingly, the second way in which the capitalisms literature impinges on Labour thinking is in its decision to go with Anglo-Americanism. Blair is seen to be in tune with Bill Clinton, and at loggerheads with some European partners, in his emphasis on the merits of the Anglo-American approach.[23] Despite his stakeholding rhetoric, the response of Blair and his colleagues to the capitalisms debate is to caution against importing institutions from Germany (or Japan): lessons learnt from abroad are one thing, but economic policy must work with the grain of Britain's culture and institutions. This was proposed even in the same speeches where company stakeholding was explored.[24] New Labour's emphasis has been on developing an Anglo-American model, extolling the virtues of flexible labour markets and building welfare around the needs of a flexible workforce, with training and education to deal with job insecurity. In his 'Mais Lecture', for instance, Blair expressed scepticism about foreign models and greater enthusiasm for the virtues of ways of operating from nearer home: 'It is not always possible or desirable to transpose institutions from one country to another. The institutions themselves will to some extent reflect different cultures and traditions.' Furthermore, Blair argues, there are reasons to doubt the superiority of the German model or the undesirability of the Anglo-American one. The USA, he suggests, has an Anglo-American financial structure yet is 'dynamic and strong'. Germany may be orientating to a more Anglo-American model, shifting away from bank finance to deal with demands for pensions from an ageing population. Why switch to the German model, is the implication, when it is switching to yours? The UK's problems, he suggests, predate the development of big institutional shareholders and may have as much to do with poor management as City short-termism. Encouraging longer-term investment is seen as important, but in a way which is in tune with British history and traditions rather than through the importation of foreign models: more through tax incentives and reforms than new institutional structures and through skills, stability and low inflation to give investors the confidence to invest long-term.[25]

So Labour's response to the models of capitalism literature seems to be a good deal more moderate than that of figures such as Will Hutton. Rather than importing models from abroad, or reforming institutional relations in a German-style direction, Blair and New Labour are committed to a more modest version of stakeholding which is distinctively Anglo-American and offers incentives for moderate change within that framework. Capitalism versus capitalism has made Blair reflect on Anglo-Americanism and the alternatives: but while learning from abroad he has decided to stick, in essentials, with what he has got. Many of Blair's speeches extolling the virtues of Britishness may reflect his own sense of patriotism and are intended as a way of mobilizing popular sentiments, social unity and common purpose. But they also reflect his concern to identify and emphasize what he sees as domestic strengths and potential that can be exploited for economic success.[26] We have raised the issue of stakeholding, the concept that was supposed to be Labour's big economic idea. But what exactly is stakeholding and what has it brought to New Labour's economics? Is stakeholding still an influence or has it sunk without trace?

The stakeholder economy

In the early days of Blair's leadership expectations were high. Demands for a big idea to guide Labour thinking and give it coherence were noisy. There were also suggestions, from those more pluralist and postmodern, that big ideas were precisely the wrong thing: singular grand narratives were gone and this was the age for many small ideas. Then in January 1996 Blair made a heavily trailed speech while on tour in Singapore. The speech announced his adherence to 'stakeholder' economics and was followed up by speeches on social policy and constitutional reform, both applying a stakeholding perspective to these areas.[27] Stakeholding was a concept which could offer the big idea for economic policy – giving it direction and something to be organized around. And possibly it could even work further afield, across the range of Labour's rethinking and policy ideas.

> The creation of an economy where we are inventing and producing goods and services of quality needs the engagement of the whole country. It must become a matter of national purpose and national pride. We need to build a relationship of trust not just within the firm but within society. By trust I mean the recognition of a mutual purpose for which we work

together and in which we all benefit. It is a stakeholder economy in which opportunity is available to all, advancement is through merit and from which no group or class is set apart or excluded.[28]

But what does this mean? In the political flak that followed Blair's conversion to stakeholding there were numerous interpretations. For Tory minister Michael Portillo it was what the Tories had already been doing: spreading share ownership, owner occupation and local control of schools, all means of giving people more of a 'stake' in their communities. Fellow Conservatives Michael Heseltine and Prime Minister John Major saw it somewhat differently: as a return to seventies-style corporatism where economic decision-making is done by partnership between government, industry and, worst of all, the trade unions. For Blair's colleagues and supporters, such as Gordon Brown and John Gray, it meant a society in which everyone was included, a one-nation idea about commonality and inclusion. For others on the Left, such as David Marquand and the trade unionist Jack Dromey, it meant corporations being accountable to a wider range of groups than just shareholders – also to employees, the local community and the wider society. And to other commentators it meant any or all of these things, or more.[29]

The idea, in fact, has a long and diverse history. It has been traced back to US settlers staking a claim on 'new' territory and to J. K. Galbraith's 1967 *New Industrial State*; it has been linked with John Kay's 1993 *The Foundations of Corporate Success*, and recent reports such as that of the Dahrendorf Commission and *Tomorrow's Company*, to mention just some examples.[30] In New Labour thinking there are two main forms of stakeholding, both referred to in the quote from Blair's Singapore speech above: corporate stakeholding and individual stakeholding.[31]

The stakeholder company

Corporate stakeholding is about the company having obligations to more than just shareholders, but also to employees, consumers, suppliers and wider communities. Such obligations would be ensured by some form of incorporation of such interests into corporate governance. And it is about these interests, in turn, having obligations to the company – shareholders' relations to companies, in particular, being more committed and long-term than is generally found in Anglo-American capitalism. This version draws to some extent on the German Rheinland model of capitalism and is one that has been advocated by John Kay and Will Hutton in different ways.[32] In the most radical versions some traditional rights of ownership are seen as being shared by owners with wider interests. In this sense stakeholding has things in common with the old socialist idea of the socialization of the company but without the baggage of social ownership with which this is normally associated. It sees the market as being more responsive to the community. It is probably partly because of these old-style socialist connotations that New Labour has drifted away from discussions of company stakeholding.

More radical stakeholders such as Hutton argue for obligatory rather than voluntary corporate stakeholding. Companies, they argue, will not respond to exhortation, especially not where the concept of obligations to a wide variety of stakeholders runs against traditional ideas of property rights as giving owners exclusive and unfettered control over what they own.[33] Hutton suggests that employees and banks could be incorporated into the constitution of the firm, and that there should be works councils with trade unions being seen as social partners. Company information and accounting should be more accessible and transparent. He suggests supervisory boards might monitor the executive board, as in Germany, with core shareholders on the supervisory board in dialogue with management on business strategy. Shareholder commitment should be increased by representation of core institutional shareholders on company and bank boards and voting rights limited to shareholders who are on the board. To encourage long-term investment, share options and bonuses could be exercised only after a minimum period, perhaps ten years' service, and there would be tax incentives for those who exercised options later. Such proposals, alongside reforms to the banking system, takeovers, audit, pension funds and so forth, would ensure that companies were accountable to a wider variety of stakeholders, that shareholders played more of a committed role and that investment was more long-term in outlook.[34]

John Kay's proposals are more liberal than Hutton's but still resort to the law. Kay says he is sceptical about proposals for changes to corporate governance, accountability to shareholders and greater transparency. For Kay, managers need to have autonomy, and democratic norms are not appropriate for the world of business. Instead he proposes a trustee model of ownership with a new Companies Act in which large companies with diffuse share ownership would have to adopt a stakeholder statute setting out corporate objectives and responsibilities. Key obligations to shareholders, employees, suppliers and customers would be institutionalized, as well as responsibilities for stability and security in employment, trading relationships and quality standards. This does not actually put wider stakeholders on company boards. These, Kay argues, should have independent directors and specified rules on consultation and on the role, functions and selection of the chief executive officer.[35]

Tony Blair certainly advocated a version of corporate stakeholding in his Singapore speech:

> Successful companies invest, treat their employees fairly, value them as a resource not just of production but of creative innovation . . . We cannot by legislation guarantee that a company will behave in a way conducive to trust and long term commitment. But it is surely time to assess how we shift the emphasis in corporate ethos – from the company being a mere vehicle for the capital market – to be traded, bought and sold as a commodity, towards a vision of the company as a community or partnership in which each employee has a stake, and where the company's responsibilities are more clearly delineated.[36]

In a number of areas Labour expresses concerns similar to those of Hutton and Kay. A longer-term perspective in industry and investment is called for. The best companies are said to be those who consult with employees and have close and long-term relations with them and with investors and suppliers. Investment in such companies is long-term and incorporates research and training priorities. All this, it is suggested, needs to be more widely encouraged. New Labour has, in the past, stated that its policy is to assess what aspects of corporate governance may require a new Companies Act and what can be pursued through voluntary codes of practice. Yet it is notable that Blair, in the quote above, sees corporate stakeholding as something that cannot be legislated on: ostensibly because changes in business culture cannot be secured by legislation. But it is probably at least as much because legislation would be seen by business and electors as a return to government interference in the running of companies. New Labour is keen, in fact, to stress that many businesses already think of themselves as stakeholder companies on their own initiative. Furthermore Labour is opposed to obligatory corporate stakeholding inasmuch as it involves importing German or Japanese models on to Anglo-American circumstances to which they do not fit.[37]

On the key issue of encouraging long-term commitment and constructive ownership on the part of institutional investors, Labour has considered promoting more constructive investment through requiring pension funds to vote in companies they invest in and institutional shareholders being required to have a code of conduct for voting policy and open voting records. A corporate tax review is intended to look at incentives for long-term investment, such as the reduction in corporation tax announced in Brown's 1997 budget and the CBI's proposal for a two-tier capital gains tax. New Labour's first budget abolished tax credits on pension fund dividends to encourage investment and introduced temporary tax allowances on new investment in small businesses. Drawing on the German experience of supervisory boards, Labour has suggested allowing two-tier boards to be set up in Britain on a voluntary basis and that non-executive directors from a wider range of backgrounds should be encouraged. Employee share-ownership schemes will be examined to encourage employee involvement in firms, and shareholders will be given a legal right to vote on remuneration packages at AGMs.[38]

The individual stakeholder

Stakeholding also has an individual form. This is less specifically about stakeholding in the corporation and more about individuals having a stake in society. It is more fully discussed in Blair's Singapore speech than corporate stakeholding: 'It is a stakeholder economy in which opportunity is available to all, advancement is through merit and from which no group or class is set apart or excluded', Blair argues there.

Individual stakeholding responds to what Blair and Brown and academics such as John Gray and Anthony Giddens see, as we have outlined above, is a world of flexibility and insecurity. As a result of rapid technological change and global competition companies have to be flexible to move with the times and match competitors. Workers no longer have a secure job for life but need to adapt and retrain between many jobs they will hold during their working lives. Rather than fighting this or living in a protectionist industrial world which has long since gone, post-Thatcherite governments should accept this scenario and make the most of it.[39] The main concern must be with balancing flexible labour markets and rapid change on the one hand with inclusion, security and social cohesion on the other.[40] Governments need to help companies adapt to this flexible world and also to find means of dealing with the insecurity and divisions it can cause for workers. Without help, flexibility, insecurity and rapid technological change may lead to the exclusion of workers made unemployed or with out-of-date skills and hence to lack of social cohesion.

This is where the stakeholder perspective comes in. Individual stake-holding involves a one-nation idea about including all individuals in society. Principally it sees particular 'underclass' groups as being excluded from society, especially from employment and the labour market: for example, the young unemployed, the long-term unemployed and lone parents. Many of these lack the skills and training which would make them employable in a changing job market and in fast-growing areas such as hi-technology industries, media, communications and information. In such an environment, individuals require the support of government, not to bail out the losers from change, but to enable individuals, more proactively, to adapt to change. To New Labour, welfare needs to be more orientated to services such as advice, training and childcare to help to get people off benefit into work. This involves a shift in emphasis, as we shall outline in the next chapter, from cash to services and from dependency and exclusion to welfare as employment and inclusion. To New Labour, state-managed full employment is no longer possible (unless redefined as re-employability)[41] but a skills-based approach can lead to more jobs and assist people back into employment during bouts out of the workforce. Individual stakeholding here is about the broadest idea of the government helping individuals to break out of exclusion and regain a stake in society – a one-nation idea about inclusion and social cohesion.[42]

Key policies for individual stakeholding are on education and training and focus on employment as the main method for inclusion. Individual learning accounts, the university for industry and welfare to work, are all intended as services for the incorporation of excluded groups into the workforce. As we shall show in the next chapter, the minimum wage and proposed reforms of the tax and benefits system to make work pay are intended to make it financially worth while for people to get out of the welfare trap and into employment.[43]

Brown argues that these sorts of policies deliver not only social justice but also economic efficiency. Exclusion is a social and economic waste. It leaves many potentially talented people out of the labour force. It is also expensive to keep people on benefits and to deal with the social costs of exclusion – crime, illiteracy, family breakdown and so on. As we have outlined, Brown believes that the information revolution requires a skilled workforce and that capital is attracted to skills. Reskilling and educating workers, therefore, provides for economic productivity as well as social inclusion. 'Education', Tony Blair argues, 'is the best economic policy there is.'[44] Social justice is at the basis of economic efficiency. Here Labour is arguing more than that economic efficiency is compatible with or can be balanced by social justice: that there can be a benign combination of the two. To Labour modernizers, what they define as social justice – the inclusion of the excluded through a skills revolution – is the *basis* for economic efficiency.[45]

All of this bears comparison with the policies of the US Democrats and the approach of US politicians such as Robert Reich, former secretary of state for labor under Clinton. Reich argues in his book *The Work of Nations* that capital is not tied by national boundaries and flows to areas which are skills-rich. Education and training are, therefore, the key to economic success. For him employers should be allowed flexibility (with limitations such as a minimum wage). Employee adaptability should be underpinned by education and skills, technological infrastructure and welfare-to-work policies, all of course very similar to the New Labour approach we have outlined. New Labour has had links with Reich and other like-minded Clinton advisers such as Larry Katz and Deputy Secretary to the Treasury Larry Summers. Welfare to work echoes US workfare policies and has even been proposed in an Americanized 'New Deal' rhetoric by Brown. And proposed changes to Britain's tax and benefits system is firmly based on North American experience (see Chapter 3).[46]

Individual stakeholding is a perspective on welfare and the role of the individual in society which emphasizes equality of opportunity (or 'endowment' equality) and inclusion rather than a more egalitarian distribution of wealth or income in society. As John Gray argues, greater economic equality was one of the defining principles of old social democracy: 'Although many social democratic parties in government were content merely to contain or moderate the economic inequalities thrown up by market capitalism, their ideal remained that of compressing income and wealth inequalities.'[47] But the idea of using progressive taxation to redistribute income to the poor through benefits no longer has a place in Labour's new stakeholding approach. The aim, rather, is to lift excluded groups back into society and increase the degree to which they have the same opportunities as other citizens. Greater equality of opportunities rather than of outcomes is the goal. Labour argue that this is a more extensive idea of equality of opportunity than the usual one: it aims at lifelong learning and reskilling and does not stop at the school-leaving age. Equality of opportunity may sometimes involve greater economic equality insofar as reincorporating groups is likely to make them better off. And it may sometimes be redistributional, where resources for stakeholder inclusion come from the better off – the windfall tax on privatized utilities, for example. But mainly, in the form it takes in New Labour policies, this is a strategy which is not about greater economic equality and redistribution. Its consequences for equality of incomes are likely to be moderate. Insofar as income equality may mildly improve, it would usually not be through redistribution. And the main rationale is, rather, greater equality of opportunities.[48]

Stakeholding assessed

Stakeholding is not an uncontroversial idea. For some it has too many meanings to be at all useful. It can mean different things in different contexts and to different people. Some suggest it is just a soundbite. Others that it merely advocates in a different language what all centre and liberal politicians have long held dear: citizenship and inclusion.[49] Individual stakeholding is criticized by the Left for moving away from socialist economic equality to liberal equality of opportunity. It leaves out economic equality in its own right; and it also fails to see how greater economic equality is required for equality of opportunity to be realized. For the Left, without economic equality Labour discards a precondition for equality of opportunity, and the basis for a politics which distinguishes the party from the Right. Others on the Left suggest that stakeholding focuses too much on employment and the workplace as the route back to inclusion, neglecting other sources of exclusion (racism or lack of democracy, for example) or other means for inclusion (social or political). Or it is too focused on the individual and sounds a bit too much like Mrs Thatcher's idea of a nation of share owners and property owners.[50]

Another set of criticisms of individual stakeholding argue that the supply side and skills cannot alone carry the burden of delivering the economic growth that Labour desires. Education by itself cannot be the economic policy that Blair hopes it can. Policies which create a better skilled workforce, it is argued, cannot tackle unemployment if there is not greater demand to create more jobs. Better training can equip the unemployed better to enter the labour market but will only lead to job queues unless more jobs themselves are made. Labour strategy should also be towards helping companies find new product markets and ensuring long-term committed investment. If demand management is not possible at a national level then it should be pursued at the level of greater supra national coordination.[51] The New Labour answer, of course, is that much of this, the push for exports and investment at least, are part of its strategy and that skills are the basis for competitive success and so can improve growth and create demand for labour. Critics might say British competitiveness is more to do with factors such as proximity to European markets, membership of the EU and low wages. Obstacles have more to do with lack of committed long-term investment. To this, Labour might reply that constructive engagement in Europe and encouragement of long-term investment are among its strategies.

As far as company stakeholding goes, some critics ask how the competing interests of different stakeholders in a company can be ranked and how likely it is that they could reach agreements in decision-making. For the Left, company stakeholding was too quickly dropped in 1997. Or, as we have seen, they feel that stakeholder structures are unlikely to be adopted voluntarily as Labour has suggested – they need legislation. Conversely the Right maintain that legislating for stakeholding is coercive and involves interference in management decision-making. If it is so good, they argue, companies will adopt it voluntarily. Labour has explicitly emphasized voluntarism, arguing that the most successful companies do adopt stakeholding principles out of choice. However, it has in the past proposed a Companies Act which would make it more open to criticisms of coercion if it were to show any *dirigisme*. Some on the Right also suggest that stakeholding is just old-style corporatism in disguise, a criticism not confirmed by the Labour proposals we have outlined. Or it is seen as an attempt to import foreign institutional models inappropriate to Britain. This, the Right say, shows particularly bad judgement when other countries are abandoning their stakeholding models for Britain's Anglo-Americanism. Stakeholding imposes rigidities and constraints on companies when the route of dynamism and economic success, as Europe is beginning to realize, is flexibility. This may be more relevant (if not undermining) to Hutton's proposals (although he argues against transplanting models) but misses the mark as far as Labour's moderate suggestions and explicit disavowal of foreign models go.[52]

Far from its being the mélange of many contradictory ideas ascribed to it, two main meanings of stakeholding seem to emerge in New Labour thinking: company stakeholding and individual stakeholding. These ideas demonstrate vestiges of old social democratic inclinations, for more long-term thinking and investment, more commitment by investors, greater accountability and wider obligations from corporations, plus a concern for the unemployed and excluded. Individuals will not or cannot act alone to remedy these circumstances: the state (or 'community') must intervene. Here equations of Labour with Thatcherism seem overdone, despite similarities in many areas. Yet stakeholding under Blair is in no way Old Labour. In its social democratic inclinations it departs from Thatcherism, yet it is noticeably post-Thatcherite, not wishing to return to Labour before Thatcher. Legal coercion and public ownership are not put forward as instruments for manipulating company decision-making. Nor is Keynesianism or an active macro-economic policy being proposed as the solution for the unemployed. Stakeholding moves away from the Old Labour goal of greater economic equality. While it proposes that individuals act best not alone but collectively (i.e., through government), it is also ultimately about individual opportunities, potential and autonomy: individuals being able to help themselves out of state dependency – the concern in particular of Labour's minister for welfare reform, Frank Field, as we shall see in the next chapter. It emphasizes the obligations that go with rights to help from the state, and accepts flexibility and dynamic global markets as things to be adjusted to rather than counterbalanced. Labour's stakeholding distinguishes it from Thatcherism, but it shows the signs of a party that has moved on to the ground set by eighteen years of Conservative rule.

Beyond Old Left and New Right

Stakeholding, then, betrays social democratic inclinations and shows the marks of Thatcherism. But it also expresses the desire of New Labour to get beyond the economics of Old Labour and the New Right. We have seen how Labour's economics are a response to changed times and different models of capitalism and we shall turn to the details of their policies shortly. But first we need to see how these are also in part a response to the perceived redundancy of Left and Right economics. Blair argues:

> I reject the rampant *laissez-faire* of those who believe government has no role in a productive economy; and I reject too, as out of date and impractical, the recreation or importation of a model of the corporate state popular a generation ago. Today the role of government is not to command but to facilitate, and to do so in partnership with industry in limited but key areas. This is not a matter of ideology but of national interest.[53]

Beyond Old Labour

In the 'Mais Lecture', Blair's most detailed statement of New Labour economics, he argues that Old Labour was too ideologically tied to public ownership and too allied to the public sector and producer interests.[54] It did not make judgements on the role of the public and private sector on sufficiently pragmatic grounds, about what works best in which circumstances. It tried to 'pick winners' in industrial policy, something which is beyond the capacity or role of government. Business is best left to business: the role for government is to assist in providing the optimal conditions for business to operate in. Labour's belief in the powers of Keynesian demand management were, for Blair, over-exaggerated and paid too little attention to the dangers of inflation. Demand management is not possible in a world where capital moves across national boundaries and demand is beyond the control of national governments. Old Labour failed to recognize the importance of supply-side training measures. Capital investment was not good enough. Under Labour and Tories in the postwar period there was too much volatility in economic policy, and inflation was too high to deliver the stable economic background against which businesses can feel confident enough to make long-term investments. Labour's old emphasis on high taxation is not viable: penal tax rates in higher brackets punish and deter success and rates in lower tax bands act as a disincentive to people to get off benefit into work. High public spending is inflationary and puts too much of a burden on income tax: governments should fund spending from within existing budgets rather than hitting taxpayers for more.[55]

Beyond Thatcherism

Thatcherism had alternatives to some of these weaknesses in Old Left economics. Some of the alternatives, argue New Labour Brown and Blair, were sound. The New Right was correct to see that inflation should be kept low and that the supply side is important for growth. The disruptive state of industrial relations needed tackling and Tory trade union legislation was mostly desirable. And Conservative Chancellor Lawson was right to focus on the medium rather than short term in economic decision-making. Yet New Labour does not want to go whole-hog down the road of New Right economics. For them, many aspects of Tory economic policy were flawed. Policy chopped and changed from monetarism between 1979 and 1983, to a mix of monetary and exchange rate targets until 1989, to a fully blown exchange rate regime until 1992 and finally to domestic inflation targets from 1992 onwards. Volatile shifts from boom to recession were the consequence of Tory policies. Such instability and unpredictability are damaging because they make businesses reluctant to invest. Political considerations played too much of a part in interest rate decisions and tax cuts which were not always economically the best thing to do at the time. Monetary and fiscal policy were not coordinated enough, tax-cutting combining with high interest rates which then had to be raised higher to slow growth and curb inflation. The Tories failed to keep macro-economic policy in a shape which would underpin micro-policy and the supply side: inflation was treated as something separate from investment, output and employment.

For New Labour, there is no turning back to the pre-Thatcher days of demand management, high inflation and stop–go policies, of public–private ideological divides, and turbulent industrial relations. Yet while New Labour's economic policy has marked important continuities with Conservative macro-economic policy (although the new Labour government argues that it will foster greater long-term thinking into its anti-inflationary policies), its approach to the economy is also to break with what it perceives as its weaknesses: New Labour is in this sense post-Thatcherite. For New Labour in particular, the supply side of the economy requires the active support of government to secure employment and social inclusion.

New Labour's new economics

Macro-economic policy

Monetary policy is dictated by the belief that in a globalized world governments have to retain investors' confidence or capital will simply flow out of the country. Expansionary economics out of tune with other European countries is not viable. Tax rates and inflation have to be kept competitive with those of other countries.[56] This is one basis for Labour's arguments against increasing income tax and for keeping inflation low. Gordon Brown made great show of the fact that the cut in corporation tax announced in his 1997 budget put the rate in Britain lower than that in main competitor economies. The key point is to maintain stability and confidence to encourage business to invest. Within this framework government can try to attack the supply side to deal with economic and social problems. Thus on taking office in 1997 Labour adopted a 2.5 per cent inflation target (with leeway for half a percent movement in either direction) to provide the bases for growth, employment and living standards. To take decision-making on this matter away from short-term political considerations, the Bank of England was given operational responsibility for setting interest rates. The overall aim is to increase business confidence in the stability of monetary policy.

On fiscal policy, Labour's approach is marked by prudency. It has adopted the 'golden rule' that public borrowing will be used to finance only investment and not consumption; and that the budget should balance over the economic cycle. New Labour has broken with an ideological approach to tax and spending. Labour modernizers argue that they do not have an ideological commitment to increase spending and taxation or to decrease them, as Labour and the Right have had respectively in the past. The aim is to pursue investment and economic growth and to tailor tax and spending to these objectives and the overall state of the economy, rather than set them up as ideological objectives in themselves. Spending, as a general rule, has to be financed by finding money within existing allocations rather than through higher income tax. Tax rises or clawbacks will be made elsewhere: the windfall tax and attacking tax breaks on health insurance, pension fund dividends and house-buying, for example. Hence Labour's policy to stick to Conservative spending limits for the first two years of government after 1997 and their financing of extra education and health spending through use of the contingency fund, spare money from the windfall tax and reallocation of lottery and defence department money. Labour aims to raise money by closing off tax avoidance and loopholes. Particular sorts of spending, for example on investment and education, are to be prioritized over other forms which are not productive, for instance social security. Spending on education, in fact, is to be increased in the future by savings on social security produced by welfare to work.

Labour's approach to macro-economics incorporates the aim to take a leading role in European integration, pledged to completion of the single market and signed up to the social chapter. On the single currency Labour proposes genuine convergence and participation at the right time dependent on a 'yes' vote in a referendum. Their stated approach is to be more constructive than the Conservatives were, yet still with an emphasis on protecting British interests. In 1975 many in the party voted against Britain's membership in the EEC and some of the most prominent pro-Europeans left in the early 1980s to form the SDP. The 1983 manifesto included a commitment to withdrawal from the EEC. Under Blair's leadership, Labour's European policy has continued a pro-European direction established under Kinnock and Smith, prompted for them in part by the social agenda put forward by Jacques Delors, president of the commission in the 1980s, and by the EC's policies on regional development and industrial restructuring. But New Labour's European policy has hardened. Under Blair, Labour has openly declared for the Anglo-American model. In 1995 economic policy documents there was a residual sign of a more interventionist view on Europe. Labour emphasized its commitment to an active industrial policy in transport, telecommunications, training, research and development and the use of structural funds to assist economic change. Labour was keen that membership of the single currency should be based on 'real' convergence criteria such as growth and employment, not just monetary targets. Labour's policy in 1995 was to support a much broader definition of the social chapter and to emphasize the importance of cooperation among the 'social partners'. But by 1997 Blair and Brown were stressing the need for the EU to follow the flexible labour market route and welfare reform. Labour was arguing for toughness on the enforcement of single market competition regulations. Any labour market regulations, including in the social chapter, must pass three tests, Brown argued: 'Did they increase productivity, did they increase employment opportunity and did they increase labour market flexibility?'[57] The 1997 manifesto stated that participation in the social chapter would be used to promote employability and flexibility, not high social costs. Once in government, Labour came under pressure, just as the Conservatives had before, on the issue of membership of the European single currency, set to start in 1999. In a statement in October 1997, Chancellor Brown announced that Britain would not join until after the next general election but that, if after that election it was in Britain's interest to join — if the British economy was in step with the rest of Europe, if monetary union was flexible enough to cope with economic change and if the single currency would have a positive impact on British investment, jobs and the City of London — then the British government would join. Brown's statement signalled that the new Labour government had no objection on principle to membership of the single currency and to economic and monetary union.

Some of Labour's macro-economics, like its micro-economics, echo the policies of the American Democrats. Gordon Brown's emphasis on a five-year deficit reduction programme has more than shades of Clintonomics: the latter are linked to lower interest rates, low inflation and increased investment in the USA, objectives Brown is keen to achieve. Operational independence for the Bank of England and tougher regulation of the City are said to be influenced by Brown's observations of the US Federal Reserve and the Securities and Exchange Commission.[58]

It is possible to see the break with demand management, interventionism and anti-privatization in Labour's new approach. But it is less easy to see any significant differences, at either an ideological or a policy level, from the previous Tory administration's macro-economic approach. Of course some Labour policies are too *dirigiste* for the Tories, interfering with the rights of business to make profits and use them as they wish: the windfall tax and the abolition of tax credit on pension fund dividends, for example. But key differences are of detail, tone and competence rather than principle. Tough inflation, prudent fiscal and monetary policy, low taxes and low public spending were all policies of the outgoing Tory administration as well as of Blair's Labour. Labour's approach to Europe is to be more constructive than the Conservatives yet also stresses the priority of Britain's national interests in European negotiations. Labour has often questioned the Conservatives' economics on grounds of competence rather than ideology.

Left critics of Labour's macro-economic approach argue, of course, that Labour handcuffed itself too much in ruling out income tax rises for five years in its 1997 manifesto: tax rises may be needed to cool down growth, prevent an overheated economy slipping into recession, and meet funding needs in education and health. Tax and spend is more desirable than the gradual privatization of these spheres. Given the extent of Labour's landslide in 1997, critics argue, the party could still have got elected if they had proposed at least a small tax rise for the very top earners, or had left their options on taxation policy open a little more. Labour, it is argued, even further undermined its already diminished manoeuvrability by handing interest rates over to the Bank of England. For other critics, Labour underestimates the role that moderate stimuli to demand can provide to supplement supply-side measures, by themselves insufficient for major job creation. Others argue that government's ability to ensure stability is limited. Furthermore, they say, there is not even a factually robust case for the argument that greater stability is the basis for growth. German and Japanese success was not built on the bases of stable economies.[59]

Public and private

Labour has not only broken the Old Labour mould in its approach to macro-economics. It also aims to get away from allegiances of the Old Left to the public sector, nationalization and government intervention and of the New Right to the private sector, privatization and deregulation. Labour styles itself as a practical party of the Centre Left or radical centre that goes beyond the public–private dogmas of Old Left and New Right. For Tony Blair the point is to make decisions on pragmatic grounds about what works best rather than on the basis of ideology. And public–

private partnership rather than public *or* private is what is to be pursued.

Public ownership played a repeated part in Labour ideology and policy in the past as we outlined above. In the late 1980s the party began to move away from pledges on nationalization. However, it was under Tony Blair that the break with public ownership as an ideological article of faith was made. After much discussion over details, Blair managed in 1995 to replace Clause 4 of the party constitution which dedicated the party to 'common ownership of the means of production, distribution and exchange'. The new Clause 4 committed the party to 'common endeavour' in pursuit of the realization of individual potential, to 'the enterprise of the market and the rigour of competition' balanced with cooperation, and to roles for both private and public sectors. Power, wealth and opportunity should, it states, be 'in the hands of the many not the few'; social justice is defined as being about help for the insecure and poor and about equality of opportunity. The balancing of various traditional opposites, such as rights and obligations, freedom and solidarity, is outlined.[60] For modernizers this rid the party of an irrelevant and outdated commitment inappropriate to the modern age. For the Left it rid Labour of what made it socialist and different from other parties and replaced it with something they could all agree on. Ted Benton, for example, argues that, 'In the end, what is definitive of socialism is not so much its value-commitments (these are almost universally shared), as its diagnosis that they cannot be realised in an economic system governed by market forces and the rate of profit.'[61] With Clause 4's shift from antipathy to capitalism to its embrace, what makes Labour different from other parties has disappeared. Either way the commitment to public ownership as an ideological principle had gone. The Tories were portrayed as the party remaining tied to ideological dogma on this issue. From now on decisions about privatization or public ownership should be made on practical not ideological grounds. In practice New Labour showed no interest in nationalization or renationalization: if anything the bias was towards bringing private business into the public sector.

There are a number of areas in which Labour suggests pursuit of public–private partnerships. Before the 1997 election Tony Blair and colleagues held numerous meetings and receptions with business people – the so-called prawn cocktail offensive – to ram home the seriousness of their commitment to working in partnership with business and securing their support. Labour policy is to appoint people from business into government – Lord Simon, the former BP chairman, turned trade minister for example, and working peers such as David Sainsbury, head of the retail chain bearing his name. Appointing figures from business as overseas ambassadors has been one way considered for promoting exports. Tony Blair scored a dramatic coup in his 1995 Labour Party conference speech demonstrating his concrete commitment to public–private partnerships by announcing the agreement with British Telecom on wiring up schools and hospitals to the internet. Public–private partnerships, through the private finance initiative, have been made to build a number of new hospitals. Hospital building is to be financed by private sector consortiums and the hospitals will then be leased back to NHS trusts.

Producers and consumers

Treasury minister Alistair Darling argues that, when choosing which system works best, public or private, 'we should be concerned first and foremost about the consumers',[62] an angle that is reflected widely in Labour policy discussions. Very often it is business efficiency and consumer interests that are the main concern of policy rethinking: employee interests appear less often – remarkable for a party formed out of organized labour and with long-running links with trade unions. Much emphasis is given to getting the unemployed on to the labour market. The minimum wage and social chapter are important for employees, but the role of the former is at least as much to make employment viable for the unemployed while the latter, when Labour signed up to it, contained only minimal directives on works councils and unpaid parental leave. Employee interests *in* employment form an area little discussed by Labour. The baton has been passed from producer to consumer interests.

This is reflected in Labour's interests in competition policy. Labour has had competition policies in the past, but never embraced so fulsomely as under New Labour, with a shift in emphasis from producer to consumer interests and accompanied by a move away from nationalization and industrial policy.[63] Labour's aim has been to take a prohibitive approach to competition policy so that anti-competitive or restrictive practices are outlawed from the start rather than challenged after they have happened. Competition authorities are to be streamlined and made more effective, for example by the amalgamation of the Monopolies and

Mergers Commission with the Office of Fair Trading and the creation of a unitary Competition and Consumer Standards Office. A wider definition of the public interest is proposed where mergers are considered by the competition authorities. Labour suggests shifting the burden of proof to the bidding company to show that merger would be in the public interest. In the financial sector consumer interests, harmed in the past by poor advice in areas such as personal pensions and endowment mortgages, should be more firmly protected by consolidation of financial regulation under a single regulatory authority. It has been proposed that the privatized utilities should be made more responsive to consumers through regulation and price-capping linked partly to profits so that excess profits are shared out between the utility and customers.

The increasing emphasis on partnerships between government and the private sector and on consumer rather than producer interests has been accompanied by a decreasing allegiance by Labour to links with the unions. Labour has transformed the role of trade unions in party decision-making, through one member one vote and reduction of the union vote at the party conference. Tory industrial relations legislation on strike ballots, union elections and picketing are to be kept on by Labour. Tony Blair has said that trade unions are one among many interest groups in society who will be treated with fairness but not favours.[64] This amounts to an ideological break with the past when Labour was perceived by itself and others as having a special relationship with the trade unions. The party was founded as the political wing of the organized working class, and continued as the party with the biggest working-class vote and a particular concern with union and employee interests. Labour had strong funding links with the unions, who cast a big vote and had their views much attended to in policy-making. Partnership now means not corporatist links with trade unions but cooperation with business. In 1997, if Labour had friends and a special relationship, it was at least as much with sections of the business community as with the unions.

Micro-economics and the supply side

Monetary and fiscal policy at the macro level, outlined above, is intended to secure the bases of stability and confidence for reforms at the micro level. Here Labour's employment strategy focuses on supply-side reforms rather than on demand management, as in the past. Labour is keen to stress that factors such as technology, investment, human capital and infrastructure should not be treated as exogenous to growth and policies on growth but as part of them. Gordon Brown emphasized this in a speech obviously not checked by spin-doctors for adherence to soundbite stipulations. Here he stressed the importance for Labour's economics of 'neo-classical endogenous growth theory'. Factors such as those just mentioned, he suggested, should not be seen as outside the analysis and politics of growth but as intrinsic to them. They are not just given but can be affected by active government intervention. In this vein Labour argues that micro- supply-side reforms are essential to economic growth and not something that should be treated as separate or best left to the market. Brown's speech on endogenous growth was written by his advisor Ed Balls. 'It's not Brown's it's Balls'', proclaimed Tory minister Michael Heseltine at the Conservative conference that year![65]

Deregulation on the supply side, for New Labour, then, is not good enough. Allowing firms to be flexible is certainly important for dynamism and innovation. But Britain cannot compete on low labour costs with less developed countries, and companies by themselves will not build the skills base for British economic success. Government has to play a role through engineering public–private partnerships on education and training which can get the unemployed back into the labour market and build the skills base for economic success, especially in new technology. The key aims and policies at the micro- supply-side level are, therefore, as have been discussed, on: education and training in a flexible labour market; encouragement of new technology; longer-term investment; policies on welfare to work; promotion of small and medium-sized businesses; and improving infrastructure, for example in transport. Crucial to solving problems at this level are a stable and low-inflationary macro-economic framework which can maintain the confidence of business and investors to invest and enter into partnerships.

Transport and the environment

Labour has committed itself to a more integrated public transport system and less use of private cars. In 1997 Deputy Prime Minister John

Prescott took on a combined department covering transport and the environment, in order to realize Labour's transport objectives in tandem with environmental aims, and environmental concern is enshrined in the new Clause 4. When it came to power, transport was one of the areas where Labour's proposals were least concretely developed. But Labour did argue for higher investment in rail, stronger enforcement of train operators' service commitments, tougher regulation and a new rail authority to combine functions currently carried out by disparate agencies and to provide greater coordination, and it suggested a new orbital rail route for London to take traffic off the roads. Labour's manifesto proposals on road transport were even less concrete than for rail: consideration for the needs of all forms of road vehicles, strong bus regulation, encouragement of bus lanes and park and ride schemes, safer cycling and walking provision, reduced vehicle excise duty for lower emission cars, a review of the roads programme, and suggestions for taxes on road space and company car parking.[66]

Labour aims to have a cross-departmental approach to environmental protection, backed up by a parliamentary environmental audit committee. It is pledged to reducing carbon dioxide emissions by 20 per cent by 2010, a far more radical goal than that of previous governments or the EU. It promises to promote cleaner, more efficient energy use and development of renewable energy sources. Programmes for home energy efficiency, such as insulation, are linked to an under 25s environmental task force for the unemployed, funded by the windfall tax. Labour aims to promote environmental technology industries, creating jobs here as well as in the energy efficiency programme. Labour announced a new food regulation agency, greater sensitivity to the needs of rural areas and, in some tension with this, a free vote in the House of Commons on hunting with hounds.[67]

On both transport and the environment, Labour came into criticism soon after taking office. A number of road building projects with environmental implications which Labour had condemned were approved. John Prescott vowed not to undermine the central part of the car in transport policy and made his commitment the very weak one of reducing two-car ownership by the end of Labour's first term of office. Greens criticized Labour for cutting VAT on fuel, a decision where social priorities overruled environmental ones. A former Labour environmental adviser argues that Labour's carbon dioxide emissions target has been watered down to be dependent on international steps rather than unilateral. Greenpeace is concerned that Labour's commitment to clean-coal power stations contradicts its pledge to reduce carbon dioxide emissions. Hoped-for green tax rises, for example on petrol, diesel and company cars, did not materialize in Labour's first budget. Without green taxes, with VAT on fuel reduced and without the balancing of differentials between higher taxes on energy conservation than energy consumption, as floated in opposition, many question how the carbon dioxide emissions targets can be met.[68]

A post-Thatcherite economics

The substance of New Labour's economic policies gives the lie to the view that under Blair Labour has become a party devoid of ideas or policies. The new policies tie in with careful thought by Labour's leaders about perceived social, economic and political changes: globalization, the information age, flexibility and insecurity – changes around which rethinking and new policies are orientated. In rethinking its economics, Labour has drawn on debates about different models of capitalism and ideas from the literature on communitarianism and stakeholding. Furthermore, as we shall see in the next two chapters, ideas such as supply-side economics and stakeholding interplay across the field of Labour policies well beyond the economy and industry.

What we have outlined also does not say much for the arguments of those, whether Conservatives or supporters of Blair, who argue that Labour is true to what it always was, whether in means, ends or both. Such a perspective shows a startlingly short political memory. Gone are Keynesian demand management, nationalization, planning, tax-and-spend policies and industrial policy as interventionist as it was in the past. Few would have predicted in the 1970s, or even 1980s, a Labour Party quite so committed to prudent economics, low inflation and stability to secure the confidence of investors. Or a party who attacked the Tories for inflationary policies and tax rises and celebrated its own confidence in cutting business taxes, mobilizing the enthusiasm of the private sector and keeping the unions at arm's length. Such notions are far distant from what Labour stood for pre-Blair. Gone, as well as means, are ends which are economically redistributional or egalitarian: in fact gone, in the explicitly stated words of Gordon Brown himself, is the Old Labour belief in greater equality in outcomes secured through changes to progressive income tax or public ownership.

Those who see New Labour as aping the Tories on economic policy have a little more to back up their arguments. On macro-economic policy, the defeated Major government and Labour under Chancellor Brown look remarkably consistent. On the fundamentals, New Labour has accepted that Old Labour was wrong and Mrs Thatcher was right, and it has moved on to Tory economic ground. It is on details, the competence and unity of the government, and the freshness and imagination of ministers to carry out what they promise, that Labour is confident that it is different. Labour's stress on community, inclusion and the interests of the many and not just the few sets a different tone to that of the Conservatives. These are reflected in new policies on welfare to work, the minimum wage (and the EU social chapter) and education and training which both mark a break with the Conservative years and which demonstrate serious thinking on long-term unemployment – and, as we shall turn to now, welfare reform.

3

Welfare and Social Policy

Fifty years on

Fifty years after the election of the first postwar Labour government, Tony Blair spoke of its welfare achievements: the creation of the National Health Service; the implementation of Beveridge's National Insurance scheme; and the commitment to full employment. The Attlee administration, Blair said, was 'the greatest peacetime government this century'. But, the Labour leader continued, times had changed: 'We need a new settlement on welfare for a new age, where opportunity and responsibility go together.' The message was clear: the world had moved on since 1945; and Labour, Blair argued, must move onto new political territory. The party's new social policies, he said, 'should and will cross the old boundaries between left and right, progressive and conservative.'[1]

As with Labour's economics, Blair was pushing at an open door. By the late 1980s, during the party's internal Policy Review, Labour's commitment to high tax-and-spend social policies came under threat. They were perceived by the modernizers in the party as an electoral liability, especially to middle-class voters in southern Britain. In the run-up to the 1992 general election, Neil Kinnock and John Smith – leader of the opposition and shadow chancellor respectively – endlessly repeated the mantra that a Labour government could only spend what it earned – a foretaste of Blair and Gordon Brown's strategy during the 1997 campaign. Once leader of the opposition, Blair promised that New Labour would 'think the unthinkable' on welfare. As shadow home

secretary, Blair had already s
his famous soundbite 'toug
As party leader he enthus
Commission on Social J
which called for a radica
Chris Smith, then shad
with thinking unthink
vately funded safety r
portedly drawn to ic
social security.[3]

not a sign of success.[4]
Labour made a virtue
education and soc
achieved without
higher taxes. S
On this, Lab
gued that b
come o
Brow
part
lo

During the 1997 election campaign Brown
government would for two years stick to the Conservativ
as set out in Chancellor Kenneth Clarke's last budget. Labour also
mitted itself to not increasing income taxes during a first term of office.
In simple terms, Labour's social policy plans would not involve any new
money (certainly not from higher income tax rates), except for the much
talked about 'windfall tax' on the privatized utilities, which would pay
for the welfare-to-work programme. In health, education and social security, extra funding would come from 'efficiency savings' and from the
phasing out of Conservative programmes; or from money sitting in local
authority bank accounts, as in the case of housing (which would, in fact,
raise public expenditure); or from the fruits of economic revival and
shrinking dole queues.

This strategy was partly a shrewd political move to avoid damaging
Conservative attacks during the run-up to polling day. In 1992 the
Tories had labelled John Smith's shadow budget 'Labour's tax bomb-
shell'. Despite its cautious public spending commitments, Labour went
into that election promising to raise pensions and child benefit levels.
These would be funded from increases to the top rate of tax and to middle income national insurance levels. In 1997 Labour made a virtue out
of what many in the party thought a political imperative. As Chris Smith
had suggested in May 1996: 'There are some who argue that the best
test of how progressive a welfare policy is, is the amount of money that is
spent on it. I disagree. High social security spending is a sign of failure,

the run-up to the general election a year on,
out of *not* arguing for extra funding for health,
al security. Reform of the welfare state could be
significant increases in public expenditure – and thus
rvices and standards could be improved in other ways.
ur parted company with the Liberal Democrats, who ar-
igher standards of welfare needed extra resources which could
ly from higher taxes. During the election campaign Blair and
went out of their way to bury Labour's image as a tax-and-spend
y. As Labour's manifesto put it: 'The level of public spending is no
nger the best measure of the effectiveness of government action in the
public interest. It is what money is actually spent on that counts more
than how much money is spent . . . New Labour will be wise spenders,
not big spenders.'

Once in government, Brown's first budget brought cheers from the
Labour benches as the 'iron chancellor' found extra resources for health
and education. But this extra cash came from the Treasury's rainy day
fund, the contingency reserve, and from the windfall tax, not from higher
taxes in other areas. The new Labour government was determined to
keep its tax pledges made in opposition.

'Flexibility plus'

Taking its cue from the Commission on Social Justice, social policy has,
as we saw in the last chapter, become the supply-side elixir which New
Labour believes will create more jobs by boosting long-term economic
growth rates. A better educated and better trained workforce, supported
by a social security system which helps the unemployed back into work,
is seen by Labour modernizers as the route not just to social justice but
to economic success as well. For New Labour, welfare, rather than im-
peding growth and individual initiative, as the New Right argues, can
actually be supportive of the market economy. British business and British workers, in the face of a global economy, need to be flexible; and they
can only be flexible, Labour argues, by being skilled: 'flexibility-plus' in
New Labour-speak. This means that people must be educated and trained
for an economy which needs knowledgeable and skilled workers who
can move from task to task, from job to job, and who will help attract

international investors to Britain. Any other form of flexibility, Labour claims, is just a synonym for low wages and job insecurity.

In the following pages we shall set out the approach taken by past Labour governments and thinkers to social policy, before assessing in detail the changes made under Tony Blair.

Old Labour and the welfare state

Social policy has been at the heart of Labour and social democratic politics since the war. The collective and universal provision of welfare services – in health, housing, education and social security – would guard against poverty, promote equality and underpin citizenship and social cohesion. Labour's social democrats believed that welfare should be provided by the state, paid for out of taxation and administered as a public service.

Much, but not all, of what we now call the welfare state was established under the Attlee administration: the National Health Service, the National Insurance and the National Assistance schemes, council housing, local authority children's departments and, underpinning it all, the commitment to full employment. The welfare state was the 1945 Labour government's 'most significant achievement'.[5] To be sure, Labour's postwar social policy built on the Liberal government's social security reforms before the First World War, the extension of these by the National government in the 1930s and the work of the wartime coalition in areas such as education. The New Jerusalem – in social security, health, education and housing – was built on the foundations of nearly half a century of piecemeal social reform.

Capitalism, socialism and the welfare state

Social policy in Britain, academically and politically, was shaped by two distinct, though overlapping, bodies of thought: Fabian socialism and New (or Social) Liberalism. Both have cast their shadows over the politics of welfare – first as saviours, then as villains. From the turn of the century, the Fabians and the New Liberals argued for active government against the nineteenth-century nightwatchmen state. The Fabians, led by Sidney and Beatrice Webb, and the New Liberals, such as Leonard Hobhouse, John Maynard Keynes and William Beveridge, believed that gradual social reform could take place within the boundaries of capitalism. Indeed, they argued that such social reform was necessary if capitalism was not to collapse into revolution as poverty, inequality and social degradation undermined the legitimacy of the social order. The Fabians and the New Liberals shared the view that free market capitalism was unstable, and that if left unchecked would create unacceptable social consequences, witnessed by the mass unemployment during the Great Depression of the 1930s. The amelioration of social conditions by government lay then at the heart of the Fabian tradition and the New Liberal challenge to *laissez-faire*.

There were of course differences of opinion on the ultimate goal: the Fabians believed that welfare reform would pave the way to a socialist society; the New Liberals (and many like-minded Conservatives) that social reform formed the basis for a middle way between socialism and *laissez-faire* capitalism. There were also marked differences on the detail of social policy: for example, on the balance of public, private and voluntary provision; on the relative merits of insurance schemes; and on the level and conditions of social benefits. But these reformers did agree that the state should take a leading role in providing welfare on a comprehensive and collective basis.

This consensus on welfare reform before, during and after the Second World War – and spanning politically all three major parties – was, as Pete Alcock writes, 'as much a matter of compromise as a meeting of minds'. Broad areas of agreement could never mask real differences of opinion on particular policies. The consensus that did exist, Alcock continues, 'was predicated upon the assumption that the state welfare reforms would support, and not prejudice, wider economic growth.'[6] By the 1970s many on the Marxist Left were arguing that the postwar welfare state had done little to advance the cause of socialism: that it was simply a means to cover the social costs of capitalism and a way to pacify and placate the working class. Whatever the merits of such claims, and whether or not the postwar social policy consensus assumed that the welfare state would support rather than prejudice economic growth, those Labour architects of the New Jerusalem believed that the welfare state was a little bit of socialism at the heart of capitalism. As the representatives of the working class, they believed that business must accept the need for comprehensive social reform – or face the threat of revolution from more radical elements on the Left. The welfare state, they thought, was built on values (need, not ability to pay) and a structure (collective rather than individual provision) which embodied an alternative way of living to that offered by free market capitalism. The welfare state would allocate resources not on the basis of property rights but on the rights of all citizens to share in the wealth of society on the basis of need. And the collective, universal and redistributive nature of welfare would, in R. H. Tawney's terms, remoralize the acquisitive capitalist society by promoting the common values of cooperation, social purpose and public service.

Citizenship and equality

The creation, then, of the welfare state stands out in Labour politics as a defining moment: when need rather than ability to pay determined access to welfare to all citizens. Since 1945, in manifesto after manifesto, Labour has been the champion of an expansive social policy: for an extension of the scope and provision of the welfare state. The provision of welfare on a universal basis was seen by postwar social democrats as the mark of citizenship in a modern society. The intellectual rationale for such claims was provided by T. H. Marshall. In *Citizenship and Social Class*, published in 1950, Marshall argued the welfare state entrenched social rights, thereby completing the development of modern citizenship begun in the seventeenth and eighteenth centuries with creation of civil rights before the law, and extended into the political sphere in the nineteenth century with voting reform. Marshall believed strongly that the eradication of poverty required a form of 'welfare capitalism'. State collective welfare services, supportive of social rights and egalitarian in outcome, should not for Marshall undermine competitive markets but should be their counterbalance. Marshall's view is thus supportive of a social policy middle way. He differed from other postwar social democratic welfare thinkers such as Richard Titmuss, who believed that the values of the market should be subordinate to those of the welfare state.

Certainly to the leading Labour revisionist of the postwar period, Tony Crosland, welfare was more than just a pragmatic set of middle way policies to support market capitalism. Within the parameters of the mixed economy and liberal democracy, he saw the welfare state as the means not just to relieve hardship and correct social need but to deliver greater social and economic equality to society. Crosland's brand of social democratic revisionism rested on the separation of means and ends. Socialist ends such as equality, Crosland argued, need not, in a much changed world, rest principally on the old socialist means of public or common ownership of property. For Crosland, Keynesian macro-economics and the mixed economy would provide the leverage over private enterprise which was both economically and socially desirable. They would, in particular, create the stable economic growth which would pay for a large state welfare system and provide full employment. But the welfare state for Crosland was not simply about doing those things that private enterprise failed to do – so-called public goods. The welfare state would act as a mechanism to deliver the socialist values of equality and social justice.

Let us examine this proposition further as it bears directly on the changes made under New Labour. In thinking about social democracy and social policy we can, as Crosland did, distinguish between ends and means; and it is worth spelling out clearly what postwar social democrats such as Crosland thought of each. Simply put: what was social policy meant to deliver (the ends)? And who or what was going to do the delivering (the means)? The simple answer was: equality and the state. But what kind of equality and what form of state provision?

Equality has two senses: meritocracy, or equality of opportunity; and egalitarianism, or equality of outcome. Crosland's view of equality is by no means straightforward. He certainly went beyond equality as simply meaning meritocracy. In fact, many postwar social democrats, such as Michael Young in his 1958 satire *The Rise of Meritocracy*, were scathing of equality of opportunity. Crosland stated that 'equality of opportunity is not enough': 'under certain circumstances the creation of equal opportunities may merely serve to replace one remote elite (based on lineage) by a new one (based on ability and intelligence).' Such an 'aristocracy of talent', Crosland argued, would be a great improvement but would not, he believed, be socially just. Equality of opportunity, Crosland concluded, should 'be combined with measures, above all in the educational field, to equalise the distribution of rewards and privileges so as to diminish the degree of class stratification, the injustice of large inequalities, and the collective discontents which come from too great a dispersion of rewards.'[7]

But Crosland was not an egalitarian in the rather narrow sense of meaning that everyone should have the same income and wealth. In an age when Keynesian economics promised economic growth and full employment – as Macmillan put it, 'most of our people have never had it so good' – Crosland believed that higher incomes would give rise to a pattern of consumption which was more equal: the law of diminishing marginal utility would see to that. But Crosland also argued that: 'the present distribution of wealth in Britain is flagrantly unjust'; and that: 'the possession of great differential wealth confers an enormous social advantage.' So, for Crosland: 'the distribution of this advantage is a matter of social concern.'[8] Crosland considered inequalities of wealth unjust where they were related to property, especially inherited, and not to work; to opportunity rather than ability; and to distortions in the tax system. He conceded that, on grounds of economic efficiency, using direct taxes to redistribute earned income further than it did already at the time was unfeasible, however much he himself thought that the then distribution of income was unjust. Rather, he thought that some of the advantages of property could be socialized, much of it through collective welfare provision: by redistributing property via the tax system to the public sector. So Crosland advocated a series of tax reforms on property (death duties, property taxes, capital gains taxes and inheritance taxes) to help pay for social provision. As to how much equality, it might be better to leave it to Crosland himself:

> I feel clear that we need large egalitarian changes in our education system, the distribution of property, the distribution of resources in periods of need, social manners and style of life, and the location of power within industry; and perhaps some, but certainly a smaller, change in respect of incomes from work. I think that these changes, taken together, will amount to a considerable social revolution.
>
> On the other hand, I am sure that a definite limit exists to the degree of equality which is desirable. We do not want complete equality of incomes, since extra responsibility and exceptional talent require and deserve a differential reward. We are not hostile, as our opponents sometimes foolishly suggest, to 'detached residences in Bournemouth where some elderly woman has obviously more than a thousand a year'. I do not myself want to see *all* private education disappear: nor the Prime Minister denied an official car, as in one Scandinavian country: nor the Queen riding a bicycle: nor the House of Lords instantly abolished: nor the manufacture of Rolls-Royces banned: nor the Brigade of Guards, nor Oxford and Cam-

bridge, nor Boodle's, nor (more doubtfully) the Royal Yacht Squadron, nor even, on a rather lower level, the Milroy Room, lose their present distinctive character: nor anything so dull and colourless as this.

But where en route, before we reach some drab extreme, we shall wish to stop, I have no idea.[9]

For Crosland, then, Keynesian-managed economic growth and taxation on wealth and property would provide the finance for a welfare state which would create more equal opportunities as well as produce more egalitarian outcomes. There is in Crosland's thinking a strong desire that public policy should be concerned both with life's starting lines (equality of opportunity) and with its finishing posts (equality of outcome).[10] Whether this remains the case to the same degree in contemporary New Labour thinking is doubtful. Moreover, Crosland, as a public servant, had little interest in making judgements on how people lived their lives – although he made it fairly clear that he would prefer it if everyone, like himself, went out and had a good time! He simply wanted society to be a richer and more equal place. He was, to use David Marquand's terms, a 'hedonistic collectivist': he was happy to use the power of the state to bring about social justice, but morally neutral about individual behaviour. This contrasted with the more austere, 'moralistic collectivism' of the first postwar Labour government, and certainly contrasts with the new wave of moralistic collectivism under New Labour – Roundheads to Crosland's Cavaliers. The moral relativism of Crosland's generation of social democrats was, moreover, infused with doubts over the claims society might make on the individual. As Marquand suggests:

> The notions that rights should be balanced by duties, that activity was better than dependence and the point of collective provision was to foster self-reliance and civic activism came to be seen as patronising, or elitist, or (horror of horrors) 'judgemental' . . . Among left-of-centre Keynesian social democrats, equality came to be seen as a good in itself, irrespective of the uses to which the fruits of egalitarian policies were put.[11]

The point of contrast with today's revisionists is clear. New Labour is concerned both with how people behave and with the opportunities they may have. It also makes plain that it believes that society – 'the community' – can make meaningful claims on the duties and obligations individuals owe it.

Social democracy in action

In Harold Wilson's 1964 government, Crosland was education minister. In a decade when equality and technology went together, Crosland's belief that spending money on education was both egalitarian and a good investment found favour. The new Labour government was committed to an expanded programme of welfare measures in health, education, housing and personal social services – and to a more progressive tax system. It was assumed that Keynesian fine-tuning would deliver a growth dividend to help pay for more welfare. But the economic problems the government faced, especially in defending the value of the pound, meant that the actual social policy successes were limited. Although, as Eric Shaw writes: 'Within the limits of the resources available, the social record of the Government was by no means as poor as depicted by its critics at the time. The real problem lay with an economic performance which failed to deliver additional resources.'[12] The rate and scope of benefits rose; and welfare spending continued to rise as a percentage of gross domestic product (GDP).[13] This was of course at a time when spending *more* on welfare was seen as a sign of success rather than failure by the Labour leadership.

When in the 1970s the Conservative Party abandoned the middle way and the policy consensus on welfare dating back to its 1951 general election victory, Labour continued to press for more welfare services and higher social benefits. Despite Labour's drift to the Left – the 1974 election manifesto called for a 'fundamental and irreversible shift in the balance of power and wealth in favour of working people and their families' – which would become even more pronounced after 1979, in 1975 it announced cuts to public spending mid-recession. Under pressure from the IMF, further reductions in public spending followed. In 1977 and 1978 the Labour government presided over cuts in welfare spending as a percentage of GDP, although some areas (housing and education) fared worse than others (social security and health). But certainly the postwar growth trend in public spending on the welfare state had levelled out.[14]

The significance for Labour's social policy of all this was that the commitment to full employment, which had underpinned the postwar welfare state, was gone. 'It was', Nicholas Timmins suggests, 'the moment which marked the first great fissure in Britain's welfare state ... The magic prescription of growth, public expenditure and full employment, paid for by higher taxation and perhaps slightly higher inflation, had ceased to work.'[15] Or, at the very least, the Labour leadership (and the proto-Thatcherites in the Tory Party) at the time believed that it had. Whether they were right remains hotly debated. And certainly it took at least another decade before the rest of the Labour Party would come round to the death of Keynesianism and implications of this for social policy. In another area of social policy, education, Callaghan's premiership foreshadowed both Conservative and New Labour policies in the decades to follow. In his speech in 1976 at Ruskin College, Oxford, Callaghan said that poor standards in British education were contributing to her economic problems. Callaghan argued that the problems education faced were less about the structure of education or how much public money was spent but on what was taught and how it was taught.

Welfare, social democracy and the New Right

The pressures of low growth and high public spending took their toll on both Conservative and Labour governments in the 1970s. Distant voices on the Right had since the 1950s questioned the logic of the social democratic welfare state; and even by the late 1960s some Labour figures were feeling the strain of an ever expanding social budget as growth rates fell. But those calling for greater selectivity, more individual responsibility and a smaller welfare state remained marginal figures in British politics. In the first half of the 1970s both the Tories and Labour remained committed to tax-and-spend social policies. That all changed when Margaret Thatcher replaced Edward Heath as Conservative Party leader following their election losses in 1974. The Right was on the ascendancy.

The well-charted rise of the New Right, a heady mix of classical liberal ideas and old style conservative ones, provided the first major intellectual challenge to the postwar welfare consensus. The New Right argued simply that the state was doing too much and that it should do less by shifting responsibility for welfare back onto private individuals and families. The universal welfare state, they argued, was a public monopoly coercive of individual liberty as well as a drain on private resources. State welfare, moreover, had created a 'dependency culture' which was having a morally corrosive effect on individuals and creating a whole host of social problems for society. The effect of the postwar social democratic welfare consensus, the New Right argued, was to accelerate Britain's relative economic decline. And those who had shaped that consensus – the Fabians, the New Liberals and the Tory Middle Wayers – were turned by the New Right into the villains of the piece. There were new gods to idolize.

Successive Conservative governments may have fallen short of wholesale privatization of the welfare state, but the agenda has been clear nonetheless. In challenging the basic assumptions of social democratic social policy, the New Right argued that wealth creation should come before welfare provision; individuals should be self-reliant rather than dependent on collective state services; freedom and choice should take priority over equality and social justice; and, wherever possible, markets rather than hierarchies should be deployed to allocate resources, whether or not assets were actually privatized or not. A whole host of social policy measures have followed from these principles, from the sale of council housing and the contracting out of local government services to the internal market in health and parental choice in education. The success or failure of these reforms is not our concern here. Rather it is the response they provoked on the Left – the central question for post-Thatcherite politics.

New Labour: rethinking social policy

Politically, the Labour Party spent most of the 1980s and early 1990s fighting tooth and nail against the social policy reforms of successive Conservative governments. Labour stood for the welfare status quo: a position essentially defined by the theory and practice of postwar social democracy. As Timmins writes: 'For more than a decade Labour simply stopped thinking constructively about the welfare state. It was, after all, their welfare state. It was soon to be clear that it was indeed under attack, and they were damn well going to defend it, warts and all – particularly against that woman.'[16] So the defence of the welfare state and the promise of extra funding for social benefits and services were the centrepieces of the 1983 and 1987 Labour election manifestos. Only during the Policy Review following the 1987 defeat was this basically defensive position questioned.

But Labour's public opposition to the Tory welfare reforms is not the whole story of contemporary Centre-Left social policy. It is useful for understanding the rise of New Labour if we recognize the increasingly critical attitude of some social democrats to the postwar welfare state – this despite studies which showed continuing public support for much of the welfare state.[17] To be sure, there had always been a steady stream of research which had pointed up the inadequacies of British social policy, in particular its supposed failure to eradicate poverty.[18] But over the past two decades, in the face of the neo-liberal assault on the welfare state, the Centre Left has begun to question the theory and practice of postwar social policy. Three questions stand out. First, who pays and who benefits from social policy? Secondly, how should welfare be delivered? And thirdly, what should social policy aim to achieve? These are the central questions for the rest of the chapter.

New Labour and social policy: who pays, who benefits?

Who pays and who benefits from the welfare state depends on what social policy is expected to achieve. Poverty relief and the redistribution of wealth and income to the poor and those in special need are three objectives. But the welfare state is also a means of social insurance (against unemployment and sickness, for example) and saving across the lifecycle (pensions, for example), neither of which is necessarily redistributional in effect. The Left has always given greatest prominence to the redistributive aspects of social policy, and has tended to judge the welfare state on whether it makes society a more equal and therefore socially just place.

The early work of one of Britain's leading contemporary social policy academics, Julian Le Grand, demonstrated that the welfare state, far from redistributing wealth to the poorer sections of the community, was actually featherbedding the middle classes, especially through health and education.[19] So whatever the grand egalitarian intentions of postwar social democracy, its practice was somewhat different. Paradoxically, Le Grand's research lent support to the arguments from the New Right: that the welfare state was helping those who could actually help themselves; and that social policy should therefore be much more selective about who benefited. But Le Grand's work also raised similar questions for the Left.

If we look at the pattern of welfare state winners and losers, we can see that the combined effects of taxes and benefits *are* mildly redistributional: taking figures for 1991, the bottom half of households are net gainers from the welfare state and the top half are losers. Different parts of the welfare state are more important for different social groups than others. Cash benefits accounted for 76 per cent of gross income of the poorest tenth of households in 1991 but only 2 per cent for the richest tenth. For even those benefits in kind such as health and education, where middle-income groups do do better, those at the bottom still do markedly better than those at the top.[20] Once the effects of the tax and benefit system are taken over individuals' lifetimes, the welfare state remains somewhat redistributional. But the figures also suggest that *the majority* of welfare benefits are self-financed: 'Nearly three-quarters of what the welfare state does looked at this way is like a "savings bank", only a quarter is "Robin Hood" redistribution between different people.'[21]

What this research into the winners and losers of social policy has done is to create a climate on the Left where hard questions could begin to be asked about the distribution of social benefits across social classes, and about the extent to which middle-income groups might be expected to pay for the benefits they receive, or even not receive them at all. With the experience of welfare reform in Australia in mind, where the Labor government's reforms in the 1980s were heavily reliant on the targeting of social benefits, some on the Left have shifted away from uncritical support for a free and universal welfare state. Despite a chorus of disapproval, Gordon Brown suggested in 1996 that child benefit for the over sixteens be means-tested so as to release funds for those in greatest need. Labour's welfare-to-work programme is heavily targeted on the young and long-term unemployed and on lone parents. New Labour has ruled out raising benefit levels across the board as a means of poverty relief (as well as ruling out a rise in income tax to pay for welfare provision). Even those commitments left after the 1987 Policy Review – increases in child benefit and pensions paid for by increased taxes on higher incomes – have disappeared. In continuing to link the state pension with prices (rather than earnings, which generally rise more quickly), and in considering proposals to focus help on poorer pensioners, Labour is implicitly assuming that many of those in receipt of social security can help themselves; and that public policy should be targeted on those who are less able to do so. In the autumn of 1997 Labour's social security minister

Harriet Harman tested the loyalty of the new government's backbenches by announcing that benefits to lone parents would be cut – a policy of the previous Conservative government which Labour had opposed – and that welfare support would be targeted on measures to help single parents back into work. In the middle of this political storm a leaked Treasury paper proposed that Labour was considering the taxing or means-testing of all state benefits, effectively reducing social security to a safety net for the poor.[22]

Labour's leading welfare guru, Frank Field, remains committed to the universalism of the welfare state, at least to the extent that it includes everyone. Field, appointed by Blair after the election to head social security reform, has admirers on the Tory Right, something which does not always endear him to Labour's Left wing. Field's ideas for a 'stakeholder' social insurance system covering social security and pensions would be compulsory and so retain its universal character. But Field is less enthusiastic about social policy as a directly redistributional tool. The welfare state should help individuals to help themselves out of dependency on the welfare state: 'There is no general groundswell amongst middle-class groups for the redistribution of wealth to the poor, particularly in the aftermath of the Thatcher years. Politicians who maintain otherwise are a public menace distracting from the real task.'[23] The point for Field is that the state of dependency on welfare, especially means-tested benefits, is a bad thing in itself. Simply raising benefit levels does nothing about this fact. In the late 1960s Field, then head of the Child Poverty Action Group (CPAG), had highlighted the 'poverty trap' many poor families faced. Today he continues to suggest that the welfare state destroys incentives for those on benefits to take jobs – the poverty trap. But he now makes a stronger case for the morally damaging effect of welfare dependency on individuals:

> almost half of the population live in households dependent upon one of the major means-tested benefits. Means tests penalise all those human attributes – such as hard work, work being adequately rewarded, savings, and honesty – which underpin a free, let alone a civilised, society. The present welfare system, therefore, reinforces this shift in morality, further eroding the fundamental law-abiding principles and wealth of the country. Lying, cheating and deceit are all rewarded handsomely by a welfare system which costs on average £15 a day in taxation from every working

individual. Again it is difficult to overestimate the destructive consequences welfare now has for our society.[24]

For Field, welfare reform should be judged not on egalitarian criteria – the rich paying and the poor benefiting – but on its success in reducing the welfare roll and on its ability to help individuals provide for old age and periods of unemployment.

Gordon Brown insists that New Labour remains committed to equality, but not any old equality: 'We cannot meet the challenge of creating both the educated economy and a just and more cohesive society without taking the idea of equality of opportunity seriously. Not hankering after an unrealisable equality of outcomes, as old Labour was accused of doing, advancing the wrong kind of equality, when the challenge is to make equality of opportunity real.' To be sure, Brown is interested in outcomes: he regards some inequalities as 'unjustifiable'.[25] And Labour attack eighteen years of Tory government for making society more unequal in terms of the distribution of wealth and income. But, to Brown, this means that 'equality of opportunity should not be a one-off, pass-fail, life-defining event but a continuing opportunity for everyone to have the chance to realize their potential to the full.'[26]

Geoff Mulgan, director of the think-tank Demos and a Downing Street policy advisor specializing in welfare reform, suggests that the Left's traditional concern with rights and distributive justice has acted as a block on innovative social policies. Mulgan's view is that the welfare state should be more active in dealing with specific problems. Whether benefits are universal or targeted is for Mulgan a redundant debate. Rather it is a question of the relative effectiveness of nationally standardized or locally customized policies: 'State responsibility', writes Mulgan, 'does not, however, imply that national systems will work best . . . Success in developing new ways of creating work and improving welfare will depend crucially on much greater scope for local experiment.'[27] Field is in favour of giving local social security offices more autonomy and power of discretion over their administrative and fraud budgets – although not benefit levels.[28] New Labour is also drawn to the idea of 'local discretion' and more 'personalized' benefit and employment services in the delivery of its welfare-to-work programme.[29]

Underlying these ideas for more local experiment and discretion is the idea of 'social exclusion'. During the 1997 parliamentary summer recess, Peter Mandelson announced in a Fabian lecture the government's intention of establishing a new unit on 'social exclusion' based in the Cabinet Office and chaired by the prime minister. Mandelson suggested:

> this modern world offers rich rewards to some and a wide range of opportunities for many more. Where these are the result of genuine initiative and creative dynamism New Labour has no quarrel. But it also contains a great deal of insecurity for a broad mass. For a significant minority at the bottom of the social ladder, who are at best on the edge of the labour force, the result is social exclusion.[30]

For New Labour, the socially excluded are poor but they are not simply the poor. Many who are defined as being in poverty relative to the rest of the society are not excluded in the same sense. The socially excluded lack the skills, capabilities and even willingness to get and keep a job – the key marker for social inclusion – and are cut off from the world of work and education. So it is the government's job to target help on the socially excluded through more education, training and the welfare-to-work programme, giving local case workers greater autonomy in helping the excluded back into society. The new Social Exclusion Unit, which was launched by Tony Blair in December 1997, cuts across Whitehall departments and so challenges the traditional departmental culture of British government. To the new Labour government, it is the socially excluded, a much narrower category than standard definitions of the poor, who are to be the beneficiaries of New Labour's social policies. But their right to help comes at a price: with rights come responsibilities. The government will fulfil its side of the bargain by helping the socially excluded find work; in return, the socially excluded must fulfil their responsibilities by doing something about their own condition.

For New Labour, who pays and who benefits from the welfare state is not to be judged in terms of economic inequalities. New Labour has finally killed off the idea that taxing and spending was a way of making society more equal. Rather, social exclusion/inclusion has become the marker against which the success or failure of the welfare state is to be judged, not the distribution of wealth and income across society. Those able-bodied persons who can help themselves out of dependence on the welfare state to independence have an obligation to do so. Only those who cannot help themselves merit a promise of special help. Indeed, helping poor pensioners and the chronically sick and disabled, Labour modernizers argue, can better be done where those capable of helping themselves do so, thereby releasing resources for those who cannot. To old Croslandites such as Roy Hattersley, this is all a bit much: welfare to work is fine for the long term, but what about the poor on welfare now: benefit levels must be raised and paid for by higher taxes on the wealthy. Social justice demands it.[31]

New Labour and social policy: delivering welfare

The second question – how welfare should be delivered – further illustrates the shifting position of the revisionist Left on social policy in the face of the free market Right. To be sure, since the 1960s many on the Left had grown wary of the 'statist' assumptions of postwar social democracy. The old New Left, born out of the split with Soviet communism in the 1950s and the rise of the new social movements in the 1960s, advocated devolved and decentralized forms of government. At a local level Labour councils experimented with neighbourhood management schemes in areas such as housing. And Labour modernizers in the 1980s such as Bryan Gould were strong supporters of the decentralization of government. New Labour modernizers share many of the sentiments of the old New Left but they have, we would suggest, taken them a step further. The leading modernizer Tony Wright suggests that: 'One of the great achievements of Labour's new thinking has been to enable it to reclaim the public service principle, badly in need of restoration and restatement, while not confusing this with old models of public service organisation and delivery.'[32]

The questioning of Labour's (and social democracy's) previous attachment to the state can be seen in two clear areas: first, how the state delivers welfare; and secondly, whether social policy should always be a matter of public, state provision (certainly in any direct sense).

Knights, knaves and pawns

Le Grand, now the Richard Titmuss Professor of Social Policy at the London School of Economics (the institution at the heart of the Fabian welfare tradition), has written of the behavioural assumptions of the postwar social democrats and their New Right nemesis which neatly captures the issues at hand. Postwar social democrats, Le Grand suggests, worked from the assumption that those public servants, schooled in the prevailing ethos of public service, who delivered social services were knights; and those in receipt of welfare – whether in education, health, housing or across the counter in a dole office – were all pawns. The goodly Fabian knights might work for the common purpose, but they treated the citizen as a largely passive pawn, easily manipulated with no input into what social policy provided or how it was provided. In that famous old phrase of Douglas Jay, 'the men in Whitehall know best'. At the heart of the New Right case against social democracy, as Le Grand shows, is that public servants and welfare recipients alike are knaves: there is an essential dishonesty among welfare players – producers and consumers. Public servants are bureaucratic empire builders, not devoted servants of the common good; and those in receipt of welfare play the system for all it's worth to further their own self-interest – the potential for fraud is endemic. For the New Right, social policy was, and still is, about constructing forms of public and private administration which turn private vices into public virtues. The introduction of the market into the welfare state has been central to this project. If self-interest is rampant, as Adam Smith argued, then knaves must be confined to competitive environments which turn egoistic behaviour to the common good. Self-interest can thus have unintended beneficial consequences for society as a whole.[33]

But what is the post-Thatcherite Left to do? Is it to go back to the old game of knights and pawns? Or is it to accept the New Right case that knaves are the norm? Or if it concedes that people are only just more knavish today than they were in the past, mainly from force of circumstance, can it devise some way of encouraging, and even forcing, individuals to be more knight-like? Field has taken the knave route: social policy should be designed to make the forces of self-interest work to the general good. 'The growth of individualism', he says, 'is not going to be arrested by talk of rebuilding community. Welfare has to be shaped so that individual wishes can simultaneously promote new senses of community.'[34] Labour's welfare-to-work proposals are also rooted in a view of the unemployed as potential knaves who face sanctions if they refuse to do something about their own condition. Other Labour modernizers, inspired by communitarianism, prefer the later option of turning knaves into knights, even if this has led to charges of social authoritarianism. The rhetoric of New Labour, especially that of Blair himself, is infused with the sense that individuals should put the care of others first – that they should be more knight-like. In practice, New Labour's social policy combines knave and knight strategies. The party's plans for the National Health Service provide a good example.

Knaves and knights: Labour and the NHS

How does Labour intend to fund a health system where demand for services is constantly growing? Labour claimed in its 1997 manifesto that the NHS 'is under threat from the Conservatives. We want to save and modernise the NHS.' On specific pledges, the 1997 manifesto promised to take 100,000 people off hospital waiting lists and to end waiting lists for cancer treatment entirely by 'abolishing' the internal market and cutting red tape. The 1997 manifesto also promised to raise spending in real terms every year. This, of course, is exactly what the Conservatives did since 1979: the annual rate of growth in spending on health after inflation was 3 per cent. Even after adjustments are made for the specific prices paid by the NHS, this figure is 1.8 per cent.[35] Labour's charge against the Tories is that they have spent too much of this money on a bureaucratic paper chase – the internal market – and that the increase in resources has not kept up with the needs of the population, especially one that is ageing. Moreover, the internal market, in particular, allowing some GPs to become 'fundholders', with the power to purchase treatments from providers (mainly the trust hospitals) while others are not, has created, Labour claims, a 'two-tier' system which benefits some patients and not others. So, Labour is putting forward two sets of arguments: efficiency ones and equity ones.

How does Labour see itself resolving these problems? Its answer in the 1997 manifesto was to 'cut costs by removing the bureaucratic processes of the internal market'. The money saved, some £100 million, Labour claimed, would be spent on patient care. Given that the government spent over £34 billion on health in 1992–3, and that the NHS was facing a debt of £200 million in April 1997, £100 million is small beer. But if we look more closely at what Labour is saying, its plans are more to reform Tory reforms rather than turn the clock back to a pre-Conservative age. So here Labour is combining knave and knight strategies to deal with a post-Thatcherite problem.

Labour's 1995 policy document *Renewing the NHS* promised to put 'the patient before the market'. But the document also made clear, as does the 1997 manifesto, that the basic split in the internal market between 'purchasers' and 'providers' will remain under Labour. The main purchasers, the GPs, would under Labour's 1995 plans 'commission' healthcare from hospitals and other health providers. To end the 'two-tier' division between fundholders and non-fundholders, all GPs would be part of the commissioning process, which would bring together GPs, nurses and health authorities to commission healthcare cooperatively. The 1997 manifesto states that 'GPs and nurses will take the lead in combining together locally to plan local health services more efficiently for all the patients in their area.' Health authorities would be the 'guardians of high standards. They will monitor services, spread best practice and ensure rising standards of care.' On the question of the NHS trust hospitals, Labour's plans in opposition were to allow the trusts to continue to manage their own affairs. Only the assets of the trusts would be shifted to the NHS. The health authorities would be left to set 'high quality standards' for trust managements.

Once in government, Labour moved quickly to announce the end of the practice whereby fundholding GPs were able to ensure speedy service from hospitals (or 'queue-jumping', as Labour put it).[36] Under the changes, hospitals can only admit patients on the basis of need, so ending, Labour claimed, the internal market's 'two-tier' character, as trusts will no longer be able to offer fundholders preferential treatment. (Although health academics have long pointed out that the NHS has never been able to deliver equity across the board: waiting times have always differed from place to place.) In a White Paper, *The New NHS – Modern, Dependable*, published on 9 December 1997, the new Labour government proposed abolishing GP fundholding, replacing it with a GP-led commissioning model. Under this model, local GPs and community nurses will form primary care groups, covering areas of 100,000 patients, which will control the purchasing of hospital and community care. They will manage a single, capped budget and will be able to spend money on the basis of local need. Trust hospitals will agree long-term agreements with primary care groups. Two new national bodies will be established to ensure consistent access to, and quality of, services across the country.

Labour argues that the commissioning model has proved successful where it has been tried out. So its plans are to extend the system to the whole of the NHS, replacing the internal market. Stephen Pollard, once head of research at the Fabian Society and now at the Centre Right Social Market Foundation, has argued that Labour's reforms amount to little more than an acceptance of the internal market: 'Arguing that Labour will abolish the internal market, while keeping the purchaser–provider split, is intellectually contradictory but politically necessary.'[37] Stripped of all the rhetoric of cooperation and accountability, Labour's plans are nothing more than to make all GPs fundholders. Labour's NHS strategy, if Pollard is right, is a knavish one – Labour's reforms amount to making the playing field more level for GPs to purchase services from providers. The 'quasi-market' character of the NHS would be retained. It is, so to speak, a policy to make life more equitable for the knaves and their patients.

In certain respects, Pollard has a point. Labour's commissioning system has similar objectives to fundholding: that is, to allow GPs to obtain services from a health provider, thereby exerting pressure on health providers more generally to deliver the right kind of treatment at the right cost. Labour argues explicitly in its 1997 manifesto that there is strength in numbers: commissioning 'will enable all GPs in an area to bring their combined strength to bear upon individual hospitals to secure higher standards of patient provision.' But, in other respects, Labour's proposed reforms to the delivery of healthcare depend on more knight-like behaviour. GP fundholders will not act alone but in concert with other GPs and health practitioners as part of cooperative commissioning units. While these units will still, under Labour's proposals, be divided in delivery from the providers of health services, the relationship between the two is conceived of by Labour as a more collaborative and long-term one. In the NHS White Paper, year-on-year 'contracts' will be replaced by contracts of a minimum of three years' duration between commissioning units and health providers. Labour hopes that this will allow hospitals in particular to make longer-term plans for health needs as demanded by the more strategic health authorities.

Labour's plans for the NHS, if they are ever implemented in full – and the NHS has certainly had its fill of reform over the past decade – would reform the Conservative reforms of the delivery of healthcare, not abolish them. But does the combination of knave and knight strategies work? Opponents argue that Labour's plans, certainly the directive that hospitals must admit patients only on the basis of need, will have the effect of making waiting times worse for everybody because GPs will no longer have the power to make hospitals more responsive and efficient – thereby reducing waiting times for all. Labour's proposals for the NHS aim to make the supply and demand of health provision a more collaborative and long-term process, which may undermine the ability of GPs to put pressure on hospitals: yearly contracts may make it more difficult for hospital administrators to plan for the future, but they certainly keep them on their toes; three- or four-year agreements might make it easier for those same administrators to think long-term, but it may also breed complacency.[38]

Exit and voice in welfare

Whether knights can be knaves and knaves knights remains to be seen. But what is clear is that New Labour and the post-Thatcherite Left have foreclosed a return to a welfare strategy based on knights *and pawns*, to the old Fabian model of welfare governance – a model built on the idea of a centralized, bureaucratic and above all paternalistic welfare state. Social policy has become critical of the producer-dominated approach to welfare in which the interests of society and those of its public servants are viewed as the same. Welfare thinking on the Left has recognized that under the influence of old-style Fabianism, as well as its own bureaucratic momentum, the welfare state grew distant from those it served, alienating and disempowering the citizen.[39] In Albert Hirschman's terms, the citizen has no 'voice' in the administration of welfare: after all, Whitehall or the local town hall knew best. Neither, many on the Left concede, does the citizen have much choice: the state has since 1945 become more and more of a monopoly welfare supplier, under the sway not of those it serves but of producer interests. So, the citizen has no voice and no 'exit' from the state in terms of meaningful choices between alternative welfare providers.[40] While remaining critical of the distributional effects of Conservative social policies, and of the definition of users as consumers rather than citizens, some social democratic social policy thinkers have embraced welfare strategies which give recipients more voice and more choice through more decentralized ('community') forms of public administration. There are continuities here with the old New Left's support for more voice (if not choice) in public services in the name of democracy. But many on the Left now go much further by engaging constructively with the 'quasi-market' reforms of the 1980s and 1990s.[41]

The work of social theorists such as Anthony Giddens, Ulrich Beck and Zygmunt Bauman has also contributed to an intellectual climate on the Left which has grown distrustful of the state as a rational, impartial paterfamilias. Indeed, in Giddens's case, his work has had a more direct impact on British politics through his contributions to, and interventions in, Centre-Left debates.[42] Giddens has argued widely that 'late modern' societies such as Britain are characterized by 'reflexivity'. Simply put, this means that the traditional role of 'experts' (or, as Bauman calls them, 'legislators')[43] has been called into question by a society where individuals have access to greater knowledge, and where they are willing and able to reflect and make decisions about their own lives. Both Giddens and Beck have argued that the modern world has undergone a process of 'detraditionalization': the old structures and relationships which in the past dominated people's lives have been eroded; and individuals, as Beck puts it, are left to 'produce, stage, cobble together their own biographies of themselves.'[44] Bauman's 'legislators' have been replaced by 'interpreters' able to guide the citizen through a postmodern world of competing explanations and value systems.

This may all seem a world away from the hard realities of social policy. But, for Giddens, the reflexive character of late modern society challenges what he calls the 'cybernetic model' of social life and social administration. This is a model of organization based on a central mechanical source of power and authority which directs matters in any given system. This has led Giddens to challenge the top-down, bureaucratic model of welfare: in a reflexive as well as an uncertain world, individuals want to take informed decisions and choices, not have them made for them by 'experts'. Postmodern social policy has in areas like education challenged the idea that the welfare state should be the same to everyone everywhere. For a postmodern society is marked by diversity and pluralism, not homogeneity and uniformity. So why should all schools be the same? And why should the state be the main provider of education? To the postmodern educationalist, the idea of 'comprehensive education' is a dated one. Leading New Labour supporters such as John Gray and Will Hutton have also supported a move away from a uniform comprehensive model to a more diverse and selective system.[45]

There is, then, a sentiment among many on the Left that the game of knights and pawns played out on uniform boards has run its course. There are strong arguments for the citizen to have a voice in social policy as well as exits from any particular welfare provider. Individuals, it is thought, should be given greater access to, and control over, the decision-making and administration of welfare. The 'producers' of welfare – those who run social service departments, NHS hospitals or local schools – must be responsible and responsive to the 'consumers' of welfare. Social workers, doctors and teachers should be 'interpreters' not 'legislators'. As the post-Fordists would have it, the welfare state needs to be 'flexible' – a point which Blair made in a speech in 1996.[46] 'Clients', patients and parents should have access to knowledge; they should have the right to express their preferences; and they should be able to make meaningful choices across a diverse range of options which reflect their own particular lives. To all of this New Labour adds that rights come with responsibilities: as patients, healthcare providers, teachers, pupils and even parents.

Labour and education: 'choice, diversity and standards'

This antipathy to the centralized, bureaucratic welfare state has seeped into New Labour thinking on social policy and has contributed to significant shifts in party policy. In health, as we have seen, Labour is reforming Conservative reforms, not abolishing them. So too in education. The view of the secretary of state at the Department of Education, David Blunkett, is that 'standards not structures' are what matter. Although Labour has no obviously preferred model of education – as say against the Conservative view under John Major that there should be a 'grammar school in every town' – Labour's policy is to retain the most significant elements of the Tory education reforms to the delivery of education in the 1980s. The Labour government will continue to allow parents to make choices about the schools their children attend. It will also continue to allow schools to control their own budgets – 'local management of schools', or LMS. And Labour will continue the Conservative policy of promoting greater diversity of education provision by encouraging schools to specialize in particular subjects, such as technology and languages. Only in respect of the 'assisted places scheme', first introduced in 1980 to pay for bright children from poor families to attend independent fee-paying schools, will Labour reverse the Conservative diversification policy on the grounds of equity. The money released, Labour proposes, will be spent on reducing primary school class sizes below thirty for all children.

In opposition, Labour's major education problem concerned what to do with those schools which have opted out of control of local education authorities (LEAs) to grant-maintained (GM) status. This issue has proved a severe test for Labour modernizers and their post-Thatcherite view of the world. Old Labour, committed not just to comprehensive education but to education run by LEAs, opposed school opt-outs tooth and nail. The dilemma of how to deal with this crucial part of the Thatcher legacy – Lady Thatcher had once expressed a wish to see all state schools become independent of local government – came to a head over the decisions of the Blairs, and later of Harriet Harman (one of Blair's most loyal modernizers) and her union modernizer husband Jack Dromey, to send their children to GM schools – and, in Harman's case, to a *selective* grammar school to boot! The charge of hypocrisy levelled against these modernizer couples in part camouflaged a gradual shift in party policy away from opposition to opted-out schools to support – as well as a shift away from support for LEAs as being the key controller of local education. By the 1997 election Labour had no plans to return GM schools to LEA control – the local authorities would simply be represented on the school governing bodies. Existing admissions policies would remain. On the fate of the remaining grammar schools in England and Wales, some 161 schools, Labour suggested in its 1997 manifesto that a ballot of local parents would decide if the demand arose. Labour does still remain hostile to a more selective admissions policy – the Conservatives ran on a platform of more selection in schooling. However, Labour offered no plans in its manifesto to reverse existing grammar school selection policies except by parental decision, although it has indicated that it will reverse the '15 per cent rule' which has seen all state schools having the right to select up to 15 per cent of their intake on ability.

But if Labour has embraced more voice and more choice in education

– thereby broadly accepting the Conservative structural reforms to schooling – where does it differ from the Tory Party? What is different perhaps is the idea that standards can be raised in the last instance by government fiat rather than by market forces. While parents will still be able to choose the school for their children, and schools will be funded on a per capita basis (so popular schools will receive more money than unpopular ones), Labour does not pin higher school standards on this internal market as the Conservatives did. But New Labour's education policies are also distinctive from Old Labour's.[47] Labour's policies emphasize what in education jargon is known as 'ethos' rather than 'environment': the success of a school depends on the quality of leadership and teaching and the values of the school rather than the class background or social environment of the pupils. There are 'effective' schools and 'ineffective' ones, or, more simply, good ones and bad ones. What is important is what you do with an intake of children, not what class or social background they come from. This was a view heavily endorsed by the head of the Office for Standards in Education (Ofsted), Chris Woodhead, under the Conservatives. So David Blunkett's decision to retain the services of Woodhead after the election reflects a continuity with the previous government's approach (and Blunkett's own views on education).

Most of Labour's education policies were previewed in opposition.[48] One of its proposed reforms, the setting up of a Standards and Effectiveness Unit, was quickly enacted once Labour won power, headed by Michael Barber. Within two weeks of the general election it was announced that the Department of Education was to use Conservative legislation to send 'hit squads' into schools thought to be failing – a policy Labour had spoken against in opposition. In Labour's first Queen's speech, a 'Fresh Start' policy was announced whereby 'failing schools' would be closed down by government ministers and reopened with a new head and senior management. This was all part of Labour's declared aim of 'zero tolerance' of low standards and a clear shot across the bow of 'producer interests' – the teachers.

Labour's education White Paper, *Excellence in Schools*, was published on 7 July 1997. Blair set the tone in *The Times* that day: 'There are many good schools in Britain, but not enough; many good teachers, but not enough, many well educated children, but not enough.'[49] On the controversial area of testing, the White Paper proposed new national tests for nine-year-olds in mathematics and the continued publication of secondary and primary school test results. Schools thought by Ofsted and the government to be failing will have to improve or face closure, or be closed and reopened under Fresh Start. LEAs will also be inspected and a Standards Task Force set up to advice on teaching methods. (And, as Blair, Blunkett and Woodhead have made abundantly clear, the government and Ofsted have strong views on what constitutes good and bad teaching methods.) In a School Standards Bill published in December 1997 the government proposed strengthening the powers of Ofsted against teacher training colleges and giving greater powers to the Department of Education over LEAs. The Bill also proposed setting up twenty-five 'Education Action Zones', in which parents, local businesses and voluntary groups might experiment in schooling free from national regulations, including the National Curriculum.

On the structure of education, the White Paper proposed that the comprehensive system be modernized under the slogan of 'diversity within one campus': Labour favours the setting of pupils by ability, an end to mixed-ability teaching and fast-track progression for bright pupils. On teaching, the White Paper proposed a new General Teaching Council to raise the status of teachers as a profession. Teacher training is to be reformed with an emphasis on numeracy and literacy. It also proposed quicker procedures for dismissing incompetent teachers and new qualifications for senior and head teachers. On parental involvement in schools, the White Paper supported the already established Family Learning schemes to promote literacy; more parental governors; and home–school contracts to cover areas such as support of the school ethos, homework, discipline and attendance. Both in the White Paper and in comments made by Blunkett soon after the election, Labour proposes national guidelines for homework, including the idea of a school–parent pledge for twenty minutes of reading every day at home; and that every primary school spend an hour a day each on literacy and numeracy.

The publication soon after the election of Sir Ron Dearing's report on university education, and Labour's response to it, is further illustration of the Blair revolution. To fund a continued expansion of university education, Dearing recommended ending fifty years of free tuition by the introduction of fees amounting to 25 per cent of university course costs – £1000 in 1997. Labour agreed: students, who could reasonably expect a lifetime of above-average earnings, should contribute to their higher education. Only those from low-income families would be exempt.

Labour went further: what was left of the old student grant should go. A loan would cover the full cost of a student's maintenance. 'We are determined', wrote Blunkett in response to Dearing, 'to ensure that there is access to higher education for all those who can benefit from it.'[50] But to finance greater access, those who could contribute towards the cost of expansion – middle-class families and university graduates – would be expected to do so. In November 1997 the Teaching and Higher Education Bill was published which included measures to introduce university fees and to phase out student grants.

The limits of government

> Old ideologies die hard. The idea that the state knows best and must monopolise service provision in case people make the 'wrong' choices for themselves is a long established tradition both among socialists and paternalist conservatives. Tony Blair's Labour Party has recognised that state monopoly is not always the best way to achieve society's ideals; instead the key lies in ensuring that the people have economic power and that this power is fairly distributed. It is that which nursery vouchers have to offer.[51]

These are not the words of the New Right. They are from the new New Left. Julian Le Grand, writing with another leading social policy professor, Howard Glennerster, treads where even Labour modernizers fear (at least in public): New Labour has already abolished the Conservative nursery vouchers scheme. But Le Grand and Glennerster do reflect the mood of many modernizers on the Left. The question of how welfare should be delivered does involve that most Thatcherite of questions: what are the limits of government?

To be sure, welfare, despite all the postwar reforms, was and is a 'mixed economy'. The state may have become the dominant player – too much so for the Right – but the private, voluntary and informal sectors have continued to play a role in welfare provision. For much of the Left, certainly within the Labour Party, this was as it should be. The state provision of welfare was seen as the best guarantor of social justice. Any erosion of the state's role was to be resisted. But the belief has grown on the Left that the state (central or local) does not actually have to be the sole or actual provider of services. Instead, it can act as the purchaser and regulator of services, willing to enter into partnerships with the voluntary and private sectors. Its role is to supervise and act as a guarantor of high quality service provision. In modernizer think-tanks such as Demos there has been a growing interest in the voluntary sector and in 'social entrepreneurs' as the instigators of social provision. The Left's statist approach to welfare, it is suggested, has 'crowded out' the work of voluntary action. This work mirrors similar interest on the Right in think-tanks such as the Institute of Economic Affairs.[52]

Again Frank Field has led the argument in the Labour Party for forms of collective welfare provision which bypass the state. He bemoans the Fabian antipathy to the voluntary sector and to their 'statist' approach to social policy. His idea of 'stakeholder welfare' in areas such as pensions, care for the elderly and unemployment benefit rests on creating new welfare institutions. In pensions, for example, Field has suggested that individuals have the choice of saving for a second pension managed either by a state corporation, a mutual society or a private company – although the saving itself would be compulsory. Labour's plans in opposition for a 'stakeholder pension' were less radical: they would act as a second pension to the state pension for those outside of the occupational pension system and would involve partnerships between the public and private sectors.[53] Before the 1997 general election the then Conservative social security minister, Peter Lilley, unveiled a plan to create a compulsory privately funded scheme which would replace the basic state pension. (Lilley, like Field, had been drawn to Chile as an example of a fully funded insurance scheme replacing a pay-as-you-go scheme – as the British state pension is.) Labour accused the Tories of privatizing pensions and – oddly for the Labour Party – of committing government to spending more money well into the next century. In July 1997 the new Labour government set up a review to examine the future of pensions under the social security minister John Denham. And, in a move which appeared to mirror rather closely Lilley's pension plans before the election, Labour announced that it would be offering tax incentives for those outside of the occupational pension net to take out a second personal or 'stakeholder' pension with mutual or cooperative societies or with employers.[54] A further taste of where New Labour will head on the provision of social security came in the summer of 1997 when Harriet Harman announced that three private consortiums had been given permission to 'shadow' different parts of the Benefits Agency with a view that, if they could demonstrate ways of providing a better standard of service, they might be given the contract to run the agency. The move was part of the Change programme started by Lilley under the last Conservative government.[55]

How welfare is delivered marks a significant shift in Labour's thinking on social policy. As the Commission on Social Justice put it: 'The polarities of the post-war period – individual versus collective, state versus market, public versus private – are giving way to a new recognition of their interdependence.'[56] This view has led Labour modernizers towards a pluralist approach to public administration. There has been a shift in emphasis from the state as a monopoly provider towards partnership with the private and voluntary sectors; to more decentralized forms of governance; and to an emphasis on individual choice, personal independence and personal responsibility.

New Labour and social policy: what should welfare do?

So far we have examined who pays and who benefits from welfare and how New Labour has shifted its position on the delivery of social policy. But what of our third question: what should social policy aim to do? This goes to the heart of the New Labour welfare agenda. For postwar social democracy, social policy was seen primarily in terms of counterbalancing free market capitalism. Social policy was about promoting social justice; and social justice involved strong notions of distributive justice which required practical measures to redistribute income and wealth. Moreover, redressing economic and social inequality was also seen as the most effective way of dealing with social problems: the causes of crime and anti-social behaviour were at root socio-economic. Most social democrats accepted that the welfare state could co-exist with an economy based on private property, especially a mixed economy in which there was a large element of state ownership, planning and macro-economic management. But New Labour's commitment to a market economy (rather than a mixed economy) has shifted the debate, and has in large part been made possible by its social policy. Here the Commission on Social Justice marks a significant development in New Labour thinking.

Social justice and economic efficiency

The Commission on Social Justice was established by John Smith in 1992. Headed by Lord Borrie and run by the Institute for Public Policy Research (IPPR) with David Miliband as its secretary, the commission provided a focus for rethinking Centre-Left social policy within mainstream Labour politics. Published in 1994, the final report's themes quickly became familiar New Labour ones. At the core of the report is the idea that welfare should be supportive of both social justice and economic efficiency: they are 'two sides of the same coin'.[57]

In certain important aspects, the report's focus on social justice reaffirms familiar social democratic themes. There are commitments to civil and political liberties and to basic needs; poverty, inequality and discrimination remain central concerns. But in other respects the report marks a step away from postwar social democracy in the distinction it draws between 'levellers', those people it suggests who are only concerned about the distribution of wealth, and 'investors', who are concerned about the conditions for promoting wealth creation in a market economy. To the writers of the report – investors not levellers – the pursuit of social justice need not necessarily be at the expense of economic efficiency – and vice versa. Social justice is conceived of as a widespread (and more equal) distribution of individual 'life chances': what has been dubbed 'endowment egalitarianism'. Traditionally, such opportunities have been seen by the Left as reflecting the class divisions in society; and these divisions as rooted in the unequal distribution of property, wealth and income. So, for the Left, something had to be done about the class structure of society and the market system which reflected that structure. They had either to be abolished (socialism), or their effects had to be counterbalanced by the state intervening in the market and redistributing wealth (social democracy).

The *Social Justice* report, however, takes a rather different view. Inequalities in individual opportunities are rooted in the stock – or lack – of individual skills and abilities, and the environment within which such abilities can be enhanced and used. In post-Fordist style, the report argues that competition and capital mobility in the new global economy create a demand for investment in new labour skills and flexibility. As we saw in the last chapter, governments may no longer have the power to manage demand to boost employment, but they can shape the supply side of the economy in such a way as to make the country more attractive to international investors and individuals more employable at higher rates of pay. In so doing, the sum total of economic activity is made greater. Social policy, then, is the means to provide labour with the flexibility it needs to find jobs in the global economy. If governments do this, not only will they bring about a more just society but they will also further the interests of the economy. And if governments fail to do this by making the right investments in welfare, they will precipitate a downward and destructive spiral of low skills, few opportunities, poor economic performance and social disintegration.

In trying to compete in the new global economy, moreover, new patterns of work will challenge the assumptions of the old welfare state – such as male full-time, lifelong working. These combined with social and cultural changes in the status and employment of women give rise to demands for a welfare system capable of dealing with the decline of lifetime employment, two-parent families and male bread-winners. Proposed measures such as 'lifelong learning', welfare to work and reform of the tax and benefits system are intended to 'promote personal autonomy and choice', giving individuals the 'confidence and capability' to manage their own lives.[58]

The central message from the Commission on Social Justice was a significant one for Labour's modernizers. The welfare state could be a help, not a hindrance, to economic development. Social justice, it turned out, could be good for business. Many of the policy ideas, such as 'lifelong learning', welfare to work and tax and benefit reform, have found their way into New Labour social policy – although some, such as the reduction of working hours, have not.

Even some who broadly welcomed the report suggested that the interdependence between the market and the welfare state, between efficiency and equality, was overplayed by the commission.[59] Leaving aside the real problem of linking them in a global economy environment, it leaves the Left vulnerable to the charge that social justice is an instrumental value and not one which was being argued for on its own merits. After all, what if social justice does not promote economic efficiency, which it might often not? What then is the commission and Labour left with? And even if the marriage of economic efficiency and social justice does pay in the longer term, who will pay for the social problems a country like Britain faces in the short term?

Social justice in practice: welfare to work

The main influence of the Social Justice Commission on New Labour can be seen in its welfare-to-work programme. Gordon Brown, the main architect of the programme, offered in 1994 a broad view on what the welfare state should be about:

> We must look hard at our own welfare system to ensure that it provides pathways out of unemployment and poverty rather than trapping people in persistent dependency. For the risks and insecurities that the welfare state was set up to combat have changed dramatically over fifty years and the welfare state has to keep up with the times. The welfare state must be about supporting people as they respond to these challenges – extending their choices and opportunities; acting as a trampoline rather than as a safety net.[60]

Trampoline, not safety net, is the positive metaphor which Labour's welfare policies in general, and welfare to work in particular, seek to portray. The broad idea behind the programme is a simple one. The welfare state should not passively deal with those who become unemployed for whatever reason. Rather, it should actively assist them back into the labour market by providing education, training and work expe rience opportunities. 'Unless we get our education system right', wrote Blair on the day the government's 1997 education White Paper was published, 'our children will not be prosperous and our country will not be just.' Education, Blair said, should be 'at the heart of government'.[61] More investment in education and training had already become part of party policy during the Policy Review, despite the unease many on the Left felt for government training schemes. Much of Labour's claim that its welfare-to-work programme is more than just another training scheme to massage the unemployment figures rests on the emphasis on the trans fer of benefit payments to education and training as well as job search programmes. In the 1997 manifesto there are commitments to 'Lifelong Learning', individual learning accounts enabling public money to be combined with contributions from individuals and from employers so as to allow the individual to buy training packages.[62] Labour proposes a University for Industry to encourage adult skills training. Labour supports proposals to extend and reform vocational qualifications made by Sir

Ron Dearing in 1996, including the widening of A-levels. Without Labour's education and training policies there is little 'plus' to its 'flexibility plus'.

The first pieces of New Labour's welfare-to-work programme were in place within two years of Blair becoming leader.[63] In the 1997 manifesto the welfare-to-work policy for 250,000 young people was one of the party's five 'election pledges'. The final details of the programme were announced by Brown in his first budget in July 1997. The four options for the young unemployed are: a private sector job; work with a voluntary sector employer; a job with a 50,000-strong environmental task force; or full-time study on an approved course. Employers are given a £60 per week rebate for six months to encourage them to take on the young unemployed. Despite criticism from within the Labour Party on earlier plans to cut benefit levels by 40 per cent, David Blunkett announced that young people who refused one of the four options would lose all their benefit for the first two weeks if they were without 'just cause'. After two weeks claimants will receive benefits at 60 per cent of the full rate. Those who refuse one of the four options a second time will have their benefit stopped for a month.[64] Employers will be required by government to offer either on-the-job training or day release for study on accredited courses.

In addition to the plans for the young unemployed, Brown announced measures for the long-term unemployed, for single parents and for the disabled – again policies which had been previewed by Labour in opposition. Under one scheme employers receive a subsidy of £75 per week for taking on those unemployed for more than two years. In addition, the government offers firms a £750 per head training subsidy. Lone parents with children in the second year of full-time education are offered advice and counselling on employment and training opportunities at job centres. In addition, Brown announced plans to train 50,000 young people as childcare assistants and for changes in benefit rules to make childcare more affordable for single parents. Money from the National Lottery goes towards setting up after-school clubs. Finally, plans were unveiled to help those on disability and incapacity benefit to find training and employment. As expected, Brown announced that the welfare-to-work programme was to be financed from a 'windfall tax' on the privatized utilities raising £5.2 billion.

The welfare-to-work measures announced by Brown are not entirely novel to Britain. In 1996 the Conservative government launched 'Project Work', a programme of interviews, 'job search' and compulsory work experience for those unemployed for more than two years. Refusal to take part in the programme led to a withdrawal of benefits. The idea of welfare to work is well established abroad. Labour (and the Commission on Social Justice before) has been able to draw on a number of schemes from across the world.[65] In Australia the Labor government's welfare reforms included a voluntary programme of training, childcare allowances and after-school clubs to help single mothers back to work (the Jobs, Education and Training, or JET, scheme); and the Job Compact programme, where the employment service found the unemployed jobs with the private sector. The United States has also provided much food for thought for Labour's welfare reformers. Bill Clinton was elected as president in 1992 on a promise to 'end welfare as we know it'. Welfare, the Clinton Democrats argued, rewarded idleness, created dependency and trapped the poor in poverty. Instead, government should help people help themselves: welfare to work.[66] One of Clinton's most controversial proposals was to stop benefits after two years in return for a guaranteed subsidized private sector job or a place on a government community service. Clinton also proposed extending the Jobs Opportunities and Basic Skills programme, set up in 1988, to provide basic education and training for the unemployed. Clinton's grand hopes for welfare reform foundered on the rocks of a Congress which went Republican in the mid-term elections in 1996. But the 'tough love' welfare strategy continued, often at state level, as Clinton allowed states to experiment in welfare reforms. One such scheme, Greater Avenues for Independence (GAIN) in California, which offers job search, education, training and work experience opportunities to the unemployed on an individual basis, crops up in Labour policy documents as an example of 'world's best practice'.[67]

There is another side to Labour's welfare-to-work programme: making work pay. There are two elements to Labour's policy: the minimum wage and the reform of the tax and benefits system to make taking a job more attractive to the unemployed. A minimum wage has long been Labour policy. New Labour argues that a legal floor to wage levels is necessary because low pay is unfair and the unemployed need incentives to take jobs. After the election the new Labour government established a Low Pay Commission under George Bain to recommend both the level of the minimum wage and any exemptions from it. In November 1997 Labour published a bill to establish the minimum wage, likely sometime in 1999. It supported a flat rate for the whole economy and all economic sectors, although it left the details of rates and whether young people and trainees would be exempt to the Bain commission. However, reports suggested that the Labour government had made clear to the Low Pay Commission that the rate should 'have regard to the wider social and economic implications' and that young people be exempt or be covered by lower rates.[68] Tackling social exclusion for New Labour includes a recognition that low paid jobs are better than no jobs at all.

Reform of the tax and benefits system is the other area where New Labour hopes to reward those who want to work. Reducing the disincentives against the unemployed taking work has long been talked about by Labour.[69] The Conservative government reduced the real value of benefits and introduced the means-tested Family Credit as an in-work benefit. Labour's 1997 manifesto stated that it would 'examine the interaction of the tax and benefits system so that they can be streamlined and modernized, so as to fulfil our objectives of promoting work incentives, reducing poverty and welfare dependency, and strengthening community and family life.' The manifesto makes reducing the starting rate for tax a 'long-term objective'. This would reduce the marginal cost of employment in lower paid work for the jobless.

Soon after their victory at the polls, Labour set up a review of the tax and benefits system chaired by the chief executive of Barclays Bank, Martin Taylor. Again, New Labour appears to be looking abroad for inspiration – in this case, to the USA. Part of Clinton's plan to reform welfare was to 'make work pay'. This meant increasing the Earned Income Tax Credit (EITC).[70] EITC was introduced in 1975, and it attempts to reduce the disincentives of taking work by giving tax credits rather than benefit handouts to poor working families. EITC is a form of tax rebate which rises to a set ceiling as earnings increase and then is withdrawn gradually as that level is exceeded. The hope in Britain is that the unemployed will take low-paid jobs because work will pay more than life on the dole: they will not lose all the extra income by paying high marginal taxes. And the government will be seen to be rewarding work, not welfare. Speaking after the 1997 budget, Brown said that EITC was superior to Family Credit: 'EITC would be unlike Family Credit in that the more you worked the more you would receive from the tax credit system. By contrast, with Family Credit, there is a cut off point so there is almost an incentive not to work.'[71] In his Autumn 1997 'green budget' Brown announced that the Taylor review would look at transforming the Family Credit benefit payment into a tax credit.

Can welfare to work work?

Despite shrinking dole queues in 1997 – there were some doubts after the election whether 250,000 unemployed young people could actually be found to fill the scheme – Labour's welfare-to-work programme received a warm welcome from both sides of industry. But the examples of welfare reform from Australia and the USA also point to problems a Labour government may face. The first are the costs and benefits of such schemes. Labour claims that, over the long term, welfare to work will save money. In Australia the JET programme, even after five years, has cost taxpayers more than it has saved. Moreover, the short-lived Job Compact ran into trouble as employers complained about unskilled and unmotivated workers for which the public subsidy did not compensate. Labour's proposals for a 'gatekeeping' service to prepare young people and the long-term unemployed for work is a response to this problem.[72]

Welfare-to-work schemes face 'displacement' and 'deadweight' problems: some of those found work will displace existing workers; and some would have found jobs anyway. Most feasibility studies of welfare to work assume significant displacement and deadweight effects, so the number of new jobs created each month is thought to be relatively modest. Even so, most studies conclude that the net effect of welfare to work over the longer term is positive in terms of higher tax yields and lower benefit payments (although a Joseph Rowntree Foundation survey of welfare-to-work schemes in 1997 suggested that, unless Labour's schemes were tightly costed, they would cost the taxpayer money rather than save them in the short-term). Part of the success of welfare to work, supporters claim, is that it increases the overall pool of skilled and employable labour. This actually expands the total number of jobs in the economy by widening its productive capacity, rather than just shifting a fixed pool of jobs between different people. But there remain arguments about whether Labour would be better targeting the older rather than the young unemployed, who are more likely to find some kind of work without state aid;

and whether a flat-rate subsidy is the best of way of encouraging employers to take different categories of the unemployed.[73]

Advocates of welfare to work also argue that the emphasis on training and 'lifelong learning' makes individuals not only more employable at higher rates of pay but also more mobile in the labour market. Lower paid jobs at the bottom of the market will lead to better paid, more skilled jobs later. As Richard Thomas, a research fellow to the Commission on Social Justice, put it: 'Our goal is a truly "flexible" labour market, which promotes efficiency, access, choice and mobility.'[74] Or, as Esping-Andersen suggested: 'if . . . the welfare state's principal activities were dedicated to maximising the life-cycle opportunities of individuals, most obviously through education and training, then our imaginary post-industrial family would know that their "McJobs" experience would be brief, and that life could improve.'[75] Some fear, however, that such a view is complacent and over-optimistic. There are fears that welfare-to-work schemes may suffer from a 'revolving door' as the unemployed move from the dole to unskilled temporary work and back again, never gaining a foothold in the more secure and better paid parts of the labour market. The McJob may be a job for life.

The second major lesson from welfare to work abroad concerns the demand side. Welfare to work is about reforming the supply-side of the economy: about increasing the quality and quantity of labour. But what, to put it simply, if there are no jobs? Supply siders, as we saw in the last chapter, make the assumption that their reforms will increase the long-term growth rate of the economy by increasing its non-inflationary productive capacity: there will, in short, be more jobs in total in the future. But what of the demand for labour? The success of the US economy is a case in point. Its supply-side welfare reforms may or may not have helped to reduce unemployment to a rate below 6 per cent in 1997. Bill Clinton, soon after New Labour's election victory, boasted that the American model of flexible labour markets and welfare reform comfortably beat all-comers. But one aspect of American success is often overlooked: the attention to the demand side of the economy.[76] Under the chairmanship of Alan Greenspan, the Federal Reserve (the US central bank) has allowed the US economy to grow at rates which would have caused apoplexy in the inflation-obsessed corridors of the Bank of England. In Britain admirers of the last Tory chancellor, Kenneth Clarke, argue that his pragmatic view of demand management prevailed over the bank's more monetarist view and, as a result, unemployment fell, especially among young people. The Fed, by contrast, is charged by Congress with managing the US economy to maximize growth and employment at low inflation. Interestingly, one of the main architects of Clinton's supply-side economics, Robert Reich, wrote at the time of Brown's first budget that welfare reform was not enough. After two supply-side suggestions, his third key to success was to 'Run the economy at full tilt. Fiscal and monetary policies should be designed to maintain adequate demand, at nearly full employment.'[77]

Finally, there are doubts about the compulsory character of Labour's welfare-to-work programme. Is it anything more than 'workfare': work for benefits? Gordon Brown has certainly shown sensitivity to the charge. Speaking after the launch of the original welfare-to-work document in 1995, Brown said that 'This is not workfare in the sense that it is understood – as the penalising of the unemployed for being unemployed, and asking people to work in return for their benefit.'[78] In his 1997 budget speech he appeared less defensive: 'With these new opportunities for young people come new responsibilities. There will be no fifth option – to stay at home on full benefit. So when they sign on for benefit they will be signing up for work.'[79] In certain respects Brown's proposals are not workfare: young people are being offered employment (or education) after six months on benefit. But in other aspects they are. The Commission on Social Justice argued that the distinctive feature of a workfare scheme was its compulsory character – no work, no benefits: 'Workfare . . . tries to make unemployment disappear by converting it into public works programmes paid at benefits plus a weekly top-up. But the long-term unemployed, like everyone else, want to work for wages, not for benefit or benefit-plus.'[80] The commission saw no mileage in a public-sector, compulsory, benefit-plus scheme. But Labour's welfare-to-work proposals are compulsory; and those working in the voluntary sector or on the environmental task force will be paid the equivalent of benefit-plus. Taken as a whole, the welfare-to-work programme is, in intent at least, more than just a scheme for manipulating the unemployment figures: there is an emphasis on real jobs (subsidized by the state), as well as job search and training measures to help people such as lone parents find jobs. But if workfare means certain categories of the unemployed having to work for their benefits, then welfare to work is a form of workfare.

Law and order

Before the 1992 general election the Tories accused Labour of being 'soft on crime'. A year later Labour's new shadow home secretary, Tony Blair, argued that the party was now 'tough on crime, tough on the causes of crime'. If Old Labour had any policy on law and order, it was one which linked rising crime to unemployment, poverty and inequality. The role of economic and social policy was to eradicate these causes of crime. New Labour still argues that 'social exclusion' is a factor contributing to criminal and anti-social behaviour. Welfare to work is part of New Labour's policy on being 'tough on the causes of crime'. But it is by no means the only element of New Labour's policies on law and order.

Before the 1970s a consensus existed between Labour and the Conservatives that law and order was beyond politics: that government could do little to influence the level of crime; and that law and order was a matter for the police and the courts.[81] From the 1970s onwards the consensus broke down as the Conservatives accused Labour of contributing to the rise in crime. The Tories questioned Labour's commitment to the rule of law, in particular as it related to striking trade unions. And they promised to amend Labour's liberal 1969 Children and Young Persons Act to toughen the law on juvenile offenders. In 1974 Labour was largely silent to these charges. In 1979 it responded by arguing that crime was related to racism, unemployment and social deprivation. Labour's 1983 manifesto had much on penal reform, non-custodial sentences and the accountability of the police. In the 1987 general election Labour blamed Conservative policies for the rising crime rates. The Tories responded by suggesting that governments had limited powers to reduce crime and that the responsibility for fighting crime lay with 'all of us', linking criminal behaviour with poor parental support and poor school discipline. In the run-up to the 1992 election Labour responded to Tory claims that it was soft on crime by calling for more police and social measures to cut crime rates.

Throughout the period from the 1960s to the early 1990s, Labour's stance on law and order was shaped by a number of associations: what David Downes and Rod Morgan call Labour's 'hostages to fortune'. The first was Labour's historic link to the trade union movement. The fight for trade union rights had long brought the labour movement into conflict with the forces of law and order. Events such as the national strikes by the National Union of Mineworkers in 1973 and again in 1984 undermined Labour's position as a defender of the rule of law – this was certainly how the Conservatives sought to portray matters. Secondly, Labour's commitment to underprivileged groups was tested to the limit during the riots which hit many British cities in the 1980s. In seeking to explain why such riots took place, Labour appeared to be condoning lawlessness. Thirdly, Labour's connection with political movements such as the Campaign for Nuclear Disarmament committed to civil disobedience again brought the party into opposition with the forces of law and order and undermined Labour's credibility as an upholder of the rule of law. Finally, the Labour government in the 1960s engaged in a programme of liberal reform including the decriminalization of homosexuality and abortion, the reduction of censorship laws and abolition of capital punishment. The period from the 1960s to the early 1990s was one in which Labour generally took a libertarian approach to social and cultural issues.

By the late 1980s a limited consensus had emerged on law and order between Labour and the Conservatives: this covered support for the police, crime prevention schemes, victim support and a policy of custodial sentences for serious crimes and non-custodial ones for minor offences. However, Labour and Tories still parted company on the causes of crime. Since 1992, and in particular since Blair became leader, Labour has been able to shake off the 'soft on crime' tag by moving beyond this limited consensus – Labour has followed the Tory lead and gone tough on crime and by moving onto territory previously occupied by the Right on the causes of crime. To New Labour, 'Recognising that there are underlying causes of crime is in no way to excuse or condone offending. Individuals must be held responsible for their own behaviour, and must be brought to justice and punished when they commit an offence.'[82]

New Labour has in large part been able to effect a shift on law and order by, as Downes and Morgan put it, dumping their hostages to fortune. It has distanced itself from the trade unions, especially striking ones, and will not reverse the tighter laws on trade union action introduced by the Conservatives in the 1980s. New Labour too has distanced itself from the civil disobedience of anti-road and other single-issue protesters in the 1990s. Moreover, under Jack Straw, who shadowed home affairs in opposition and was appointed home secretary by Blair after 1

May, it has distanced itself from the law-breaking or 'anti-social' socially excluded. In 1995 Straw proposed a crackdown on 'squeegee merchants' cleaning car windscreens at traffic lights. Labour proposed two new measures: Community Safety Orders and Child Protection Orders – the former a restraining order for 'chronic, anti-social behaviour', the latter a curfew for children under ten unsupervised late in the evening.[83]

The substance of New Labour's policies, and the support from Blair and Straw for 'zero tolerance' policing from New York, 'broke strikingly with Old Labour thinking, which stressed broad social and economic measures and welfare support to control minor deviance.'[84] For New Labour, public order is the first priority. In *Tackling the Causes of Crime*, Labour painted a grim picture of the cycle of crime and social decay – and provided a revealing insight into its thinking on the cause and effect of criminal acts:

> The rising tide of disorder is blighting our streets, neighbourhoods, parks, town and city centres. Incivility and harassment, public drunkenness, graffiti and vandalism all affect our ability to use open spaces and enjoy a quiet life in our own homes. Moreover, crime and disorder are linked. Disorder can lead to a vicious circle of community decline in which those who are able to move away do so, whilst those who remain learn to avoid certain streets and parks. This leads to a breakdown in community ties and reduction in natural social controls tipping an area further into decline, economic dislocation and crime.[85]

In this 1996 policy document Labour listed the causes of crime in the following order: 1) poor parenting (including poor supervision, 'harsh, neglectful and erratic discipline', 'parental discord', parents with criminal records, low family income and social disadvantage); 2) low school achievement, disruptive behaviour at, and truancy from, school; 3) drug and alcohol abuse; 4) unemployment and recession; 5) care in the community; 6) homelessness; and 7) lack of facilities for young people. Policies to deal with these causes included: parental responsibility orders; measures to 'hit drug dealers hard', as well as more treatment for drug users and education on the effects of drug use; educational policies to raise standards in schools; the welfare-to-work programme to increase opportunities for the unemployed; a goal to provide more services for the mentally ill; and the release of money from the sale of council houses.

Finally, New Labour has dumped the last hostage to fortune, a liberal approach to the criminal justice system. Three months before the general election, *The Economist*, bastion of old-fashioned liberalism, described New Labour as 'a poor defender of liberty'. In opposition Straw had failed to obstruct Tory Home Secretary Michael Howard's Crime Bill imposing minimum sentences on the judiciary, and had only at the eleventh hour supported the liberal opposition to the Police Bill which gave more extensive powers to the police to break in and bug homes and offices. *The Economist* described Straw and Howard as 'partners in crime'.[86] During the pre-election period, in a remarkable reversal of political roles, New Labour accused the Conservatives of failing to reform the criminal justice system in ways which would make prosecution and punishment quicker, especially for young offenders. Playing to the galleries of Middle England, as well as the council estates of inner-city Britain, the election campaign saw Straw and Howard trying to outbid each other on being tough on crime and criminals – new laws, tougher policing and quicker, longer sentences. Labour's 1997 election manifesto boasted: 'Labour is the party of law and order.' Labour promised the electorate more police on the beat, a crackdown on youth crime, 'effective sentencing', 'zero tolerance' of anti-social behaviour and crime, and a new crime of racial harassment and racially motivated violence.

The emphasis on 'zero tolerance' was evident in a Crime and Disorder Bill published in December 1997. The new bill also marked a break with Labour's liberal approach in the 1960s to the criminal justice system, especially regarding young offenders. Introducing the bill, Home Secretary Jack Straw said: 'It's about implementing a zero tolerance strategy. It's not a magic wand. There are no magic wands about dealing with human behaviour'.[87] Under the proposed act, child safety orders and curfews will be introduced for the under tens linked to crime and anti-social behaviour; parents of delinquent children will be subject to new court orders, and the law stating that children aged between ten and fourteen are incapable of telling right from wrong will be abolished. Anti-social behaviour orders will be introduced for the over tens. The bill also includes measures to replace cautions for young offenders by a single final warning and for reparation orders to make young offenders apologize and compensate their victims. Under the proposed legislation judges would have greater powers to extend sentences of sex offenders and those committed of violent crimes and ban sex offenders

117

from vulnerable areas. The bill also proposed a new offence of racial aggravation.

After the election the new Labour government went back on some of its pre-election law and order rhetoric. Straw reneged on his promise that Labour would implement the Crime Act in full: plans for mandatory prison sentences for burglary and drug offences have been shelved, although mandatory life sentences for repeat sex offenders and those involving violence have been retained. On the Police Act, however, the Home Office code drawn up under Straw appears to negate the liberal amendment requiring the permission of a judge before police have powers to raid or bug a home or office.[88] The central question for New Labour's post-Thatcherite law and order policy is whether its 'tough on crime, tough on the causes of crime' soundbite will reshape the ground established by the Conservatives in the 1980s and 1990s, namely that crime is an 'individual pathology' shaped largely by the family and that any attempt to 'explain' criminal acts is to condone them and to deny individual responsibility.

Labour's communitarianism: from social democracy to social authoritarianism?

The charge of social authoritarianism is often thrown at New Labour. Out with Old Labour's liberal approach to the criminal justice system has gone its more general sixties permissiveness. Under the influence of North American communitarianism and English ethical socialism, Labour modernizers have reacted to what they perceive as the rights-claiming and 'anything goes' culture of the period. The basis for the charge of social authoritarianism can be found in the character of the communitarianism New Labour espouses.[89]

First, Labour's communitarianism is strongly laced with ideas of reciprocity: helping the poor and unemployed gain that stake in society is conditional on them doing something about their own condition. The welfare-to-work programme involves significant elements of compulsion and makes rights to welfare more conditional on the 'responsibilities' of welfare recipients. Secondly, alongside welfare to work is an emphasis on moral entreaty to cure society's ills: 'The only way to re-build social order and stability', wrote Blair, 'is through strong values, socially shared, inculcated through individuals, family, government and the institutions of civil society.' Blair went on to deny that this meant a 'lurch into authoritarianism or attempt to impose a regressive morality'.[90] Yet, thirdly, this does involve a politics based on a conformist idea of the 'strong community'. Labour espouses firm, even punishable, ideas about the duties and obligations citizens owe the community. Labour's communitarianism is about there being common duties and values to which we all adhere. And, fourthly, there is regressiveness. The content of these duties and values, what Blair has called the 'new social morality', is heavily marked by conservative values, crowding out the more progressive and pluralist ethics of much recent Centre-Left thinking. On family policy, schooling and law and order, New Labour has taken policy positions which are marked by conservative values – on the role and shape of the family in society; on teaching methods; and on the causal explanatory chains for criminal acts. Progressive values on such matters get proportionately less space, especially when *both* main parties now increasingly shun them. Fifthly, there is something prescriptive about New Labour's approach as well. In a way no longer thought possible for the economy, New Labour in government looks set to be interventionist on social matters. The 'strong community' looks dirigiste. There is a reliance on legislative solutions to what are presented as ethical threats. Whatever the problem – bad behaviour in schools, noisy neighbours, children on the streets in the late evening – New Labour seems poised to reach for the legal pen. In their first days of government it was prescriptive moral verdicts on issues such as cigarette advertising, the sale of alchoholic soft drinks and curbs on handguns and foxhunting which aroused some of the cries of bossy social authoritarianism. And New Labour appears to see few problems when it comes to legislating for individual behaviour, yet has fought shy of doing the same for corporate responsibility: this will be left to voluntary solutions.

Labour modernizers deny the charge of social authoritarianism. Tony Wright acknowledges that:

Some people may feel uneasy about Labour's emphasis on community and responsibility, thinking that at best it is irrelevantly nostalgic and at worst dangerously authoritarian. If understood properly, it is neither. It does not deny the importance of experiment and diversity, or the fact that the community is made up of a plurality of communities, nor does it involve the state poking around in people's private lives where it has no business. But it does involve a challenge both to the possessive individualism of the New Right and to the thin rights-based liberalism of some of the Old Left: neither can provide the basis for a new politics of community and responsibility which redraws the balance between rights and duties, individual purposes and shared purposes, me and we.[91]

New Labour policy may also be seen to remain within the boundaries of a modern liberal tolerant and progressive society. When speaking on the family, Blair always adds the qualifications that he does not want a return to 'Victorian hypocrisy about sex, to women's place being only in the kitchen', or to politicians 'preaching to people about their private lives'. Leading Labour modernizers, such as Patricia Hewitt, present progressive views on family policy. Jack Straw remains a liberal on many social questions, such as race relations, the gay age of consent and the ban on gay and lesbian people in the military. Blair accepts that abortion is a matter of conscience.

For those who defend New Labour against the charge of social authoritarianism, legislating on moral issues is what governments are for. The real issue here may not be that Labour has got too moralistic at the expense of liberal permissiveness (within limits moralism is what governments are for) but that it has become more conservative and less progressive in the *content* of its moralism. Defenders might also argue that Labour was elected on a popular vote to pursue a moral agenda. Or they could argue that Labour's *social* authoritarianism does not match the *political* authoritarianism of Lady Thatcher's partial use of government power against left-wing opposition in the trade unions and local government. Labour may in practice mix centralized presidential leadership and social moralism, but does so in combination with democratic reforms which will increase devolution of power, accountability and transparency. Our conclusions from the last two chapters support the case that Labour is less social democratic. And it certainly looks more moralistic and conservative than it has in the past – but more socially *authoritarian*? How much is its conservative moralism counterbalanced by greater democracy in its approach to constitutional and political reform? This is the concern of our next chapter.

4

Government and the Constitution

The challenge facing us is that which confronted the Victorian reformers of the last century who, almost uniquely, gave Britain democracy without revolution. It is to take a working constitution, respect its strengths, and adapt it to modern demands for clean and effective government while at the same time providing a greater democratic role for the people at large.

Tony Blair, in *The Economist* (14 September 1996)

New Labour, new politics?

Labour's conversion to the cause of constitutional reform is a relatively recent one. Up until the late 1980s the dominant view within the party was that constitutional reform was a waste of time. There were more important matters for a Labour government to address, such as poverty and unemployment. But Neil Kinnock's Policy Review from 1987 began to change Labour's approach to the constitution. Abolition of the House of Lords had long been party policy. By 1989 the Policy Review had made a proposal to replace the Lords with an elected second chamber, the principal function of which was to safeguard human rights legislation. This was seen as a better way of securing individual freedom than a formal bill of rights, with which leading modernizers such as Roy Hattersley remained uneasy because of the power it would vest with the judiciary. While also rejecting reform of the electoral system in favour of proportional representation (although there was growing support for PR inside the party), Labour's Policy Review nailed the party's colours to

121

the cause of devolution. By the 1992 general election Labour was campaigning for elected parliaments or assemblies for Scotland and Wales (something which Kinnock had fought against in the 1970s) and regional government for England, as well as a Charter of Rights, a Freedom of Information Act and reform of the House of Lords. Labour also left open the issue of electoral reform, having set up a commission under Raymond Plant to study the merits of PR.

The Policy Review, then, sowed the seeds of constitutional politics in the Labour Party; and as the post-Kinnock reform of the party took shape, first under John Smith, then under Tony Blair, the seeds have grown – and, under the Blair administration, look set to bear fruit. In 1996, Blair wrote that a Labour government's constitutional programme would aim: 'to strengthen the rights and obligations of citizens; to take decision-making closer to the people; and to improve the democratic credentials of Westminster.'[1] The 1997 manifesto promised devolution for Scotland and Wales and regional government for England; greater powers for local government; elected mayors for London and other major cities; the abolition of the voting rights for hereditary peers in the House of Lords; freedom of information legislation and open government; the incorporation of the European Convention on Human Rights into British law; and a referendum on electoral reform. Labour's 1997 election campaign ran on the theme of 'trust': the Tories couldn't be trusted and a New Labour government could. Labour would be a cleaner act. It would reform the machinery of British government by making government more open, more accountable and less prone to sleaze. And a New Labour government would only make promises it could keep. It would be a government more in touch with the people.

Compared to the proposals from those old stalwarts of constitutional reform the Liberal Democrats, Labour's constitutional programme is cautious. In 1997 the LibDems offered a written constitution in place of Britain's uncodified one; a British Bill of Rights; sweeping changes to both the House of Commons and the House of Lords; and, of course, PR. Despite their differences, Labour and the LibDems published a joint constitutional report covering the substantive areas of agreement between them two months before the 1997 election. Taken together, the measures proposed by the two parties were, according to the constitutional expert Vernon Bogdanor, 'of a sweep and scope quite new in British politics'.[2] As political commentators struggled to find some clear shade of water between government and opposition in the run-up to polling day, it was the constitution which provided it. On the one side stood the Major Tories, steadfastly defending the constitutional status quo and accusing the opposition of tempting the break-up of the United Kingdom; on the other side, Labour and the LibDems, united in their condemnation of 'Tory sleaze' and the centralized British state, and both pressing for substantial constitutional reform.

The levers of power

New Labour's constitutional politics also mark a clear divide with Old Labour, Left or Right. Labour's postwar reformers, according to David Marquand, would have found New Labour's constitutional plans 'frivolous at best and dangerous at worst'. Marquand suggests that, 'For most of their history, British social democrats have been as enamoured of the ancient traditions of Britain's parliamentary state as have their rivals on the right . . . social democratic thinkers gave much more thought to what the state should do than to what it should be.' Marquand argues that, in the context of the period – British institutions had stood the test of war – such a view is understandable. And any residual desire to reform the British state evaporated once Labour took office: 'Labour ministers discovered – or thought they had discovered – that, in good hands, the Westminster model could be the engine of a social revolution. For social democrats of Crosland's generation, the point of political activity was to get back into the engine room and reach for the levers. There was no need to worry about the finer points of its design.'[3]

To be sure, Labour, like the Conservatives, engaged in intense and divisive debates after 1945 over Britain's place in Europe, in the Atlantic alliance and in the rest of the world. With the revival of nationalist sentiment within the United Kingdom in the 1960s, some Labour figures became converted to the cause of devolution, although Labour as a whole remained a unionist party. The 1960s also saw the design of Britain's ship of state draw fire from the re-emergent Marxist Left. It attacked Labour for believing that the existing levers of power could deliver socialism. Throughout the 1960s, and right through the 1970s and early 1980s, British Marxists such as Ralph Miliband – father of Blair's policy adviser David – condemned Labour for lacking a theory of the state.

Winning an election and forming a government was one thing, they argued. Using the 'capitalist state' for socialist ends was quite another. Politics reflected the class structure of capitalism – the state did so no less. Many on the Left of the Labour Party took up these arguments. A Labour government, they suggested, democratically elected and committed to a socialist programme, faced opposition from unaccountable sources of power not just in the business world but from within the state: in the civil service, in the judiciary, in the police, military and secret services. These unaccountable elements of the state, the Left argued, would have to be brought under 'democratic control' if a Labour government was to do its job.[4]

British capitalism, the constitution and stakeholder democracy

In Marquand's view, postwar social democracy had no real conception that the levers of power are not neutral instruments but help to shape the whole culture of public and private policy-making: for him, the design of the ship of state does matter. The institutions and conventions of the British constitution have impeded the modernization and long-term success of the economy, and served to prop up an unacceptably individualistic and unequal form of capitalism.[5] The advent of neo-liberal Thatcherism in the 1980s served only to exacerbate these features of the British economy and society. The task for social democracy in the 1990s is, for Marquand, to accept the time-bound character of postwar Labour politics and to move to a much more constitutionally inflected politics to turn the tide on Thatcherite individualism.

Such a view is shared by contemporary writers such as Will Hutton. In *The State We're In*, Hutton argues that Britain's economic problems result from underinvestment due to the character of the City of London – Britain's financial institutions demand too much profit too quickly. According to Hutton, British financial capitalism is shaped by Britain's constitutional form: 'The City of London and Whitehall and Westminster are symbiotic; one could not exist without the other, and none could have become what they are today without the others' support.' For Hutton: 'the semi-modern nature of the British state is a fundamental cause of Britain's economic and social problems.'[6] To reform the British constitutional state – to control the power of the executive; to devolve, decentralize and make more democratic and accountable the institutions of government – is to alter the framework within which economic and social decisions are made, thereby changing the character and outcome of those decisions, making them longer-term, more collaborative and more attuned to the needs of the real economy and society. Writing in David Miliband's early blueprint for New Labour, Hutton suggested that markets must be socially controlled and directed by new democratic public agencies:

> not the static democracy of mass parties representing electorates in national parliaments, but a much more engaged democracy reviving the life of the citizen at work, home and play, offering a multiplicity of sites for association and community. There needs to be a whole new interlocking web of public agencies, ranging from training boards to development banks, from transport institutes to science laboratories, to which are delegated the job of setting boundaries to market behaviour.[7]

Hutton's message in part reflected an academic revival in institutional thinking across the social sciences and which was finding a political audience in journals such as the *Political Quarterly*. Economic behaviour, it was suggested, could not be abstracted from the social and institutional world around it. Indeed, the social and institutional environment was crucial to shaping economic action. To those constitutional reformers such as Marquand and Hutton – and to early New Labour modernizers – significant political action was required to alter the institutional arrangements which provided the framework for British capitalism.[8] 'The capitalist free market is a marvellous servant but a disastrous master', wrote Marquand.[9] The point, then, was to make the economic servant do more of the political masters' bidding.

Marquand and Hutton spent much of the mid-1990s urging Labour modernizers to take up the baton of radical constitutional reform, reform which they believed could deliver a dynamic yet socially just form of capitalism. Writing with Tony Wright, Marquand argued:

> Labour's institutional revolution should go wide and deep, taking in all those institutions whose unreformed condition blocks the path to a more decent, dynamic and democratic society. Financial institutions have to be harnessed to the needs of the real economy. Company structures should be remodelled to incorporate the interests of an enlarged range of

stakeholders. The privatised utilities need to be reorganised as public interest companies. New institutions are required to run a reformed welfare state. The public schools have to be opened up. The institutions of professional power must have clearer and stronger public accountability.[10]

Such a view of constitutional reform embodies the idea of a 'stakeholding democracy'. As Paul Hirst suggests: 'Stakeholding extends the scope of democratic principles from the political sphere to the institutions of wider society. It treats members of such institutions as if they were citizens and includes those having affected interests within the scope of such membership.'[11] Stakeholders imagine reform of the British constitution as extending deep inside the corridors of Westminster, Whitehall, the local town hall and beyond. The principle of democracy in stakeholding challenges unbridled authority everywhere: inside companies, between buyers and suppliers and producers and consumers, and inside the welfare state, the civil service and all public and private institutions. Real citizenship means being better represented, participating and having a voice in the decisions taken by those in authority, whose power, ultimately, rests on the consent of the stakeholders, the citizen body. The political agenda of stakeholding suggests that power should be dispersed, sovereignty shared and authority negotiated through multiple forms of representation.

These ideas for a radical constitutional politics embodying the idea of stakeholding were present at the birth of New Labour; they were alluded to by Blair in a 1996 speech to the Singapore business community; and they remain part of the modernizers' milieu. For nascent New Labour, searching for new models of social democracy in the early 1990s, they provided both a radical critique of British institutions after thirteen years of Conservative 'majority rule' and an alternative to Old Labour's 'levers of power' politics. Blair and New Labour certainly wanted to get their hands on those levers. But they also wanted to modernize them. 'Contrary to the Tory canard', wrote Blair in 1996, 'constitutional reform is not an issue for the "chattering classes", irrelevant to most people. Properly done, it will go to the heart of public concerns. It is important not only for its own sake, but because it makes possible the attainment of other vital goals: a stronger economy, better transport, good schools and crime prevention.' Constitutional reform is not, Blair argued, a 'distraction': 'The role of left-of-centre parties around the world and down the ages has been to extend democratic power, while the right has struggled to reduce it. But in any case economic reconstructions and democratic renovation are not alternatives. They go in tandem.'[12]

The excesses of Thatcherism (and the sins of the sixties)

For the new generation of constitutional writers, then, the central problem with Old Labour was its blindspot to institutional reform: it just couldn't see that the Westminster model of government itself was a stumbling block to social and economic reform. Worse, the character of the British state, with its powerful central institutions, was lauded and, moreover, reinforced by Labour governments.

Indeed, the possibility of Labour using the British state for radical socialist ends on only the slimmest of popular mandates caused waves of panic among Conservatives such as Lord Hailsham in the 1970s. Britain's famously unwritten constitution hands enormous power to governments with a majority in the House of Commons. It was partly the fear that, with the breakdown of the postwar consensus, the conventions which kept governments in check would not hold that led Hailsham to label the powers of the prime minister and the cabinet an 'elective dictatorship' in his 1976 Dimbleby Lecture. A number of leading Conservatives and neo-liberals were united in calling for a written constitution to act as a check on government. But most Conservative reformers lost their interest in the constitution after 1979 once it became clear that the 'elective dictatorship' might deliver 'Thatcherism' just as easily as socialism.

As Hailsham had turned to constitutional politics in the face of a radical minority Labour government, so Labour turned to constitutional reform after nearly a decade of Thatcherite omnipotence had, Labour believed, trampled all over civil liberties, minority rights, trade union rights, local government and even, when the votes were counted, the wishes of more than half the electorate. As Gillian Peele writes: 'Labour's general approach to enhancing the powers of individuals and reforming aspects of the British state was clearly different by the 1990s from a decade earlier, reflecting a major change of mood amongst the party's activists and voters towards constitutional radicalism as a corrective to the perceived excesses of Thatcherism.'[13]

The commitment of Labour modernizers to constitutional reform is heavily marked by the experience of Thatcherism. The increasingly regional pattern of voting across the United Kingdom in the 1980s – Scotland and Wales became almost Tory-free zones but were still governed by Conservative governments hell-bent on implementing radical policies like the 'poll tax' – gave cause to the devolutionists; the curtailment, and in some cases abolition, of local government powers made the case for the decentralization of government irresistible; and what were seen as a series of attacks on fundamental civil liberties – Clause 28 outlawing the promotion of gay lifestyles, the banning of trade unions in the government's defence establishment GCHQ, anti-trade union laws more generally and the increase in powers for the police – were taken by Labour modernizers as demanding what many liberals had always argued for: a bill of rights.

Rights . . .

Kinnock's Policy Review coincided with a rise in interest in the British constitution beyond the political centre ground occupied by the Liberals and the Social Democrats.[14] The Institute for Public Policy Research, closely linked to Labour and the wellspring for much modernizing thinking, published in 1991 a draft constitution, which included a bill of rights, support for PR and an elected second chamber. The constitutional reform group Charter 88 drew support from leading Labour figures such as Robin Cook (and many beyond the normal political circles) as well as the more traditional liberal figures for its comprehensive programme of constitutional reform including a written constitution and a bill of rights. These were needed, the reformers argued, to entrench positively in a body of fundamental law the rights and liberties of citizens, as well as the principles, structure and limits of government. 'In the name of freedom', Charter 88 claimed, 'our political, human and social rights are being curtailed while the powers of the executive have increased, are increasing and ought to be diminished.' The civil liberties of citizens are under threat, the charter members argued, because British law defines freedoms negatively – a person can do as they like as long as no law exists to prevent them from doing it. In a political culture where parliament is sovereign, and no formal constitution aside from convention exists to restrain government and the legislature, the freedom of the

128

citizen, they suggested, is tenuous: governments in principle have free rein to encroach on the liberties of the citizen. So the people need positive rights enshrined in law; and the power of government should be checked and be subject to greater scrutiny.

Despite the party's traditional hostility to the judiciary, Labour modernizers have increasingly advocated policies which put more power judges' way. Under John Smith, the incorporation of the 1953 European Convention on Human Rights, to which the British government was a signatory but which it had never made part of domestic law, became Labour policy. This has remained so under Blair. The 1997 manifesto states: 'The incorporation of the European Convention will establish a floor, not a ceiling, for human rights. Parliament will remain free to enhance these rights, for example, by a Freedom of Information Act.' The manifesto suggests that Labour will supplement the convention through further anti-discrimination legislation. Once in government, Labour moved to consider further legislation against discrimination on grounds of race, sex or religion. And in the autumn parliamentary session a Human Rights Bill incorporating the European convention was introduced into the House of Lords – and at once provoked controversy amid claims that the proposed legislation amounted to a *de facto* privacy law which threatened press freedom.

The Human Rights Bill will give the judiciary the power of scrutiny over the laws passed by Parliament. What would in effect be a new British bill of rights has some influential supporters among Britain's senior judges. The incorporation of the European convention will protect civil liberties through the creation of a body of fundamental law against which all laws passed by Parliament would have to pass – judged by judges. Lord Irvine, the Labour Lord Chancellor, said in 1995 that calls for judges to have the power to resist an act of Parliament was 'judicial supremacism' which would in principle undermine the sovereignty of Parliament – something he could not support. Instead, Irvine suggests, judges should only have the power to rule that a statute was in breach of the convention. Where that was the case, it would be up to Parliament to change the law. This, Irvine says, 'would be a very British compromise'.[15+]

Labour's record in opposition, when shadow home secretary Jack Straw supported much of the law and order legislation from the Conservatives (significant parts of which fell foul of the European Convention on Human Rights as well as the human rights provisions of the United

Nations Covenant), raises the rather odd situation that a government committed to a bill of rights might find itself in breach of its own legislation. Britain's record in front of the European Court of Human Rights in Strasbourg – forty-three adverse judgements is a record among the signatories – might be repeated in the domestic courts when the European convention is incorporated into British law under Labour.

. . . and obligations

Labour's conversion to the law to protect individual freedom and civil liberties has come at a price under Blair's leadership of the party. Writing in 1996, Blair suggested that 'Democracy can flourish only as part of a rich culture of rights respected and duties performed. Most of the rights and duties relate to community life beyond the sway of the politician or the ordinary scope of the courts. But the duty of the state's constitution to safeguard freedoms, and encourage the performance of duties, remains profound.'[16] Under the influence of North American communitarianism and contemporary English ethical socialism, New Labour has taken up a critical position on the modern liberal view that 'rights trump' – that individual rights take precedence over other ethical claims. New Labour perceives postwar social democracy as being too eager to extend the scope of individual rights without any corresponding concern with the responsibilities attached to rights and the duties individuals owe as members of families and communities. Moreover, Labour modernizers see the postwar rights-claiming culture as part of a more general libertarian sentiment on the Left – stretching from Crosland to the New Left – which had little interest in how people behaved, save that individuals should find personal liberation and happiness. These were, as it were, the sins of the sixties. In Marquand's terms, the political culture of the Left was 'hedonistic' rather than 'moralistic'.

Blair is certainly a proponent of such an interpretation of the postwar Left; and he is unyielding in his advocacy of a more ethical politics.[17] As we saw in the last chapter, much of New Labour's social policy has at its root the notion that society has become too accustomed to claiming rights and that too little recognition has been given to responsibilities. Reform of the welfare state should force people to accept responsibilities and acknowledge duties and obligations. But when Blair suggests that it is 'the duty of the state's constitution to safeguard freedoms, and encourage the performance of duties', does he envisage a bill of rights including a list of duties as well as rights? And if so, which duties, what obligations? Britain would certainly be alone in the democratic world in doing such a thing.

The state and the community

New Labour has followed the general trend in party thinking since 1987 that a written constitution is unnecessary to protect civil liberties and to restrain the powers of central government. Instead, the concentration of power under the British constitution is thought best dealt with through devolution and 'reinventing government'.

The 'excesses of Thatcherism' cemented a view of state power which many on the Centre Left had long held and which in small part has fed into New Labour thinking. The old New Left, which grew out of Western communism's break with the Soviet Union in the 1950s and the new social movements in the 1960s, was deeply suspicious of the state and bureaucratic forms of governance and had little sympathy for Old Labour's 'levers of power' politics. The New Left was generally libertarian in outlook, attracted to personal liberation and keen to entrench rights, especially for minority groups. The New Left was attracted as well to devolved and decentralized forms of public administration to match its commitment to a pluralistic view of society and citizenship. Some on the New Left took up the cause of devolution. Others were strong advocates of local government and 'community action'. The old New Left also viewed the Westminster model of representative democracy as a source of political alienation, preventing citizens from participating more fully in the government of their own lives. Real citizenship required more participatory and direct forms of democracy. The Athenian polis, not the mother of parliaments, should provide the intellectual inspiration. Like the contemporary stakeholders many of them have become, the old New Left wanted democracy to spread beyond the narrow confines of Westminster to the rest of the economy and society, establishing public spaces where the life of the country was discussed and where decisions were taken.[18]

Echoes of the New Left can be found in New Labour. In a Fabian pamphlet, Blair set New Labour against 'statist socialism', praising the New Left for their 'sensitivity to the abuse of political as well as economic power'.[19] New Labour policy statements are replete with ambitions to devolve power, decentralize public administration, democratize decision-making, make government more accountable and involve citizens more in the government of the country. The central metaphor for this shift away from state forms of socialism is 'community'. Individuals, as part of a wider community, are capable of acting together to do the things they could not do alone. So, for New Labour, collective action *per se* is not dead, only the forms such action once took. Attached to the idea of community is greater democracy, mainly by making political processes more open and accountable – restoring *trust* – but also involving an idea that devolving and decentralizing government makes it more democratic. In his John Smith Memorial Lecture, Blair suggested that Labour would aspire to 'a politics in which we are giving power back to the people . . . Our ambition is to create a young Britain with a new politics which treats people as full citizens, gives them greater power over government.'[20]

But is New Labour's embrace of community window dressing for the same old levers of power? In his 1995 *Spectator* lecture, Blair suggested that 'The risk of community becoming merely a synonym for government is met by reinventing government. Co-operation, to secure desirable social and economic objectives, need not happen through central government, operating in old ways. Indeed, often it is better if it doesn't.' The speech then went on to outline new ways in which a Labour government might act, such as public–private partnerships, localized crime prevention schemes, more power to local government and a bigger role for the voluntary sector in delivering services. Labour's interest in 'reinventing government' along such communitarian lines marks a shift in politics which, in ambition at least, would leave more to voluntary endeavour, whether by individuals, families or other non-state institutions in civil society. For Labour, this has meant a positive commitment to private enterprise and the market economy. Rhetorically at least, it also marks an interest in other institutions in civil society capable of becoming agents of collective action. As we saw in the last chapter, across a whole series of policy areas – welfare to work, social security, the management of schools and the NHS – Labour is now supportive of decentralized and devolved forms of public administration and of the involvement of the private and voluntary sectors in the provision and delivery of welfare services.

Shorn of 'community', New Labour's general approach to public administration has much in common with the broader managerial movement to 'reinvent government' in Britain and the USA – and which informed many of the reforms to public administration by Conservative governments in the 1980s and 1990s (such as the civil service 'Next Step agencies'). 'Reinventing government' places emphasis on consumer rather than producer interests; outcomes rather than inputs; partnerships between the public, private and voluntary sectors; the regulation rather than direct delivery of services by government; and decentralized forms of governance, including markets.[21] But 'reinventing government' does not simply equate with privatization. As Robin Butler, head of the home civil service and cabinet secretary under both the Major and Blair governments, put it, privatization was one policy option but 'it is not *the* answer . . . the ownership of a good or service is less important than the dynamics of the market institution that produces it.'[22] This pragmatic approach to public administration underpins New Labour's attitude to government after what it perceives as Thatcherism's dogmatic attachment to the market and Old Labour's equally dogmatic attachment to the state. As the Labour modernizer Geoff Mulgan argued in 1993:

> the changing balance between public and private sector, state and market solutions, cannot be separated from the organisational forms and competences which each brings to bear. It is with these, and with public and private organisations' practical ability to recognise and solve problems in everything from energy to prisons and from universities to childcare, that any useful argument now has to begin.[23]

Post-Thatcherite government, in short, is a matter of horses for courses. Before looking in detail at some of Labour's proposals to 'reinvent government', it might be useful to add three caveats. First, there is certainly an element of vagueness – perhaps even evasiveness – in some of Labour's statements on government. 'The power of the community', 'the enabling state' (Brown) or 'the collective power of all used for the individual good of each' (Blair), or even 'the strength of common endeavour' (the new Clause 4), may sound good in small chunks, but the devil, as

133

always, is in the detail. To have any meaning, these soundbites must be attached to public policies which set out concrete institutional arrangements. In the absence of any, it is difficult to see how community can mean anything but government. Secondly, Labour's commitment to devolved forms of governance – whether in schools, devolved parliaments or local government – needs to be studied carefully alongside any possibility that central government's reserve powers may negate decentralization of authority. This is especially true in terms of the 'rate capping' of local government. Thirdly, we need to question whether there is a commitment to political pluralism to match the institutional pluralism in New Labour thinking. Does Labour's commitment to the sovereignty of Parliament and Westminster majoritarian politics weaken its claim to be offering a 'New Politics'?

Given these things, it would be reasonable to suggest that a Labour administration might *do less* as a government. Certainly it might not want to do those things which postwar social democrats did or aspired to. But, more importantly, it might over the medium term roll back the frontiers of the central state, giving greater powers to local and regional government, and allow individuals and institutions in civil society the space to do more, especially in terms of the provision of welfare. This indeed would be a radical, post-Thatcherite agenda. And it might, we suggest, be the only way in which community *did not* become merely a synonym for government.

Devolution: Scotland, Wales and Northern Ireland

The United Kingdom of Great Britain and Northern Ireland is a unitary state. But, as Bogdanor points out: 'in Britain, unitary has never meant uniform, for the British administrative system has long been highly asymmetrical in order to accommodate Scottish and Welsh identities within the framework of a multinational state. So it is that retention of Scottish and Welsh identity has proved perfectly compatible with membership of the United Kingdom.'[24] Despite the sovereignty of the Westminster Parliament, the asymmetrical character of the British state is clearly visible: Scotland has its own legal system, schools and established church. Before devolution, executive affairs north of the border were run by the Scottish Office. But Scotland had no legislature – only dedicated standing committees and the Scottish Grand Committee to scrutinize and debate bills relating to Scotland. Pre-devolution, Wales too had an executive – the Welsh Office – as well as a Welsh Grand Committee to hear and debate Welsh bills. However, neither was as well established or as powerful as its Scottish counterpart. This administrative diversity – with its underlying cultural and historical roots – leads Bogdanor to prefer the 'union state' to unitary state. It also, he believes, provides the real rationale for devolution, the 'transfer of powers at present exercised by ministers and Parliament to regional or sub-national bodies which are both subordinate to Parliament and directly elected. Devolution is thus a process by which Parliament transfers its powers without relinquishing its supremacy.'[25]

Devolution was last on the Labour Party's political agenda in the 1970s. Faced with little in the way of a parliamentary majority, the Labour government after 1974 looked to the Scottish and Welsh nationalists in the Commons for support. The Scottish Nationalist Party (SNP) and Plaid Cymru had since the early 1960s seen their support rise within the electorate, and in the two 1974 general elections the nationalists saw support turn into real electoral gains. With the Liberals, they held the balance of power in Parliament. Labour moved to introduce devolution legislation as a way of keeping the nationalists on the government's side. Its first attempt in 1976, which covered devolution for both Scotland and Wales, fell on the floor of the Commons. Separate bills were then introduced for Scotland and Wales and both became law in 1978. The bills contained provisions for referendums on devolution – and both were amended to include qualified majorities (40 per cent of the *electorates* would have to vote 'yes' for devolution to happen). This proved the stumbling block for Scottish devolution. In March 1979, 52 per cent of Scottish voters affirmed devolution. But, on a turnout of 64 per cent, the 'yes' vote was only 33 per cent of the electorate – and so the motion fell. Matters were more straightforward in Wales: on a turnout of 59 per cent, 80 per cent voted against devolution for the principality.

The experience of the devolution debacle in the 1970s has not been lost on New Labour. The Labour government has sought pre-legislative mandates for Scottish and Welsh devolution with referendums using simple majorities. In Scotland, as was expected, the referendum held on 11 September 1997 showed a clear majority for a parliament with tax-varying powers.[26] In Wales the 18 September referendum result was on a knife-edge right up until the last votes were counted, with the 'yes' campaign scraping home with a 0.6 per cent majority. The Labour government learnt a second important lesson from the 1970s. Instead of long lists of powers to the devolved authorities, as the legislation in the 1970s included, New Labour's devolution pro posals set down the powers that Westminster will 'reserve', leaving the rest for devolution.

New Labour has not had an altogether easy ride on devolution. There remains a strong residual scepticism and, in some cases, outright hostility, to devolution within the party. However, the Policy Review in the late 1980s made firm commitments to devolution. These were repeated in the 1992 manifesto which committed a Labour government to the immediate creation of a Scottish parliament and the setting up of a Welsh assembly within five years. No referendums would be required. Labour also supported and participated in the Scottish Constitutional Convention, which brought together the political parties and other interested groups in Scotland. The convention, dominated by Labour and the LibDems after the Scottish Tories and the SNP declined to participate, published a report in November 1995 calling for the creation of a Scottish parliament, elected by PR and with a remit covering the work of the Scottish Office. The convention proposed that the parliament should have tax-raising powers. Again, no referendum would be necessary.

All of this appeared to be Labour policy until the summer of 1996, when the Labour leadership was preparing the final draft of the party's pre-election 'Road to the Manifesto', which was to be put to the vote of Labour Party members. As one report put it: '[Blair] is determined to fight the election on a manifesto that is not just intellectually sustainable and unambiguous, but fireproof from Tory attack.'[27] As a result, the so far referendum-less policy was overnight amended to include referendums on both a Scottish parliament and its tax-raising powers.

Reports of similar divisions between senior Labour figures over devolution were to resurface once the party took office. The matter chiefly concerned the parliament for Scotland. Although there remained opposition from within the Welsh Labour Party to the plans for an assembly in Cardiff to take over the executive work of the Welsh Office, the absence of legislative powers make Welsh devolution relatively straightforward – and, some add, a waste of tax-payers' money! But, for Scotland, the legislative powers of the Edinburgh parliament raise a problem common to all unitary states considering some measure of devolution: why should Scottish MPs at Westminster be able to vote on matters concerning only England when MPs representing English constituencies cannot vote on Scottish affairs, which would be dealt with by the separate Scottish parliament? This is known as the West Lothian question, after the former seat of the veteran Scottish Labour MP Tam Dalyell, who has been one of the most persistent opponents of devolution for Scotland. It may be true that, short of federalism – where political power is shared by central and regional government – there is no 'solution' to the West Lothian question. But there is certainly a *modus operandi*. Indeed, the West Lothian question has already been put to the test, between 1921 and 1972, during which Ulster was governed from the Stormont assembly, and, apart from the odd warning from Harold Wilson to the Ulster Unionists in the 1960s, caused few constitutional hiccups.[28] Indeed, the bipartisan policy on Northern Ireland between Labour and the Conservatives before the 1997 general election suggests that, while the West Lothian question certainly exists, the claim that there is no workable 'solution' to it is bogus. The West Belfast question is conspicuous by its absence.

One way of dealing with the West Lothian question is to reduce the number of Scottish MPs sitting at Westminster. Scotland is already over-represented in the House of Commons in terms of MPs per head of population. Labour's White Paper on Scottish devolution, *Scotland's Parliament*, published on 24 July 1997, proposed that the number of Scottish members be reduced by about twelve. Under pressure from leading English Labour ministers, Donald Dewar, secretary of state for Scotland, had to agree that the law which guarantees a minimum of seventy-one Scottish seats in the Commons be repealed. The redrawing of Scottish constituencies is unlikely to take place until after 2004.

The final proposals for Scottish devolution centre on a 129-member parliament with tax-raising powers. The parliament is to be first elected in 1999 and will begin work in the year 2000. Although no quotas will be established, the government wants selection panels to ensure the fair representation of women, ethnic minorities and disabled people (the same is true for the Welsh assembly). Electors will have two votes: one for a constituency MP and the other for a party list. So the new parliament will contain an element of PR. Members of the Scottish parliament will sit for a four-year fixed term. A Scottish executive will be formed by the majority party, led by a first minister. This Scottish government will be responsible for education, health, law and order, the environment, local government, transport, agriculture, sport, the arts and other policy areas not reserved by Westminster. Those policy areas reserved by Westminster are economic policy, social security, employment legislation, defence and foreign affairs, security and border control, ethical issues and the constitution. (The Scottish parliament could thus debate full independence but it could not declare it.) Disputes between Westminster and Edinburgh will be referred to the Judicial Committee of the Privy Council.

Scotland will continue after devolution to receive its block grant from London. The Scottish parliament will have powers to raise or reduce the basic rate of income tax by three pence in the pound. It will determine the spending priorities of its public programmes, and will be free to raise short- but not long-term loans on its own. Significantly, the Scottish parliament will be audited by the UK Comptroller and Auditor General: value for money will be a matter for central government. And, of course, as this is a matter of constitutional devolution not federalism, Westminster will remain sovereign.

Labour's proposals for Scottish devolution were widely recognized by supporters and opponents alike as marking a significant transfer of powers from the central Westminster–Whitehall state to a new state north of the border. The same cannot be said about Labour's plans for Welsh devolution. There may be good reasons why this should be the case. Before devolution, the Welsh Office had far fewer powers than the Scottish Office. Most of the work of the Welsh Office covered the execution of laws made in London. Moreover, unlike Scotland, with its own legal and education systems, Wales requires little separate legislation. In the run-up to the referendum, supporters of Welsh devolution argued that the relatively minor status of the Welsh Office did not preclude any assembly in Wales taking on more powers in the future.

Labour's proposals follow this logic by offering executive, not legislative, devolution for Wales. The White Paper *A Voice for Wales*, published on 22 July 1997, proposed that a forty-seat assembly would take over the executive functions of the Welsh Office. It will have no tax-raising powers. Elections will be on a two-vote constituency/party list formula, and members of the assembly will sit for a four-year fixed term. The assembly will elect a leader from the majority party who will head an executive committee of ten members. Westminster will retain control over national issues such as economic policy, foreign affairs and social security, as well as all primary legislation. The new Welsh assembly will have certain powers over secondary legislation, that is, the settling of the details of laws first passed by Westminster. The main powers of the Welsh assembly will be over the block grant from the Treasury to Wales (in 1997, around £7 billion). The assembly will allocate resources from this budget and so will have particular powers over areas such as health and education, as well as transport, planning and regional economic development. It will also determine the future of the quangos in Wales, which after the assembly is established in May 1999 will be under its control. Unlike the secretary of state for Scotland, whose role will diminish significantly once a Scottish parliament is established, the secretary of state for Wales will remain a major figure acting as an advocate for Welsh affairs in the British cabinet. Under the proposals, Wales will continue after 1999 to send forty MPs to Westminster.

The Labour government also supports devolution for Northern Ireland. This is based on the bipartisan policy established by Blair which marked a shift away from the 1980s, when the Labour Party supported a policy of a united Ireland by consent. Under Blair, Labour has moved to a unionist position which seeks to reconcile the 'two traditions' of nationalism and unionism. Its policy is to accept that Ulster will remain part of the United Kingdom, although the Irish government in Dublin will have a formal role north of the border as part of the 1985 Anglo-Irish Agreement. Labour also supports the creation of a devolved legislative body to govern the province, with various guarantees to the nationalist Catholic minority that any new Ulster government will not be dominated by the Protestant unionist majority.

How significant are Labour's proposals for Scottish and Welsh devolution? Do they mark a step towards a federal Britain – or even the break-up of Britain altogether? Tory and Labour opponents of devolution alike were quick to paint the creation of a Scottish parliament in particular as, in Tam Dalyell's words, 'a motorway, without exit, to a separate Scottish state'.[29] Nationalists in Scotland and Wales hope that this is true. Devolutionists disagree. They argue that the creation of a Scottish parliament and a Welsh assembly are the best means of avoiding the break-up of the union by addressing the legitimate aspirations of the peoples of Scotland and Wales for some measure of self-government. Once established – and the Welsh assembly may evolve into something more powerful – devolution, supporters claim, will calm nationalist sentiments and expectations rather than inflame them. Moreover, devolution will go some way to devolving power away from the over-centralized British state, as well as making the existing forms of regional public administration more accountable and democratic – and even perhaps more effective.

Labour's policy is unequivocally devolutionist. The 1997 manifesto states: 'Subsidiarity is as much a principle in Britain as it is in Europe. Our proposal is for devolution not federation. A sovereign parliament will devolve power to Scotland and Wales. The Union will be strengthened and the threat of separation removed.' On this, Labour clearly parts company from the LibDems, who are committed to a federal United Kingdom where sovereignty is shared across central and regional government rather than concentrated in one body – the Westminster Parliament. But Labour's plans for devolution taken as a whole – and these include a policy for rolling devolution to regional bodies in England – might create what Bogdanor calls a 'quasi-federal state', as significant legislative and executive power is stripped away from Westminster and devolved to regional governments.[30] Labour's White Paper on Welsh devolution may point the way as it puts an essentially regionalist rather than nationalist case, more concerned with the decentralization and democratization of regional public administration than with nationalist demands for self-determination.

Devolution: England

As the new Labour government set about persuading the electors of Scotland and Wales on the merits of devolution, John Lloyd wrote that 'renovation of the Union, now so urgent, is in danger of leaving out England.'[31] It is certainly true that, in 1997, the focus of Labour's devolution plans was on Scotland and Wales, as well as its attempt to broker a deal in Ulster. But Labour does have a programme for the devolution of power to the regions in England. In 1992 the party campaigned on a policy of creating a new regional tier of government in England. In a 1995 consultation paper, *A Choice for England*, Labour proposed creating 'regional chambers', consisting of the nominated representatives of local councils and acting as the 'regional voice' of local government.[32]

This was necessary, Labour believed, to make more accountable and democratic the already growing body of regional government, principally the ten Integrated Regional Offices (IROs) coordinating the regional work of the major central government departments, and supporting a wide cast of non-elected quangos. The regional chambers would also add substance to the regional coordination already undertaken by local authorities. *A Choice for England* emphasized the 'rolling' character of regional devolution – a model which has found favour in Spain since 1980. Step one, it suggests, would be the setting up of regional chambers in each of the IRO regions, the function of which would be 'strategic coordination' over areas such as economic development, transport and the environment, and 'democratic oversight'. Step two would be the creation of directly elected regional assemblies – and would be optional. Local government and the public, via a referendum, must want it. A further precondition would be the reorganization of local government into unitary authorities (see below). These assemblies would have no tax-raising or legislative functions, but there was the suggestion that many of the executive functions of the IROs and quangos might be given to the directly elected assemblies. This two-step policy was endorsed the following year[33] and in the 1997 election manifesto.

London, Labour argues, is a special case. A directly elected assembly (step two) will be created if the people want one to fill the void left by the abolition of the Greater London Council in 1985 – although Labour is keen to emphasize that it has no wish to re-create the GLC, most of the powers of which have been devolved either to the London boroughs or to city-wide quangos. Soon after the election in 1997, the environment minister and deputy prime minister, John Prescott, announced the Labour government's plans for London ahead of a referendum on reform in May 1998. Labour's consultative Green Paper included plans for creating a US- or continental-style mayor for London. The London mayor would be directly elected and would head a Greater London authority covering the thirty-two London boroughs and the City of London, charged with planning for the capital in areas such as transport; for giving the City 'strategic direction'; and for taking a leading role in the capital's culture, tourism, sport and media. The mayor would be responsible for the authority's budget. The elected assembly, consisting of unpaid members sitting for three- to four-year terms, would have the power to scrutinize the budget, decisions and appointments made by the mayor. London, Prescott said, would be the forerunner for English regional government in general, including the possibility that other big cities may have their own mayors.

Labour's plans for English regional devolution have been attacked, just as the party's proposals for a Welsh assembly have been, as pointless additions to local government – costly bureaucracies with little real power. Labour is careful to play down the expense of the new assemblies and emphasize their strategic and democratic character. And it is in this respect that Labour's proposals have a certain coherence to them. Few can deny that the past decade has seen a mushrooming of new local and regional agencies – what Desmond King calls the 'new local governance system'[34] – many of which have taken powers away from local government and few of which are accountable to the electorate in the way local authorities are. The past decade has also witnessed the growth in regional economic development bodies, such as training and enterprise councils and urban development corporations. These have largely bypassed local government, having direct links with central government agencies. As party policy documents argue, Labour's proposals seek not to reverse these trends but to restore and extend the role of local government and local democracy in regional governance. What is less clear is the extent to which a Labour government sees the creation of regional government in England as allowing for regional policy-making, and the diversity of policies which would inevitably happen, not just regional administration.

Local government

Certainly, in consultation documents and policy speeches, New Labour is committed to the rhetoric of policy pluralism when it comes to local government. In his 1996 John Smith Memorial Lecture, Tony Blair said: 'I want to enable local communities to decide more things for themselves through local councils.' A policy document presented to the 1995 party conference states: 'there is no universal solution to the problems faced by local communities . . . The essence of local government is that it is local, coming up with practical local solutions to particular local problems or making the most of local opportunities.' To do this, Labour proposed in 1995 that Parliament place on local councils a statutory duty 'to promote the overall social, economic and environmental well-being of the communities they serve'. Councils would be granted 'a new power of community initiative giving them greater freedom to respond to local needs'. The document also suggested that, 'while central government should set standards and have fall-back powers to use in extreme situ-ations, central government should cease its detailed interference in the day-to-day affairs of local councils.'[35] Labour also proposed that local government be reorganized wherever possible into unitary author-ities – a necessary step, as we have seen, to directly elected regional assemblies and followed the 'reinventing government' route, support-ing the idea that local authorities should oversee the delivery of services, and be the guarantor of their quality and value for money, without ne-cessarily doing the providing.[36] To this end, Labour proposed in addition that compulsory competitive tendering should be abolished.

On accountability, Labour suggested that a third of councillors should come up for election every year, and that local authorities should be more accountable to local electors through the publication of a council's audited performance plan, as well as attempts to increase public consul-tation and participation through techniques such as 'community forums', 'citizen juries', user groups, advisory panels, public hearings and opinion polls. On the crucial issue of finance, Labour proposed that central gov-ernment retain its right to allocate funds to councils, but that the busi-ness rate should be set locally, not by central government; that the 'capping' system on council spending by central government be reformed; and that local authorities be permitted to invest the money from the sale of council houses and other capital assets.

The tone of the 1997 manifesto, while retaining the emphasis on de-mocracy and local accountability, is far less decentralist. Central govern-ment will reserve powers to limit 'excessive council tax rises'. The policy to allow local authorities to set the business rate may only happen 'after consultation with business'. The national Audit Commission, which audits local government, will be given additional powers 'to monitor per-formance and promote efficiency: On its advice, government will where necessary send in a management team with full powers to remedy fail-ure.' The champion of local civic democracy against central government, Simon Jenkins, suggested that these reserve powers undermined Labour's claim that it was 'breathing new life into democracy'.[37]

Since the election, Labour has continued its policy towards local government of talking softly but carrying a big stick. Gordon Brown's first budget provided extra funds for hard-pressed local education authorities; but he also told them what they must spend it on. The phased release of local authority capital receipts was started; but the Conservative capping regime would remain subject to review. David Blunkett's Department of Education sprang into action using Tory legislation to send in hit squads to 'failing' schools and LEAs. But the government also announced a 'best value' initiative which would pilot alternatives to competitive tendering: strict economic criteria will be replaced by broader measures of success, including the effectiveness and quality of service.[38]

Steve Richards, political editor of the *New Statesman*, suggests that the Labour government is genuinely ambivalent about how much real power to devolve to local government: 'There is a general recognition from ministers that there are real risks in giving greater responsibilities to councils, although in principle that is what they would like to do.' To New Labour, local government must, in Blair's words, 'understand that they have to use power with prudence and responsibility.'[39] The key to Labour's policy on local government is accountability – which was, paradoxically, what lay behind the Conservatives' 'poll tax' to replace the property-based rates system. But instead of making everyone pay, as the 'poll tax' did, New Labour's strategy appears to be aimed at making local government more responsible by making local councillors more accountable and responsive to the voters for the money they spend. By 1997 around 80 per cent of council funding came from, and was determined by, central government. The remaining finance raised locally was also limited by Whitehall under the capping regime. Real power would mean increasing the proportion of that money raised locally and handing local councils real control over the size of their budgets. Labour's proposals for more frequent elections, policy panels and local referendums are aimed at breaking through and establishing the basis for greater local accountability and, crucially, responsibility. After announcing the Labour government's financial settlement with local government, which stuck to the previous Conservative government's spending plans but which relaxed council tax capping limits, John Prescott wrote:

> I have told councils that they may spend more money; this is not to permit them to be irresponsible, but to allow them to be responsive to their voters. I have also said, very clearly, that however much they propose to

spend, they must consider whether local taxpayers can afford it. This is not an opportunity to return to the days of spiralling local taxes. The more responsive councils are, the easier it will be to progress to the removal of capping in the next year or so.[40]

Europe and foreign affairs

So far we have dealt with New Labour's policies on devolving power within the United Kingdom. Now we shall turn briefly to Europe. How much power is the Blair administration willing to concede to the European Union? Can New Labour balance a commitment to being positive inside the EU while remaining steadfast behind the sovereignty of the Westminster Parliament?

Under Blair's leadership, Labour's European policy has continued in the broad pro-European direction established under Neil Kinnock and John Smith. Long gone are the days in the 1980s when Labour's policy was simply withdrawal. But, under Blair, Labour's policy on Europe has also broadly followed the path taken by the Conservatives. The tone may be more positive and constructive but the substance is similar. First, as we saw in Chapter 2, New Labour has come down firmly on the side of flexible labour markets, welfare reform and free trade. Blair and Brown have been highly critical of Britain's continental partners for burdening their economies with regulations and for advocating public-sector job-creation schemes. Even on the issue which did divide Labour from the Conservatives at the last election, the social chapter, Labour adds: 'We will use our participation to promote employability and flexibility, not high social costs.'

New Labour has also come out strongly against a federal Europe. Partly out of fear that the party would be outflanked by the Tories on Europe, Labour during the 1997 election campaigned on a tough but constructive line. A Labour government would fight for British interests inside the EU. The manifesto offered little comfort to Conservative Party strategists eager to paint Labour as the lap-dog of continental European powers: 'Our vision of Europe is of an alliance of independent nations choosing to cooperate to achieve the goals they cannot achieve alone. We oppose a European federal state.' On the constitution of the EU, the 1997 manifesto called for greater openness, democracy and value for money within

EU institutions. It opposed any significant increase in the powers of the EU and supported the enlargement of the community to the east and south. Labour insisted that the national veto be retained 'over key matters of national interest, such as taxation, defence and security, immigration, decisions over the budget and treaty changes'. A Labour government would consider only a limited extension of Qualified Majority Voting (a weighted system of voting which does not require unanimity among member states) 'in areas where that is in Britain's interests'. At the 1997 Amsterdam summit of the European Union, Prime Minister Blair won an opt-out for Britain over EU plans for the abolition of internal border controls: Britain under the deal retains control over visa, immigration and asylum policy.

Labour's constructive Euroscepticism during the election campaign was not simply reactive to potential Tory attacks. Labour policy had in the mid-1990s been marked by an opposition to federalism and the extension of powers to the EU, by support for the enlargement of the EU, and by a foreign and defence policy shaped by membership of the North Atlantic Treaty Organization and by Britain's independent nuclear weapons: Labour was clear that cooperation among member states on foreign and defence issues did not mean the creation of a common policy; and that the Western European Union should be the European wing of NATO, not the start of an EU armed force.[41] Labour's new foreign secretary, Robin Cook, started his period in office by arguing that Britain's foreign policy needed a 'new direction': an ethical dimension, on human rights and arms control, especially the sale of arms to repressive regimes, after the years of Tory realpolitik. But, despite Cook's moral mission statement for the Foreign Office, the new Labour government continued to fulfil the traditional British foreign policy role as the most loyal ally of the United States, especially in the Middle East.

New Labour's European policy is certainly more sceptical than many Labour modernizers might wish. There is a strong pro-European camp of Labour modernizers who see the advent of a more democratic Europe as opening up the possibility of a new federal constitutional settlement.[42] There remains strong support for Britain joining the single currency, even if Gordon Brown has ruled out Britain's membership this side of the next general election. And many Labour modernizers continue to find the continental model of capitalism attractive, just as an earlier generation of revisionist British social democrats did.

146

Government, Parliament and the people

The case for the devolution and decentralization of government and public administration in the United Kingdom ultimately rests on a view of the British state as over-centralized and undemocratic. The creation of a Scottish parliament and a Welsh assembly, and the rebuilding of local and regional government, are at heart means of devolving power away from Westminster and the Whitehall ministries, allowing new or existing sources of political authority to pass laws and make executive decisions about where money is spent and how services are delivered. To be sure, there remain question marks over certain aspects of Labour's proposals, especially as they deal with the powers of local government. But still, Labour's reform of the British constitution is informed by the view, as the 1997 manifesto put it, that 'Our system of government is centralised, inefficient and bureaucratic.' Britain is ruled by an 'elective dictatorship' which, over the course of eighteen years of one-party government, has become sleazy, complacent and corrupt.

Sleaze, open government and Commons procedure

Labour's 1997 election campaign ran on the theme of 'trust'. The Conservative government had broken their 1992 election promises, especially on taxes; members of that government had given inaccurate accounts to Parliament on the sale of arms to Iraq; and individual Tory MPs were up to their elbows in financial sleaze as they accepted 'cash for questions' in the House of Commons. John Major had proved a weak leader of government because he wouldn't do anything about it. Labour promised to make government more trustworthy by reforming its machinery: making government more open, more accountable and 'cleaner' by reviewing the funding of political parties. Labour also campaigned to restore the public's trust in politics by promising only what was reasonable and what could be delivered.

Whether all of the mud thrown at the Major government should have stuck is beyond the scope of this book. Certainly, it is worth remembering that Major did open the doors of government a chink. In 1992, soon after winning the general election, he published 'Questions of Procedure for Ministers' (QPM), variously described as 'tips for beginners' and 'a highway code of government'.[43] Major also made public the membership of cabinet standing committees and the heads of the security services, and set up the Nolan Committee to examine the charge of sleaze in government.

'Unnecessary secrecy in government', Labour's 1997 manifesto cautioned, 'leads to arrogance in government and defective policy decisions.' Labour campaigned on a Freedom of Information Act and an independent National Statistical Service. A White Paper on open government had been expected before the summer recess in 1997. But a Downing Street spokesman was quoted as saying that ministers needed 'more experience of government'.[44] On parliamentary procedure, Blair wrote in 1996 that 'We need to improve the way we scrutinise and debate legislation, how MPs hold the executive to account, how we organise the legislative programme and how we deal with European legislation.'[45] After the election the new Labour government moved quickly to change the format of prime minister's questions, and Ann Taylor, Leader of the House, set up a review of parliamentary procedure. Labour's 1997 manifesto committed the new government to the implementation of the Nolan recommendations on standards in public life and placing an obligation on all political parties to declare their sources of income above a minimum figure.

Labour's victory in the 1997 general election also brought about a remarkable change in the number of women in Parliament: 120 across all parties, of which 101 are Labour, compared to sixty-three during the 1992 parliament. Labour had established in 1993 a policy of women-only shortlists. This required that in each region half the candidates in target seats and in seats where there was a Labour MP standing down had to be drawn from women-only shortlists. The policy was ruled illegal in January 1996. Once in power, a new women's cabinet sub-committee was set up and a women's unit in Harriet Harman's Department of Social Security. This fell short of the cabinet-level job previously promised by New Labour, although not in the manifesto. The role of the unit was to monitor policy-making across all Whitehall departments and ensure women are on the political agenda. Of concern to many of the women MPs, especially the new young women Labour MPs, was the importance of changing the culture of Parliament and policy-making from an adversarial boys' club to a more cooperative, women-friendly place.

The new Labour government also moved quickly to reorganize, and consolidate the powers of, the central machinery of government: namely Downing Street and the prime minister's private office, press office and policy unit, and the Cabinet Office and its standing committees. Much of the attention – and the furore – surrounded the appointment of Peter Mandelson as 'minister without portfolio' inside the Cabinet Office to coordinate the work of government departments. Attention was also drawn to Blair's press secretary, Alastair Campbell, who ordered that all ministerial interviews and statements be cleared with his office first. The view of the new Labour government was that the centre of government (the 'core executive') – in particular, Downing Street and the Cabinet Office – was too weak under the last Conservative government. Speaking after five months in power, Mandelson said: 'The job of the centre of government is to make sure departments work together: failure of government machinery means failing the people who elected us.'[46] So the new Labour government proposed to beef up the centre by creating a coordinating role for Mandelson and by establishing a strategy committee of the cabinet chaired by the prime minister and including the deputy prime minister, the chancellor and the foreign secretary. In an interview in *The Times* on 1 December 1997, the Lord Chancellor, Lord Irvine, suggested that it was this most historic of offices of state which could provide a coordinating role within British government, ending, as Irvine saw it, the 'turf wars' between Whitehall departments.

The new character of the Blair administration was reinforced at the end of July 1997 with the publication of the administration's ministerial code – an updated QPM. With so many allegations of sleaze before the election, inevitably much of the attention was drawn to the notes on the conduct of ministers relating to misleading statements to Parliament (they must resign), personal gifts and private interests. But the more significant parts of Blair's QPM concerned the powers of Downing Street. These required that all major interviews, media appearances, speeches, press releases and policy initiatives by ministers be cleared by Downing Street in advance. And all media contacts by ministers were to be logged.

Political commentators were divided on these changes. Three months after the new administration took office, Peter Riddell, political editor of *The Times*, wrote:

> Goodbye Cabinet government. Welcome the Blair presidency . . . [The ministerial code] sets out in a formal code of conduct . . . the biggest

centralisation of power seen in Whitehall in peacetime . . . Either a Prime Minister trusts those whom he appoints to ministerial office, or he does not . . . So much for Cabinet ministers being independent heads of department with their own responsibilities . . . Moreover, such centralisation will, in practice, be impossible to sustain.[47]

Simon Jenkins affirmed this view.

If ever there was a Cinderella passage in a manifesto, it was Mr Blair's attack on the over-centralisation of government, its bureaucracy and lack of accountability under the Tories . . . Against all academic analysis, he seems to believe that Downing Street is not a strong institution of modern government, but a weak one. Cabinet government must not be pluralistic or open, but regimented from the centre. The centre must equally be ready for total war. This aggressive philosophy of government is bold. It defies the maxim that absolute power corrupts.[48]

But *The Economist* cautioned against over-reaction. Many of the things the new Blair government was doing were common practice, such as the checking of ministerial statements and coordinating the presentation of policy across departments. Moreover, the new arrangements might, as Mandelson suggested, just be 'more effective and decisive'. Nor did *The Economist* see a conflict between New Labour's commitment to devolution on the one hand and strong government from the centre on the other:

Mr Blair's intention is that the government should disperse those powers which it is not best placed to exercise directly, but that it should use effectively those powers it retains. Mr Blair's drive to control his government may raise doubts over his willingness to devolve real power to regional assemblies and local government, but it certainly does not preclude him from doing it.[49]

The House of Lords

Reform of the House of Lords should cause New Labour few problems. After all, the best, and perhaps only, defence of the Lords as Parliament's second chamber is that 'it is there and perhaps also because it works after a fashion.'[50] For a party of the Left, the abolition or reform of the Lords and the hereditary principle should lead to no loss of sleep. The conservative attachment to tradition and the principle of 'if it ain't broke don't fix it' should hold little sway over a radical, modernizing government. But the weakness of the Lords in the British constitution is also strangely a source of strength for this most arcane of institutions. The fact that the Lords cannot mount any real challenge to the authority of the Commons means that, if Labour were to establish a second chamber with real power and democratic legitimacy, it would be creating an institution which could mount a challenge to its unbridled authority.

This in part has meant that Labour has never given particular priority to reform of the Lords. During the Policy Review, Labour proposed a second chamber, elected by PR, which would act as a guarantor of fundamental rights. This was still Labour's policy under Blair in 1995. But by early 1996 policy on the Lords had shifted. In his February John Smith Memorial Lecture, Blair suggested that, while the party favoured an elected second chamber, the abolition of the hereditary principle might be the start to a longer process of reform: 'Surely we should first make the House of Lords a genuine body of the distinguished and meritorious – with a better, more open and independent means of establishing membership – and then debate how we incorporate democratic accountability.' This became the core of Labour's policy at the 1997 general election.

So, under Blair, Labour's position on reform of the House of Lords changed. There were, party managers pointed out, practical reasons for this. Outright abolition of the Lords would clog up the parliamentary timetable, especially as it is the convention that all constitution bills are taken on the floor of the House of Commons. The new Labour government's policy on the Lords was not made any clearer by the absence of any proposals in its first Queen's speech. There was speculation as to whether the delay to reform would become permanent, dependent on the Lords behaving themselves and abiding by the Salisbury convention established in 1945 whereby Tory lords will not oppose any measure which had been included in a Labour manifesto. Since being elected, Blair has used the House of Lords to bring businessmen into government and generally to forge closer links with the business community by making top businessmen such as George Simpson, managing director of General Electric, and Andrew Stone, joint managing director at Marks & Spencer, 'working peers'. New Labour's policy on the House of Lords

151

is open to the accusation that what is proposed is a giant quango in the sense that all members will be appointed. And there is no clear view from New Labour about what powers a reformed second chamber would have.

Electoral politics and representative democracy

Blair makes no secret of his opposition to proportional representation for elections to the House of Commons (i.e., for choosing the British government), believing that it can hand too much power to small parties and undermines the principle of strong government. Writing in 1996, Blair stated:

> It is not, as some claim, a simple question of moving from an 'unfair' to a 'fair' voting system. An electoral system must meet two democratic tests: it needs to reflect opinion, but it must also aggregate opinion without giving disproportionate influence to splinter groups. Aggregation is particularly important for a Parliament whose job is to create and sustain a single, mainstream government.[51]

Official Labour policy is neutral on electoral reform. The 1997 manifesto proposed a commission on reform and a referendum. This position reflects in part the depth of support for PR not just in senior party circles, notably Robin Cook, but also more broadly among Labour modernizers in the IPPR, Charter 88 and the Labour Campaign for Electoral Reform.

Labour's interest in electoral reform, like so much of its constitutional proposals, grew out of the experience of Thatcherism. Eighteen years of radical Conservative government, and four general election victories, were delivered on less than 50 per cent of the vote. To the Liberals and Social Democrats in the 1980s, Britain's first-past-the-post elections were unfair: the number of seats they won were always disproportionately less than the votes cast. The Labour Party, of course, had been a beneficiary of this lack of proportionality, turning minority votes at the ballot box into Labour government majorities in the Commons. But, towards the end of the 1980s, it struck many in the Labour Party that they might never win at the polls on their own. Before the 1992 election there was much talk of tactical voting to maximize the anti-Tory vote, even pacts between Labour and the LibDems.

During the Policy Review a commission under the political philosopher Raymond Plant was set up to report to the party on electoral reform. By the 1992 election the Plant Commission had ruled out the form of PR favoured by the LibDems, the single transferable vote (STV), on the grounds that local constituency MPs would be lost (an argument which supporters of STV deny). Later the Plant Commission went on to reject the additional member system (used in German elections) and favoured instead the supplementary vote, a form of the alternative vote system. These latter two are not in fact proportional systems. Under the supplementary vote system, electors have two votes which they place in order of preference on the ballot paper. The second preferences are taken into consideration if no candidate wins 50 per cent of the votes. But the outcome does not make the number of seats proportional to the number of votes cast, as STV and AMS do to a much greater extent. Hence the supplementary vote is a 'majoritarian' rather than a proportional system. As with first past the post, it takes as much notice of where votes are cast as how many are cast.

If the Plant Commission did not exactly solve Labour's problem about electoral reform, it did prompt the then party leader, John Smith, to commit any future Labour government to a referendum on the issue. And, despite Blair's opposition to PR – and while Labour still thought that it might need the support of LibDems to form a government – Smith's promise remained party policy at the 1997 polls. But the Labour leadership's opposition to PR for general elections has not prevented Labour supporting PR for other elections in the UK. Both Scottish and Welsh devolution will involve the additional member system of PR. The new Labour government also agreed that, by 1999, elections for the European parliament in Britain will come into line with the rest of Europe by using PR. As John Lloyd writes: 'The citadel of Westminster is surrounded by PR forests – creeping like Birnam Wood, in the last act of *Macbeth*, ever closer to the walls.'[52]

Despite the emphasis on constitutional modernization, reform of the electoral system is not a high priority for the new Labour government. In December 1997 the prime minister announced a commission under the Liberal Democrat peer (and founder member of the SDP) Lord Jenkins to consider alternatives to first past the post. Blair, as we have

153

seen, remains committed to a voting system which he believes delivers strong government – the classic defence of first past the post. The terms of reference for the commission on voting reform reflect this: the commission 'shall serve the requirement for broad proportionality, the need for stable government, an extension of voter choice and the maintenance of a link between MPs and geographical constituencies'.[53] For Raymond Plant, electoral reform goes to the heart of pluralist politics – and New Labour's commitment to it. Plant, writing in 1995 when there was some doubt whether John Smith's commitment to a referendum on electoral reform would hold, suggested that 'Pluralism is part of the vocabulary of New Labour. Surely the time has come to try and institutionalise such pluralism and not see it as one policy option among others.' New Labour's policies on devolution and even local government indicate a commitment to what Plant calls 'inter-institutional pluralism' – the dispersal of political power away from Westminster and Whitehall. But Plant wished that the New Labour leadership would go further and commit itself to 'intra-institutional pluralism': 'which means having an electoral system which is more representative of society as a whole and which will create a parliament in which the executive has continually to seek greater consent for its policies.'[54]

Away from electoral reform, New Labour has shown an interest in supplementing Westminster representative democracy in ways which might be read as a move towards a more pluralist and participatory form of politics. The use of referendums for major constitutional questions appears to have become a constitutional convention in itself – although they may have something to do with dealing with internal party divisions more than anything else. For its supporters, the referendum offers an opportunity to break the stranglehold of political parties over politics, giving individual voters a voice on specific policy questions. To its opponents, the referendum undermines the principle of representative democracy – and where it is used before a bill comes before Parliament, as in the case with devolution, creates a pre-legislative straightjacket for Parliament, thereby strengthening the powers of an already powerful executive. At the 1997 poll Labour promised four: two on devolution and one each on PR and joining the European single currency. Labour has also made local public demand the acid test of stage two of its plans for devolution for the English regions.

But Labour goes further in wanting government to be more 'responsive' to the people – an astute tactic from a government with an eye on a second term in power. Blair wrote in 1996 that 'Other democratic innovations, such as citizens' juries, are being piloted with some success to assist decision-making in the NHS and local government. Informed public participation is the key, complementing not replacing established decision-making by elected representatives.'[55] In mid-July 1997 the new Labour government announced plans for a 'people's panel': a 5000-strong focus group to test the public's reaction to government policies.

Modernization, pluralism and sovereignty

New Labour has nailed its colours to the modernization of the British state. It seeks to decentralize institutions, update arcane conventions, to make more collaborative the adversarial style of government, and to rid British politics of the sleaze which it said had crept into government after eighteen years of Conservative rule. New Labour would not just clean up politics, but it would restore the people's trust in government, bringing a modern and open style to politics. Ministers would call each other by their first names and wear lounge suits, not black tie, to City banquets. Labour would keep its promises to the voters: its manifesto was a 'contract with the people'; its 'ten commitments' the party's 'bond of trust with the people. They are specific. They are real. Judge us on them. Have trust in us and we will repay that trust.' The new Labour government's first political storm in the autumn after the election was, ironically, on the very issue on which the party had campaigned hardest: sleaze. The disclosure of a £1 million donation to the Labour election fund before the election from the head of formula one motor racing, Bernie Ecclestone – and the offer of a further £1 million after the election – smacked of 'cash for favours', as the Labour government proposed to exempt formula one from its ban on tobacco advertising and sponsorship. The charge was hotly denied, but enough mud stuck to tarnish New Labour's 'Mr Clean' image. To some, Blair's pre-election claim that Labour would be 'tough on sleaze and tough on the causes of sleaze' rang hollow after the affair; to others, including Blair himself, it was just poor political judgement.

New Labour, moreover, would keep in touch with the popular mood and help to express it. The death of Diana, Princess of Wales, in 1997 cast Blair as the populist leader. As the news broke of her death, Blair spoke with apparent emotion, prefiguring widespread displays of public grief. He called her the 'people's princess' and negotiated a public funeral incorporating members of the charities she represented and ordinary people she met. Blair's own 'compassionate' agenda and concern 'for the many and not just the few' seemed in tune with a public mood which responded to the princess's perceived like-minded humanitarianism and popular touch. His first Labour conference speech as prime minister came weeks after Diana's death. Labour, Blair claimed, expressed a 'giving age' of greater compassion.

'Trust' provided New Labour with the perfect theme with an electorate thought ready for a change of government. 'Trust' is a variant of that old New Left theme 'legitimation'. The Left once thought that the capitalist state faced a 'legitimation crisis' as it found it harder and harder to generate the resources to do the things that the voters expected it to do. In the 1980s another gap in legitimacy opened up as Thatcherism enforced 'majority rule' on an unrepresentative minority vote. (Less than 50 per cent supported the Tories at the polls but they ruled as if they really did have an absolute majority.) There were, moreover, some who believed that the whole legitimacy of the old political order was being undermined by the forces of globalization. The notion of sovereignty, the rock on which Westminster parliamentary government is built, had been shattered.

The politics of New Labour are clear. They will fill the legitimacy gap by modernizing not just government but the economy and the welfare state. This will bring better public services at no great extra cost. New Labour has said it will restore people's trust in government by bringing it closer to them, making it more representative and responsive, and enforcing new standards of conduct for those in public life. New Labour says that it acknowledges the forces of globalization and that government must work within such limits, not cling to old methods. The legitimacy of government, the people's trust in politics, will be restored through radical modernization.

Politically, New Labour has cast its net widely. In his speech to the 1997 Labour Party conference Blair listed his heroes: '[they] aren't just Ernie Bevin, Nye Bevan and Attlee. They are also Keynes, Beveridge, Lloyd George. Division among radicals almost 100 years ago resulted in a twentieth century dominated by Conservatives. I want the twenty-first century to be the century of the radicals.' New Labour's one-nation politics is in style inclusive, reaching beyond the boundaries of class as well as across party divides. Before the 1997 election Labour joined the Liberal Democrats to publish a joint policy document on constitutional reform. And after victory Blair extended the hand of government to the LibDems, offering Paddy Ashdown and senior colleagues places on a cabinet committee on constitutional reform.

But Blair has always made it clear that winning an election as a single party was New Labour's goal. And while he could never be accused of believing that the Labour Party was the sole font of human knowledge – the new government set up too many policy reviews with non-Labour members to think that – he has established an administration which is marked by a strong centre. Effective this might be; but it must also exclude when the hard policy choices that Blair recognizes have to be made are made. Moreover, Blair's disinterest in reform of the electoral system suggests that New Labour remains committed to majoritarian government and has a limited interest in sharing power in the way a pluralist politics would require.

Further, the modernization of the British constitution which the Labour government has put into motion has definite limits, the most important of which is the sovereignty of the Westminster Parliament. This position provides a clear framework and boundary for Labour's policies on devolution and Europe. There is little in New Labour's devolution proposals or elsewhere that sovereignty within the United Kingdom might be shared, or that those institutions which share in the government of the country might better have an independent constitutional guarantee. These areas have been declared out of bounds. To this extent, New Labour still believes in the old levers of power.

5
Post-Thatcherism

What's new about New Labour?

The picture we have painted of Labour's rethinking in its economics, social policy and politics is a complex one. In this chapter we shall outline different interpretations of New Labour. Then, proceeding to our own view, we shall examine whether New Labour holds the same values as Old Labour or whether it has become a Thatcherite party. We shall argue that New Labour is post-Thatcherite, showing how it compares with other European social democratic parties on this score.

What's new about what Labour, if anything? There are at least four possible interpretations of what Labour has become. According to the first, it is little more than skin deep: a marketing and media creation by the party's own Dr Frankenstein, Peter Mandelson. (The hope is that one day the monster will turn on the master, according to script.) The party which was a PR shambles in the early 1980s, staggering along behind a Conservative Party with a huge campaign budget and an image moulded by the advertising agency Saatchi and Saatchi, has now taken presentation and style to new heights. According to this interpretation New Labour is a PR show. It is style devoid of substance, created by the war room and spin-doctors of Labour's specially created media HQ at Millbank. The soundbite has replaced the real substance in Labour thinking; the 1997 manifesto was empty of meaningful commitments.

There is some truth in this interpretation. New Labour has made media presentation more important in British politics than ever before. It realized that its electoral problems were to do not just with the unpopular substance of its policies, but also with its appearance in the public eye. Under Mandelson, Labour had its media image finely cultivated, right down to parliamentary candidates' haircuts and clothes, leaflet images and coordinated soundbites in speeches. Focus groups were developed to test the acceptability of party policies to voters and obtain a closer understanding of voters' wishes. Labour focused on immediate rebuttal of Conservative attacks, pressure on journalists and editors to accept Labour's agenda and the importance of winning over high-circulation tabloids to the party. These marketing techniques and media presentation were brought in for electoral reasons, to break out of a reliance on waning class-based political allegances, and to capture the middle ground and win office.[1]

But as an encapsulation of what New Labour is all about this reduction to a media and marketing ploy is sorely lacking. While accepting the importance of the electoral numbers game, our argument is that there is a complex but definite substance to New Labour. Scratch the surface and there is something deeper. The message has changed, not just the messenger. Ideas are important to New Labour's identity and what it does with political power. The philosophy and policies of British social democracy have been carefully rethought. They have been sensitively presented to us, but with substance in the philosophical underpinnings and matching policies outlined in detail in this book. It may be stylized in presentation, and driven by electoral calculation as much as ideological imagination, but substantive it is.

A second interpretation of New Labour is that it does have substance, but that its substance is nothing new. This was the approach of the Conservatives' 1997 election campaign. Tony Blair was featured in posters with devil-like gleaming red eyes: 'New Labour, Old Danger'. Behind the slick presentation and moderate promises, the Conservatives suggested, lay a hidden raft of old-style Labour policies: high taxation; European-style state regulation; the manipulation of government by trade union barons; the return of hidden left-wing extremism. New Labour is just Old Labour in disguise.[2]

Certainly some social democratic inclinations towards intervention and social priorities have remained. And Labour's tone on community, exclusion and social justice echoes sentiments from its past. Tory critics may be right, then, that some Old Labour impulses have survived the Blair revolution. But in general we have shown how flawed the 'New

Labour, Old Danger' view is. A great deal of what Labour stood for in the past has genuinely been jettisoned. Much of what has been put in its place is, for Labour, quite new. Across a whole range of areas, New Labour has broken with the past. Keynesian demand management to maintain full employment has been replaced by tough anti-inflationary fiscal and monetary policy. On the supply side, nationalization and government planning have given way to flexible labour markets, welfare to work and 'education, education, education'. Welfare policy is up for radical reform.

Perhaps the Conservative presentation of New Labour as Old Labour in disguise was predictable enough and should be disregarded as electoral scare tactics. Yet there is a pro-Labour version of it, the third interpretation of New Labour. As we have outlined, Blair and the modernizers are fond of suggesting that times have changed and that new means are required for achieving old values. The values endure and remain: community, equality and social justice. But new policies are needed to deliver them. Globalization, for example, has radically challenged the power and direction of national policy-making.

This line of argument has a fine pedigree among Labour revisionists, from Tony Crosland to Neil Kinnock. But for some, such as critics on the Left, Tony Blair is understating his own radicalism when he presents New Labour as being about new means to achieve the old ends. Old ends have gone out the window as well as old means. Public ownership was not just a means but also an end – the very thing which defined socialism as different from capitalism – and this has gone. Equality and the critique of capitalism have vanished. Social justice is not, for New Labour, about economic redistribution but individual opportunity. What distinguished Labour from other parties has been replaced by a catch-all idea of social justice. To G. A. Cohen it was Old Labour's belief in egalitarianism and community regulated on the basis of need which set it apart ideologically. These values, Cohen argues, were 'the only values which the Left affirmed as a matter of principle and which the Centre and Right reject as a matter of principle.' With these gone, the clear red water which separates Labour from other parties has diminished.[3]

Some of those who take this view argue that New Labour is now no more than Thatcherism Mark II, the fourth interpretation of the new party we wish to outline.[4] Labour is seen on this interpretation as having made a huge U-turn on the big policy questions – the economy, social

160

policy and defence – whether as a cynical attempt to win power or out of genuine ideological conviction. The Thatcherism Mark II view suggests that New Labour has adopted the neo-liberal economic policies of the Right – flexible labour markets, privatization, financial prudency and tight fiscal limits. Labour has embraced an Anglo-American view of entrepreneurialism and individualism as the basis for economic success. In social policy the drift towards neo-liberalism and conservatism is seen to parallel that of its economics. Labour is now combining authoritarian conservative and neo-liberal prescriptions on parenting, education, and the reform of the welfare state. Socialist goals such as equality and collectivism have gone in favour of liberal concerns such as individual opportunity and self-help. New Labour has moved to the right and occupied neo-liberal territory. This forms the basis for a new consensus in British politics between Left and Right, Labour and the Tories, leaving no electable alternative to voters who do not like this agenda. Labour's anti-Tory rhetoric, on this view, is a question of political manoeuvring rather than reflecting hard differences in ideas.

Our argument in this book does not fit any one of these four interpretations we have outlined. Labour *has* shifted to the Right. But some of their emphases and policies remain more recognizably of the Left. Labour as Thatcherism Mark II, therefore, misses the novelty of New Labour and the way it has reacted to Thatcherism rather than simply imitated it. Yet what is clear is that New Labour does mark a decisive break with Labour's past, not simply in terms of policies but in value terms as well. This leads us to our second main concern of this chapter – with what has happened to Labour's old values.

Old Values? Equality and community

The modernizers' 'New Times, New Means, Old Ends' approach to dealing with Old Labour has successfully carried the day; first over Clause 4, then over much of the rest of the party's postwar social democratic legacy, and finally at the polls. Tony Blair argues that this is a story of Labour ditching old means of public ownership, demand management and state welfare to adapt to new times. Old socialist values, meanwhile, remain in place. But we have argued that values which were part of Old Labour's ideology have been diluted or redefined. New Labour's stated ideas involve shifts in ends as well as means. This can be seen in the cases of both equality and community, two central values that New Labour argues it has kept on from the past.

First, equality. There are egalitarian elements in Labour's ideas. Gordon Brown has argued that New Labour's egalitarianism is not about equal outcomes or equality of opportunities merely at school. It is about lifelong equality of opportunity, in education and the labour market: an equality of opportunity that really means it.[5] Labour's supply-side economics and welfare reforms are about giving excluded citizens, particularly the young and long-term unemployed, greater equality of opportunity and a stake in society. Raising standards in failing schools and improving literacy are intended to equalize opportunities for those who have been left behind educationally.[6] These policies are geared primarily towards inclusion and more equal opportunities.

If the primary justification of such policies is inclusion and equal *opportunities*, small changes in *economic* inequality between the bulk of society and the excluded might also be a consequence of their success. By the unemployed getting into work the degree of income inequality between them and the rest of society could be reduced. As a result of more equal individual *opportunities* economic and social *outcomes* might become more equal. Moreover, there are mildly *redistributional* elements in policies such as welfare to work. The one-off levy on the 'excess' profits of privatized utilities used to fund schemes for the unemployed involves a reallocation of resources from profitable businesses to assistance for the poor.

However, Labour's commitment to the labour market route to social inclusion may just as likely have a neutral or even negative impact on economic differentials. Labour's sensitivity to the level of the minimum wage suggests it believes that a low-paid job is better than no job at all. Furthermore, many of the Labour government's policies have no redistributional effect. They aim to narrow the gap between the excluded and the rest, but not by redistributing resources from the rich to the poor. Educational reform and a drop in the basic rate of tax are intended to be inclusionary. Moreover, the major means for promoting greater redistribution and economic equality in society – public ownership and changes in progressive taxation – have been ruled out. The loss of means such as public ownership or more progressive taxation undermines Labour's ability to achieve its old ends. Changes in means, as such, cannot be divorced from changes in ends. So, with Labour's main old routes to economic redistribution gone, direct economic egalitarianism of a consistent redistributional sort has been ruled out. What are left are one-off redistributions; a form of equality primarily about opportunities; and a much diminished scope for greater equality of income or wealth.

Just as the meaning of equality has been redefined, the same redefinition of Labour values has happened in the case of community. This has been the case in a number of ways. First, community has changed from having a class to a one-nation meaning. When Blair talks of community here he does not mean the working-class community, but the whole nation, all included, with a common purpose. Secondly, community has shifted from involving social rights and help by the paternalistic state for the poor. Now it is more heavily tinged with ideas of rights being conditional on responsibilities, with larger areas for self-help. The shift of emphasis in welfare policy to individual opportunities and responsibility, and in public services more generally to choice, has moved the focus from community to the individual. Thirdly, Labour is more concerned with a moralistic community – society held together by strongly shared values – and less than it was with cohesion secured through common universal experience on a socio-economic level, through greater economic equality and the welfare state. Moral duties are to play a bigger part in holding society together than collectivist welfare institutions which are undermined by greater emphasis on pluralism and selective and non-state provision. Fourthly, the content of those values as they pertain to areas such as parenting, education, welfare and crime are more conservative and less progressive than they were for Labour in the past. And fifthly, the requirement for community responsibility is directed by Blair more at the individual and less at the business corporation, usually the Left's target for concerns about lack of responsibility to the community. So Blair argues that community is one of those values that is still held dear by New Labour and which puts it in line with its traditional concerns. But we have argued that there has been a shift in Labour's communitarianism to a revised meaning: increasingly conditional on duties, morally prescriptive, conservative and focused on the individual. This is at the expense of a less conditional, rights-based, redistributional, collectivist and socio-economic communitarianism, more progressive in content and aimed to a greater extent at business

163

responsibility to the community. Community as a value has shifted under New Labour from more traditionally social democratic meanings. Revisions of meaning in the cases of both equality and community have diluted the extent to which New Labour still holds to such traditional Labour values.[7]

Labour's right turn

So the emphasis on New Labour retaining its old values is misleading. But has it then thrown in the towel to Thatcherism? If Labour's modernization is in part about leaving behind its own past, it is also about what has taken its place. Labour's shift away from old social democratic means and ends has been accompanied, as we have outlined in this book, by a shift to greater neo-liberalism and conservatism in its economics and social policy. The values as well as the means have changed.[8]

In its economics, Labour in the past certainly long held to a pragmatic acceptance of markets counterbalanced by collectivism and intervention in a mixed economy. It was envisaged that the economy should combine private ownership and markets with public ownership and state intervention. However, pragmatic acceptance has turned under Tony Blair into positive celebration of the free market. The market economy more than the mixed economy is now seen as the basis of economic success. The role of the state is not to pick winners, manipulate demand to maintain full employment or set down industrial policy. It is to lay stable bases for business to pursue success in its own way. The place for nationalized industry has gone and the spread of market principles and private provision in health, education and welfare has increased.

Social policy, in the form of supply-side skills and training and welfare to work, has become linked with the success of British capitalism rather than being seen as a counterbalance to it. Social policy was about collectivist institutions such as the welfare state. The institutions of social policy – the health service, tax and benefits, the education system – were seen as embodying principles which were collectivist and counterbalanced those of the market. They had a different logic to the market and were intended to bale out its losers with benefits and counteract its inegalitarian dynamics through free, universal and common provision of health and education. Labour's social policy is now increasingly about providing skilled workers access to the labour market and supplying the basis for a skills-led economic renewal for British capitalism: education as an economic policy. Tony Blair is not the first Labour revisionist to link social justice with economic efficiency: but in his hands the idea of social policy underpinning capitalist success goes beyond older Labour formulations of it providing a counterbalance or complement between the two.

New Labour has also challenged the rights-based universalism of the postwar social democratic welfare state. Labour increasingly envisages that health, education and social security should be provided differently by diverse agencies rather than commonly by the state. Labour now sees rights to welfare as more conditional on citizens fulfilling prescribed responsibilities than in the past. And there is a greater emphasis on individual provision of welfare. There is also a greater conservatism in social policy thinking on education, the family and law and order. Whether social conservatism was part of the private beliefs of Labour ministers in the past or not, it has never been part of its explicit public philosophy in the way it is now. In all these respects, in short, Labour's *ideology* places less emphasis on social democratic norms and gives an increasing role to economic liberalism and conservatism in its economics and social policy.

Not the son of Margaret: post-Thatcherism

But our interpretation of New Labour as shifting from social democracy to neo-liberalism and conservatism does not amount to an equation of New Labour with Thatcherism Mark II. We do not see Tony Blair as the 'son of Margaret'.[9] New Labour is not Thatcherite, but 'post-Thatcherite'. It has left behind the pre-Thatcher days of Old Labour and accepted much of the terrain left by Lady Thatcher. Yet it takes this as a starting point beyond which there are elements which make New Labour different from and beyond Thatcherism. Three components make New Labour a 'post-Thatcherite' party.

The first is, as we have shown in this book, that New Labour has abandoned much of what defined Old Labour. By leaving behind Old Labour Blair has become a post-Thatcherite man – no turning back to the days before the 'Iron Lady'. To be sure the contrast with Old Labour needs to be drawn with care. Ross McKibbin, for example, argues that

165

'New Labour has willy-nilly adopted not the best but much of the worst of Old Labour. And very Old Labour: the Labour Party under Mr Blair more closely resembles the party of Ramsay MacDonald and Philip Snowden than one kitted out for the Nineties'[10] – in other words, ortho-dox, treasury-dominated economic policy. Eric Shaw takes issue with the whole notion of Old Labour. He suggests that Labour modernizers draw an inaccurate picture of the party's past for strategic reasons. The concepts of Old and New Labour have allowed modernizers to assert 'the superiority of the modernizing view by definitional fiat – new is better than old, being modern than being traditional – relieving them of the more onerous task of demonstrating the validity of their ideas by the more conventional means of reasoning and substantiation.' Yet if Old Labour is seen as referring to postwar rather than earlier Labour, as in the focus of this book, then we have shown that there is a break. And, whatever the strategic motivations for modernizers' emphases on the Old/New dichotomy, Shaw himself draws attention to the fact that there is a post-Thatcherite break with the Old: 'What modernising actually meant was never defined but it can be best understood in terms of two concepts: a *detachment* from Labour's established values and objects and an *accommodation* with established institutions and modes of thought.'[11]

The second aspect of New Labour's post-Thatcherism is that it not only leaves behind Old Labour but accepts important aspects of the Thatcherite agenda. For Labour modernizers, Thatcherism had the merit of perceiving that the world had changed; and that the old social demo-cratic politics, which both Labour and the Tories shared, no longer had any purchase in the late twentieth century. Labour modernizers argue that many Conservative reforms were constructive. Labour has conceded considerable ground to Thatcherism on major policy questions – the economy, unions and the welfare state. The difference is that, in the face of a divided and poorly led Conservative Party, they could now carry them out better (controlling inflation and managing public finances, for example). Such shifts have underlined the Thatcherism Mark II inter-pretation. Yet such an interpretation falls short because New Labour is not only attracted to Thatcherism but also repelled by it.

This leads to the third aspect of New Labour's post-Thatcherism. Thatcherism provides the terrain or starting point for New Labour. But New Labour goes beyond this. For supporters of Labour modernization such as John Gray there is no turning back: 'Social democrats have failed to perceive that Thatcherism was a modernising project with profound and irreversible consequences for political life in Britain. The question cannot be: how are the remains of social democracy to be salvaged from the ruins of Thatcherism? but instead: what is Thatcherism's successor?'[12] Blair's response to postwar social democracy has, in part, been communitarian. But communitarianism also provides Blair and New Labour with an antidote to Thatcherite individualism. New Labour accepts but also departs from Thatcherism. Successful economies, it is argued, cannot live by competitive individualism alone. Economic success requires the government, in partnership with the private sector, to provide the underpinnings for economic growth. Despite its embrace of the market economy, New Labour's politics are hostile to what Blair has called the 'politics of self'. Communitarianism is about rebuilding the social cohesion and moral fabric undermined by years of Tory individualism and *laissez-faire*. Much of Labour's economic and social policies are about communitarian inclusion. Divisions must be replaced by the inclusion of all in one nation: government for 'the many not the few'. Communitarianism gives Labour a tone which differentiates it from that of its Thatcherite predecessors, and provides a framework for policies which in intent aim to bring about greater social inclusion.[13]

New Labour, conservatism and community

New Labour shares some common ground here with conservative thinkers. Conservatism has never been entirely at ease with liberalism. Indeed, since the collapse of communism and the experience of the New Right, it is neo-liberalism as much as socialism which has been the target of some conservative guns. The alliance between neo-liberals and conservatism has suffered somewhat in recent times. The conservative hostility to liberalism begins with the overwhelming importance given to the individual and individual choice in liberal thinking. The neo-liberal revival in the 1970s focused on the market aspects of individual freedom, and the limited role of the state in decision-making in the market. More libertarian neo-liberals did argue the case for individual freedom in all walks of life (including on questions such as drug legalization and sexuality). But most neo-liberals focused their attention and their attacks on infringements of liberty in the market place. Because of this, many conservatives were happy to be in alliance with the neo-liberals against common foes: socialists, social democrats and, in the USA, Democrats. They were able to live with Lady Thatcher's blend of neo-liberal conservatism, especially as it put into practice many of their key arguments (e.g., the National Curriculum in education).

But conservatives have always had doubts about what is perceived to be the neo-liberal obsession with free markets and individual choice as the arbiter of modern society. To conservatives, economic freedom is one thing, but freedom as the rule for all social interactions is quite another. How, conservatives ask, is free choice in the market place to be kept there and not allowed to roam freely through the rest of society, leading to atomization and fragmentation? In 1996 the conservative philosopher Roger Scruton wrote on the British Conservative government of the day:

> In many people's eyes it is now the Conservative Party which stands for social fragmentation, in the interests of the individual and his profit, while the opposition represents the healing force of community and compromise . . . No one doubts the value of economic freedom or the spirit of enterprise, but the exclusive emphasis on these things looks like so much self-serving rhetoric on the part of those whose only interest is profit, and where concern for the community goes no further than the search for customers. In itself, and severed from the institutions which limit it, the market may pose a threat to traditional forms of social life, to custom, religion and morality.[14]

Scruton argues that the Tories must find a 'coherent philosophy of community' or lose their traditional supporters to Labour. John Gray is one conservative thinker who has done just that: his support for New Labour reflects his view that the Conservative Party in the 1980s became a prisoner of neo-liberal dogma. Post-Thatcherism, then, is as much an issue for the Tories as it has been for Labour.

Other Tories, such as the Conservative MP David Willetts, share Scruton's concern that the individual and market forces are not the be all and end all of political thinking. Willetts the conservative communitarian shares Blair's philosophical critique of modern liberal thinking. He draws on similar communitarian sources, although combining them with traditional Tory notions of community rooted in Hegel, Burke and Carlyle. According to Willetts, the reconciliation in the real world of community and free markets is the mark of good conservative thinking. What Willetts does not like about Blair's New Labour is that, in his view, it remains committed to a strong sense of equality, to old ideas about regulating markets and society by the state and to a prescriptive and over-demanding rather than organic communitarianism.[15]

But in fact New Labour does share common ground with modern conservatism in a number of areas. Both hold that there is such a thing as society which is more than just individuals – an observation based on a common communitarian view of society. They see society as comprised of a web of obligations, which may override individual freedom: obligations among individuals in communities and between the citizen and the state. Conservatives and Labour are united here in criticizing an over-emphasis on rights-claiming and welfare dependency and in emphasizing interdependency in society. They have a shared view of moral order as based on shared values and traditions which transcend individual morality: ethics are not rooted in individual choice and individualism is corrosive of social cohesion. And they agree that there is a Good Life which is more than the individual plans of individual people – although they may differ, as well as agree, on what exactly constitutes the good life.

So in its critique of Thatcherism, New Labour shares some commonalities with conservatism. In Labour's discourse on social justice there has been a shift to greater emphasis on opportunity and fairness which few Tories would dissent from. There are, to be sure, differences in approach as well as in policy. In particular, New Labour's constitutional radicalism at the 1997 election stood in stark contrast to the constitutional conservatism of the Major Tories – a conservatism not shared by leading Tories such as Lord Hailsham in the 1970s; and, as increasingly seems likely, by the Hague Tories in the 1990s.

Post-Thatcherism: Britain, Europe, USA

So Tony Blair argues that there is no going back to Old Labour and he thinks that much of what Thatcher did was valuable. But, starting from this Thatcherite ground, changes have to be made guided by sentiments which are often far from Thatcherite. Labour is defined by Thatcherism but goes beyond it: post-Thatcherism. The idea of post-Thatcherism may help us to understand how New Labour sits among the constellation of social democratic parties in Europe and elsewhere. As we outlined in Chapter 1, Labour is widely seen as having been behind its sister European social democratic parties in the modernization process of the 1980s. It was attached to allegedly archaic commitments such as Keynesian tax-and-spend strategies for full employment, public ownership, unilateral disarmament, close links with the unions and a less than fulsome embrace of European unity. In the 1990s, however, Blair is seen by some supporters as having leapfrogged European social democracy.[16] Labour has not so much, on this view, joined the fold of European social democracy as left it behind. New Labour has been transformed from Europe's ugly duckling into the model for renewal.

When Blair addressed European socialists in Sweden weeks after his election victory, he spoke against 'rigid regulation and old-style intervention'. At a European level, he said: 'our aim must be to tackle the obstacles to job creation and labour market flexibility.'[17] At the summit of the European Union in Amsterdam held a little more than a month after the general election, Gordon Brown argued that Europe's dole queues could only be shortened by more flexible labour markets, welfare reform and cuts in red tape for small and medium-sized businesses. On the social chapter, Brown said that any new labour market regulations would have to pass three tests: 'did they increase productivity, did they increase employment opportunities and did they increase labour market flexibility?'[18] These plans were at odds with those of the newly appointed French socialist prime minister, Lionel Jospin – backed by his Gaullist president, Jacques Chirac – which included extra funds to create employment and measures to tighten labour market regulation. Hugo Young suggested that Blair might be fluent in French but that he and Jospin did not appear to be speaking the same language.[19]

Many themes of the modernizing social democrats of the 1980s in Europe have been echoed by Blair: public ownership as an outdated means rather than an end; the compatibility of economic efficiency with social cohesion; the decline of national economic solutions and full employment; and the need to react to unemployment by improving the skills and mobility of labour on the supply side rather than through old-style demand management. However, British Labour in the 1990s is seen by many as having modernized with a more radical and willing accommodation to the Right than its continental compatriots wish to make.[20]

European social democracy's embrace of the market has been taken further by Blair and the British modernizers, involving a commitment to flexible labour markets a step beyond what more interventionist continental social democrats would like to contemplate. Social policy is being marked by a conservatism and uninhibitedness about welfare reform outstripping that of other social democrats. Blair as the most radical modernizer of European social democracy, a model for others to follow, is an image many of his acolytes would like to believe in.

Blair's New Labour *is* more readily liberal in its economics and conservative in its social policy than some of its European counterparts: it is more comparable to the American Democrats in these areas. Clinton and Blair have shown greater enthusiasm for flexible labour markets than some European social democrats. Both are concerned with balanced budgets. New Labour's welfare-to-work proposals owe much to American workfare programmes. Both Clinton and Blair put emphasis on a better educated workforce. And Labour's crime and drugs policy is comparable in many respects to that of the Americans, as are ideas such as hit squads in schools and elected mayors.[21]

Some European social democrats, however, seem to show a greater interest in more traditional social democratic concerns for job creation, intervention and state welfare. Only days after the 1997 election victory of Blair's new model party, the French socialists were elected on promises of 700,000 new jobs, a reduction in the working week without loss of pay and a plan to commit the European Union to link coordinated job creation programmes to the single currency. The French promised to boost wages, increase the wealth tax, repeal tough immigration laws and stop planned privatizations. They were certainly more moderate on areas such as renationalization, the overall tax burden and public spending. But the older Labour-style commitments caused some unease in the economically more liberal New Labour. Since their 1997 election the French socialists have been forced, under economic and political pressures such as EU convergence criteria, to look for ways of watering down their more traditional social democratic promises: limiting some public spending plans and balancing the budget. But their rightwards shifts remain less radical and wholehearted and more reluctant than Blair's.

The German social democrats at the same time were led by the more traditionalist Oskar Lafontaine. The man more willing to carry out Blair-style reforms in the SPD, Gerhard Schroder, premier of Lower Saxony, was waiting in the wings for his chance at the leadership. Schroder was much quieter on Kohl's plans to cut personal and business taxes, for example, than Lafontaine, who voiced his opposition. Despite this, SPD policy has moved economically in a neo-liberal direction and towards greater conservatism on social policy and crime with echoes of Blair's thinking on flexible labour markets, welfare to work and toughness on criminal justice. But again the move has been slower, more forced and with less conviction than Blair's. Swedish and Norwegian social democrats are seen, like the French and Germans, to be attached to ideas and polices which are increasingly old ones, certainly in comparison to what can be found in the British, Dutch and southern European social democratic parties.[22]

How might this apparent greater comparability of New Labour with the American Democrats than European social democrats be explained? Why might European social democracy beyond Britain have, until 1997 at least, modernized along more traditionally social democratic lines than New Labour? One explanation for the different roads of modernization taken by the British and other European social democratic parties might be that the latter have simply not modernized as radically as New Labour. They are still stuck in an Old Left mould which Labour in Britain has rejected. The other European parties will have to adapt further to new times if they are to be successful. In other words, British Labour is more advanced in its modernization. Blair's appeals to fellow social democrats to adapt to new times or decline suggests he may adhere to an interpretation along these lines.[23]

A second possible explanation for the differing routes of modernization of British and other social democratic parties might be that other European social democratic parties have, in fact, modernized *further* than New Labour. Unlike Blair, they have realized that neo-liberalism has been shown to be a failure and is dead and that collectivist, interventionist policies are more relevant for post-neo-liberal times. Tony Blair is out of date in being tied to liberal economics which are no longer workable. Lionel Jospin, the French socialist leader, is said to share a view along these lines.[24]

However, a third possible explanation returns us to our theme of post-Thatcherism. Here the different parties are seen not as having advanced at further or lesser stages of modernization but rather as having taken different routes of modernization relative to their cultures and historical political experiences. They cannot be compared on an old/new continuum because they have come through different experiences, cultures and histories.[25] According to this explanation, New Labour has been influenced by Britain's traditions of individualism and limited government. In particular it has been marked by the reconstruction of the economic and political landscape by Thatcherism. Its post-Thatcherism is important. Blair and the US Democrats find a lot in common because they share the same Anglo-American traditions, and because the USA, like Britain, went through a radical right neo-liberal experience under President Reagan. European countries beyond Britain are, however, seen as having different, perhaps more centralist or collaborative, cultures.[26] Many also did not experience, to the same degree, the neo-liberal experiments attempted in the USA and Britain. Where modernization involves a move to the centre of the political spectrum, that centre has been dragged less far to the Right in places like Germany and France than in Britain.

Blair, in short, is seen as having gone down a *different* Anglo-American road to other European social democrats, rather than as being in *advance* or *behind* them in terms of modernization. European social democracy is seen as adopting a more European model, less influenced by neo-liberalism, rather than a more regressive or progressive one than Blair's. This explanation emphasizes Labour's post-Thatcherism and Anglo-American culture as influences on its own path of modernization. This is seen to be what it shares with the US Democrats, with whom in policy terms it seems most comparable. And it is what distinguishes it from more collectivist and interventionist social democracy in countries such as France. In this explanation of comparative experience, the significance of post-Thatcherism gains added importance.

So New Labour's ideas have broken with Old Labour; accept the Thatcherite terrain yet are repelled by it. We have argued that this conjunction of characteristics is best described as 'post-Thatcherism'. But what does post-Thatcherism mean for the old categories of Left and Right? Do they still usefully describe the polarities of British politics? Or do 'Left' and 'Right' need to be replaced by new concepts for making sense of contemporary politics?

6

Beyond Left and Right?

At the turn of the twenty-first century there is much talk of a sea change in politics, not just in Britain but right across the Western world. We live, it is suggested, in new times: dominated by globalization; shaped by the new information technologies; culturally postmodern; a world of uncertainty and risk; sceptical of the old enlightenment faiths; new times in need of new ethics; politics in search of ideas beyond Left and Right. The old ideologies which gave meaning and hope to postwar Britain – social democracy, then Thatcherism – have crashed. Today, as Geoff Mulgan puts it, 'we are thinking in the echo of these crashes.'[1]

This may be so much end-of-century *Angst* which we might be forgiven for treating with a degree of caution. But to ignore it would be to miss how this grand millennial thinking has entered the current political vocabulary in Britain. Tony Blair has used it to explain, justify and give an identity to New Labour. For him, the politics of old Left and Right are dated: New Labour is beyond Left in repudiating state socialism and old-style social democracy; and beyond Right in rejecting neo-liberal Thatcherism. According to Blair, New Labour is something quite new. What was initially new thinking on the Centre Left has become a politics of the 'radical centre', transcending, rather than bridging, the old divisions between Left and Right.[2]

Few can deny that politics at the end of the twentieth century has taken an unexpected turn. The collapse of communism and the dominance of neo-liberal and conservative ideas has shifted the whole terrain of political debate and policy-making. But as we move into a new century, is politics in Britain and elsewhere entering a period where the old

boundaries between Left and Right, forged in the eighteenth and nineteenth centuries and consolidated in the twentieth, have become irrelevant, politically and analytically? Is New Labour (and the New
Democrats in the USA) the sign of new political times, when ideas and
policies resist the old categories? Has post-Thatcherism taken New Labour to a new politics or to the death of politics? Has it taken Labour
'beyond Left and Right' or just 'beyond Left'? In this concluding chapter we shall look first at claims that Labour has developed a new synthesis which is 'beyond Left and Right'; then at the argument that politics
after Thatcherism is pragmatic and beyond ideology; then at claims that
Labour's new politics have sealed a right-wing consensus in British politics just 'beyond Left'. We shall conclude that post-Thatcherism is not
any of these: Labour's ideas continue to be defined by the old divides,
they are still ideological, defined by a rightwards shift but not reducible
to it.

Radicalism and conservatism: from emancipatory
to life politics

Anthony Giddens in his book *Beyond Left and Right* argues that the
relevance of the Left–Right divide as a guide to the meaning of politics
is being diluted by two developments.[3] One is that Left parties used to
be seen as radical and Right parties as conservative. Now, he argues, a
rearticulation of these identities is taking place. Mrs Thatcher showed
with her resolute neo-liberal approach that the Right can be radical. For
more than a decade a right-wing Conservative government was more
interested in remaking society than with conserving the traditions and
institutions of the status quo. Furthermore, since Giddens's book, Labour has shown, with its concern to restore moral cohesion, 'one-nation'
inclusion and standards in education and the family, that the Left can
become conservative. In other words, Left and Right are no longer so
closely tied to radicalism and conservatism respectively. The traditional
attachments of Left and Right in these senses are no longer so applicable. A second change, Giddens argues, is that 'emancipatory politics' has
given way to 'life politics'. Politics no longer has the economic, rights
and equality orientation that 'emancipatory politics' had in the past. Politics is now more a question of 'life politics' – about identities, quality of

life issues, the private sphere and civil society. Left and Right divisions in emancipatory politics are being outdated by a shift in political concerns to the sphere of life politics.

Giddens's book was written before Blair became leader of the party, but New Labour seems, to us, to fit these characterizations in part. Labour is concerned to make only modest commitments for change. It seeks to promise only what it can deliver. The aim is to regain the trust and confidence of a public fed on a diet of unrealistic and unfulfilled promises from governments. Furthermore, Labour has, in its moral communitarianism, incorporated a conservative content quite new to dominant Labour thinking. And this followed a period of Conservative government noted for its radicalism. A lot of New Labour's politics, in short, is conservative both in ambition and content.

As for the shift from emancipatory to life politics, Labour has lost interest in economic dirigisme and redistribution. In the face of perceived globalization it has resigned itself to accepting the nature of the economy as it is and establishing stability and security within it. Responsibilities and moral cohesion have received an emphasis at least equalling that of rights, and Labour's policies do not, on the whole, promise redistribution towards greater economic equality. Its politics are orientated to moral cohesion and the responsibilities of the individual citizen. This shift seems to have brought Labour onto greater common ground with the Conservatives.

So Giddens's idea of left-radicalism and right-conservatism identifications being reorganized seems to have some relevance to the changing ideas of New Labour. Labour has taken on board conservatism in a way unprecedented for the British Labour Party. It is not especially radical – in fact Tony Blair makes a virtue out of being modest and prudent in his promises. And in terms of the move from emancipatory to life politics there has been a shift from social democratic emphases on economic redistribution and rights to a greater focus on the individual citizen and her or his responsibilities. There is a relatively novel willingness to make judgements on individual lifestyles and pass legislation on citizens' responsibilities.

Transcending Left and Right

A similar argument to Giddens's has also been put by John Gray and, perhaps influenced by Giddens and Gray, by Blair himself.[4] This is that Labour has moved on to a new configuration ideologically which is neither Left nor Right but something new. Labour is no longer a 'Left' party in the old sense; its ideas are no longer shaped by old ideological conflicts. The Tories are the party of ideology. Labour is seen as a party which has gone beyond Left and Right to either a new *synthesis* or a new *transcendence*. This either puts Left and Right together into a synthesis that goes beyond them; or it has moved on to a set of ideas which break with all the old dichotomies to offer something completely new in itself. As Gray puts it: 'The place we occupy is not a halfway house between rival extremes. Our position is not a compromise between two discredited ideologies. It is a stand on a new common ground.'[5]

Certainly all the talk of 'New Labour', 'New Britain', 'New Politics' and the 'third way' conveys Blair's aspirations in this direction. For Gray and Blair this synthesis or transcendence is often talked about in terms of communitarianism and stakeholding: perspectives not coloured by divisive class loyalties but by an inclusive one-nation outlook which is identifiably neither Left nor Right. A one-nation approach allows New Labour to address issues such as the gap between rich and poor (especially in terms of opportunities), social inclusion and fairness while avoiding Old Left ideas such as egalitarianism. Communitarianism and stakeholding are ideas which place a premium on social inclusion for all – for giving everyone a stake in society (notably through employment opportunities) – ensuring they have autonomy as individuals but also responsibilities as members of the community. In the labour market, the main channel for inclusion, New Labour's policies attempt to marry flexibility with security. New Labour is a political project which is neither obviously individualist nor collectivist. It combines liberalism's emphasis on individual autonomy (achieved through employment opportunities, for instance) and communitarianism's requirement for responsibilities (the requirement to accept a training place, for example) without being either one or the other alone. In short, it is a politics which, in attempting a synthesis of Left and Right, actually transcends these divides outright.

Certainly Blair has made an intriguing and often successful attempt to combine terms of political debate previously divided: the individual and the community; autonomy and responsibility; equality and liberty. Political thinkers and politicians have been bitterly divided over these opposites through the ages. Those who have tried to bring them together have often been accused, as Karl Marx said of John Stuart Mill, of trying to reconcile the irreconcilable. Yet Blair is a thoughtful politician who has formulated a sometimes meaningful combination of the old opposites and developed policies to foster both in reciprocal relationship. He has had the political will to break with ideological one-sidedness by combining the concerns of Left and Right. Alongside the inevitable rhetoric that such claims often involve, Blair has constructed a political programme informed by such ideas of reciprocity – and certainly New Labour's approach proved popular with the voters.

This combination is more than just a mix. Individualism and communitarianism may be juggled alongside one another: all as of equal validity as one another – some values applicable in some spheres and some in others (for example, individualism in the private sphere, civil society or the market; responsibility in the public).[6] But they are also combined: individual autonomy and rights (in welfare and education, for example) connected in exchange for community responsibility (to take a training place or ensure homework and attendance requirements for your child, for instance). Blair's perspective sees them as more than just co-existing, as connected. Rights are conditional on the fulfilling of responsibilities.

But does this constitute a new synthesis or transcendence which goes *beyond* old divides of Left and Right, as Giddens, Gray and Blair seem to suggest? We would argue that it is not a new politics which leaves these divides behind, but one which attempts, with some success, to combine them in a balance between both poles. New Labour does not go beyond individual autonomy and community responsibility but says that, if individuals wish to have the rights associated with citizenship in the community, they must also accept the responsibilities that go with them. Rather than a synthesis or transcendence of opposites into something new, this is a balancing of opposites, an attempt to combine them into interdependence with one another or mutual reciprocity – a balance of the old rather than a surpassing of them. So the new politics is a management of the old opposites: both are still there in tension with one another. Although this involves no less admiration for the dexterity of the task, it is not a reconciliation, synthesis or transcendence.

In fact it is probably impossible to reconcile, synthesize or transcend the old dichotomies. They are enduring divides, expressing essential tensions between opposed impulses. Equality and liberty, individualism and community: these can sometimes support one another, but inevitably they will also always erode each other to some extent. Greater economic equality can provide the resources to increase poorer people's autonomy. At the same time, more often than not, it reduces the liberty of those subject to economic redistribution. Liberty, meanwhile, can be a threat to equality. And the divides involve essential questions to do with the organization of human societies. It is not possible to escape from questions about the equality of humans, or their freedom to pursue their own ends, or of individual rights and responsibilities to their fellow citizens. These are essential, necessary and enduring questions on which Left and Right have always divided. For this reason, Left–Right dichotomies are still relevant as categories for making sense of ideas and policies in the political world. It may be possible to combine and balance the dichotomies of such divides but not synthesize or transcend them.

What can be done, however, is a management or compromise of the opposites. They can be mixed and juggled in co-existence alongside one another – some values applicable in some spheres and others in others. And they can be balanced and combined together – the approach we argue Blair, despite his more radical talk of transcendence, has taken: a balancing of Left and Right, but not a move beyond them. The problem for New Labour in government is that not all values and policies are mutually supportive, at least not all the time; and 'hard choices', as Tony Blair calls them, will have to be made between them. But does this mean, then, that politics is now more pragmatic than ideological?

A fight without ideologies

Some conservatives have regarded their own politics as driven by practical matters rather than ideology: as Macmillan put it, 'by events'. Today, if anything, it is Labour which accuses the Tories of being the party of ideologues: of dogmatic market individualism.[7] Tories, for their part, have seen Labour as expedient: leaving their beliefs behind and willing to ditch or advocate anything that will win votes. Tony Blair has talked of himself and US Democrat President Bill Clinton as leaders of a new generation who prefer reason to doctrine: a generation that 'is strong on ideals but indifferent to ideology, whose instinct is to judge government not on grand designs but by practical results.'[8] For Blair, Labour is beyond old Left and Right dogmas such as public and private, and makes decisions on such divisions on practical criteria. In the 1997 Labour manifesto Blair says:

> We will be a radical government. But the definition of radicalism will not be that of doctrine, whether of Left or Right, but of achievement. New Labour is a party of ideas and ideals but not of outdated ideology. What counts is what works. The objectives are radical. The means will be modern.[9]

To critics of Labour as technocratic, its embrace of liberal market economics and welfare reform leaves it vulnerable to the charge that politics, as in the 1950s, is merely a matter of good administration – politics has become a 'fight without ideologies'. Its own policies are technically better than those of the Conservatives – a party divided, corrupt and weakly led – rather than of a qualitatively different kind. The former Labour deputy leader Roy Hattersley claims of Blair that 'He has built a Government which is untainted by dogma. Tony Blair is taking the politics out of politics.'[10] What, according to the critics of a technocratic Labour, does this leave the party representing? What does Labour believe in? Why should voters choose it rather than the Tories except on the grounds of leadership and good management?

Labour modernizers in reply claim that what it now stands for ideologically lies in traditional values such as equality and community – retained despite the change in means for achieving them. But there are problems with such a response. First, equality and community, we have argued, have been redefined to mean something rather different to what they did in the past. And if values such as community and social justice become so broad that they cease to exclude, what then is distinctive about Labour? Secondly, New Labour wants to have its cake and to eat it too: to be a party of values but not of ideology; still to stand for old Labour ends yet transcend Left and Right. But is it really possible that New

Labour can be both guardian of old values and midwife to the new ideology-less politics?

There is something in the view of New Labour as a technocratic project. New Labour shares common ground with the Conservatives to a far greater extent than it has for a long time. Moreover, one of Labour's central claims under Blair has been its superior leadership qualities and its competence to manage and make hard choices in government. Labour would be a clean and efficient act after the Tories. It would certainly be one free of the ideological zealotry which marked Thatcherism. Labour's message to the voters was clear: the party could now be trusted to run the country.

Yet New Labour *is* an ideological project. Its communitarian politics are an ideological break with social democracy and neo-liberal conservatism. Led by Blair, New Labour has marked out a picture of what we should do and how we should live. It is a vision which departs from the statist and egalitarian social democracy of the postwar period. It is more interventionist on economics than Thatcherism; and more socially conservative than liberalism. In many respects the infusion of new thinking into Labour politics in the 1990s makes the new Labour government a more ideological administration than many of its predecessors. Previous Labour governments, after all, were often marked by pragmatism and a reluctance, albeit often born by events, to put into practice what they had promised in opposition – and certainly what the socialist ethos of the party might appear to demand. By contrast, New Labour has a set of ideas and corresponding policies which it actually wishes to pursue in power *and* feels it can.

But if Labour is not 'beyond Left and Right', yet also not purely pragmatic, is it the case that its ideology is now just 'beyond Left'? For some British politics today is characterized by a consensus on the Right to which New Labour has now signed up.

A new consensus?

Many characterizations of British politics see the postwar period up until the economic upheavals of the 1970s as distinguished by a consensus between Left and Right. This led thinkers to talk of an end of ideology in this period, of the decreasing relevance of Left–Right divisions or of

181

government being about technocratic administration rather than ideological divides. The consensus was social democratic. Within it there were disagreements on detail. But Labour and Tories alike believed in Keynesianism, full employment and a universal welfare state: the consensus rested on a 'middle way' between state communism and free market capitalism. Conservatives and Liberals believed that, left to its own devices, free market capitalism was unworkable. The economy needed more than a nightwatchman state. Socialists and social democrats, while believing that planning and the welfare state would form the basis for a socialist society in the future, saw the middle way as a practical step in that direction.

After nearly two decades of radical Tory government, recent advocacies of the 'beyond Left and Right' theme suggest that a new consensus is now in place. While the old 'middle way' leant to the Left – 'we are all socialists now' – the new consensus leans to the Right – 'we are all capitalists now', and we all believe in responsibilities, standards and morality. So there is a new neo-liberal and conservative agenda. Differences – on the constitution and the minimum wage, for example – are within a consensus on the free market economy, radical reform of the welfare state and conservative moralism in social policy. And the consensus which now embraces Left and Right, Labour and Conservatives, is in large part the result of the Labour Party moving onto what was Tory territory. Some might suggest that 'beyond Left' rather than 'beyond Left and Right' would be a better description of it.[11]

Does this consensus on the Right make the Left–Right dichotomy no longer relevant for describing British politics? Is the convergence so much as to render Left–Right differentiations redundant? One reason to suggest not is that the realignment has developed along Left–Right lines. The realignment has been in a shift by Labour from the Left to the Right. It has not been *between* or *beyond* Left–Right divisions but along the lines they set out – from one side of the spectrum in the direction of the other. Left and Right still serve as explanatory devices for showing what direction and form the alignment has taken.

Secondly, as we have suggested, within the ideological consensus on the free economy, a reformed welfare state and conservatism in social policy there are key differences. In terms of emphasis, Labour highlights social justice, the plight of the excluded and the need for fairness and social cohesion, for example. There is a difference in tone from the

Tories here. There are concrete differences on details of economic policy – the minimum wage and Labour's windfall tax, for example. Many of these differences, however minute, break down along Left–Right lines. While the epicentre of British politics has shifted to the Right, some of the Labour government's day-to-day decisions and policy details are to the Left of this. This undermines the claim that just 'beyond Left' is a good description of what has happened to Labour.

Thirdly, for some Labour modernizers and Labour-supporting Centre Left thinkers, more traditional social democracy has been retired rather prematurely. There remains a clearly identifiable social democratic politics to the Left of Blair. Will Hutton is one of a number who feel that Keynesianism is not dead, that the fiscal crisis of the welfare state has been overstated, and that greater radicalism of a traditional social democratic sort is possible for a Labour government. For Hutton and other critical supporters of Blair, there is a conservatism, especially in New Labour economics, which is too timid, too fatalistically accepting of the globalization thesis, too enamoured of Thatcherism, and which fails to attack inequalities with sufficient vigour.[12] Once you go beyond New Labour, in short, 'Left' seems to be of even more relevance. And this includes socialists even further to the Left than Hutton. So if Labour has not transcended Left and Right, not relapsed into pragmatism, nor simply succumbed to the Right, what does the advent of New Labour mean for divisions of Left and Right? The answer lies in its post-Thatcherism: its definition by Thatcherism yet departure from it.

Politics after Thatcherism

We have described in this book a cleverly designed project, moulded to face particular perceived economic, political and social circumstances. We have argued that several common interpretations of New Labour are wrong. New Labour has substance: it is not just a politics of style and the soundbite. There are elements of Old Labour still there; but Tony Blair hardly constitutes a dangerous devil in disguise. He has genuinely discarded much of what he regarded as unworkable or made Labour unelectable. In doing so he has not just discarded old means, but also redefined old values. Labour has liberalized its economics and made its social policy more conservative in ways which carve a chasm between itself and the party thinking of the past. Yet New Labour is not just Thatcherism Mark II. There are too many differences of philosophy, emphasis and policy to justify such a tag.

New Labour is defined by coming after Lady Thatcher and its ideas are marked by Thatcherism. It has broken with old social democracy and accepted many of the Thatcherite reforms. It has accommodated to the shift to the Right in politics that Lady Thatcher engineered. Yet New Labour is also a reaction against Thatcherism. This has implications for Left and Right. In the direction it has forged for itself New Labour combines Left and Right rather than transcending them. It mixes acceptance of Thatcherism with a reaction to it through communitarian sentiments. As such, while pragmatic, it is not just that: it is driven also by ideological belief. It is defined by, but departs from, Thatcherism – moved to the Right but with anti-Thatcherite emphases. New Labour's politics are defined both by Right and by leftwards inclinations which are beyond old Left. These are the politics of post-Thatcherism.

Notes

Introduction

1 Tony Blair, 'How I will follow her', *Daily Telegraph* (11 January 1996).
2 Umberto Eco, *Reflections on The Name of the Rose* (Minerva, London,1994), p. 67 [first pubd in Britain in 1985].
3 Blair, 'How I will follow her'.
4 Stuart Hall and Martin Jacques, 'Blair: is he the greatest Tory since Thatcher?', *The Observer* (13 April 1997).
5 William Rees-Mogg, 'Ring out the old, ring in the new', *The Times* (2 May 1997).
6 Tony Blair, 'The Rights We Enjoy Reflect the Duties We Owe', *The Spectator* Lecture, 22 March 1995.

Chapter 1   From Old Labour to New Labour

1 David Butler and Gareth Butler, *British Political Facts, 1900–1994* (Macmillan, London, 1994).
2 Giles Radice and Stephen Pollard, *Any Southern Comfort?* (Fabian Society, London, 1994).
3 Tony Blair, speech to the Party of European Socialists' Congress, Malmö, 6 June 1997.
4 See Stephen Padgett, 'Social democracy in power', *Parliamentary Affairs*, 46, 1 (1993), pp. 101–20; see also Frances Fox Piven, *Labour Parties in Postindustrial Society* (Polity Press, Cambridge, 1991); William E. Paterson and Alistair H. Thomas, *The Future of Social Democracy* (Clarendon Press, Oxford, 1986); Richard Gillespie and W. E. Paterson (eds), *West European Politics*, 16,1 (1993).
5 See Eric Shaw, *The Labour Party since 1945* (Blackwell, Oxford, 1996).
6 Stuart Holland, *The Socialist Challenge* (Quartet, London, 1975).

7 See, for example, Evan Luard, *Socialism without the State* (Macmillan, London, 1979).

8 See Ian Bradley, *Breaking the Mould?* (Martin Robertson, Oxford, 1981); Shirley Williams, *Politics is for People* (Penguin, Harmondsworth, 1982); David Owen, *Face the Future* (Jonathan Cape, London, 1981).

9 For the SDP, see Ivor Crewe and Anthony King, *SDP: The Birth, Life and Death of the Social Democratic Party* (Oxford University Press, Oxford, 1996). Peter Riddell's comment is made in a review of Crewe and King, 'Enjoying the political afterlife', *The Times* (13 November1995). See also Alex de Mont, 'The SDP and Owen: Lessons for Blair', *Renewal*, 3,4 (October 1995), pp. 17–23.

10 Finkelstein, who ran the Owenite Social Market Foundation, went on to run the Conservative Research Department at Central Office. Adair Turner, another SDP old boy, went on to head the CBI.

11 See *The Political Theory of Possessive Individualism* (Oxford University Press, Oxford, 1962).

12 David Marquand, *The Unprincipled Society: New Demands and Old Politics* (Fontana, London, 1988), pp. 223–4.

13 Last point made by Marquand in 'Reaching for the levers', *Times Literary Supplement* (11 April, 1997), pp. 3–4.

14 David Marquand, 'After socialism', *Political Studies*, 41 (1993), pp. 43–56. Marquand's initial enthusiasm for New Labour cooled by 1996: see Marquand and Tony Wright, 'Labour and the intellectuals', *Political Quarterly*, 67, 1 (1996), pp. 1–3; 'New Labour needs a new world view', *The Observer* (7 April1996); 'Tony and the Tories: this is what we mean', *The Observer* (7 July 1996) (with Will Hutton, Frank Field, John Kay and John Gray).

15 Alain Touraine had made the announcement in 1980; it was repeated by Ralf Dahrendorf in 1989 after the fall of communism. See also Robin Blackburn, 'Fin de siecle: socialism after the crash', *New Left Review*, 185 (January/February 1991).

16 Andy McSmith, *Faces of Labour* (Verso, London, 1996), p. 362.

17 London, 21 July 1994, in Tony Blair, *New Britain: My Vision for a Young Country* (Fourth Estate/New Statesman, London, 1996), p. 25.

18 Blair is the first to acknowledge this debt: see his acceptance speech, 21 July 1994. For Kinnock's legacy, see *Contemporary Record* 8,3 (Winter 1994), 'Neil Kinnock and the Labour Party, 1983–92: symposium'.

19 Shaw, *The Labour Party since 1945*, p. 176.

20 Tudor Jones, *Remaking the Labour Party: from Gaitskell to Blair* (Routledge, London, 1996), pp. 119–20. See also Kinnock's own account in *Contemporary Record*, 8,3 (Winter 1994), pp. 535–54; and Jones's 'Neil Kinnock's socialist journey: from Clause Four to the Policy Review', ibid., pp. 567–88.

21 Labour gained 10 million votes (against over 13.5 for the Conservatives) and won 271 seats (against 376 for the Tories): Butler and Butler, *British Political Facts*, p. 219.

22 For more details, see Shaw, *The Labour Party since 1945*; Gerald Taylor, *Labour's Renewal: the Policy Review and Beyond* (Macmillan, London, 1997); Richard Heffernan and Mike Margusee, *Defeat from the Jaws of Victory* (Verso, London, 1992); Colin Hughes and Patrick Wintour, *Labour Rebuilt* (Fourth Estate, London, 1990); Martin Smith and Joanna Speer (eds), *The Changing Labour Party* (Routledge, London, 1992); Steven Fielding, *Labour: Decline and Renewal* (Baseline, Manchester, 1995).

23 Roy Hattersley, *Choose Freedom: The Future for Democratic Socialism* (Penguin, Harmondsworth, 1987). See also Barry Hindess, 'Liberty and equality', in Hindess (ed.), *Reactions to the Right* (Routledge, London, 1990) for discussion of Hattersley's arguments for equality as freedom.

24 Raymond Plant, *Equality, Markets and the State* (Fabian Society, London, 1984); Bernard Crick, *Socialist Values and Time* (Fabian Society, London, 1984); Norman Dennis and A. H. Halsey, *English Ethical Socialism: Thomas More to R. H. Tawney* (Clarendon Press, Oxford, 1988); David Selbourne, *The Principle of Duty: An Essay on the Foundations of Civic Order* (Sinclair-Stevenson, London, 1994); Tony Wright, *Socialisms*, 2nd edn. (Routledge, London, 1996). Blair appeals to both the New Liberals and the ethical socialists as inspiration for New Labour. See, for example, *Let Us Face the Future: The 1945 Anniversary Lecture* (Fabian Society, London, 1995).

25 Bryan Gould, *A Future for Socialism* (Jonathan Cape, London, 1989); Giles Radice, *Labour's Path to Power: The New Revisionism* (Macmillan, London, 1989).

26 Jack Straw, *Policy and Ideology* (Blackburn Constituency Labour Party, 1993).

27 Jones, *Remaking the Labour Party*, p. 133.

28 Shaw, *The Labour Party since 1945*, p. 202.

29 Colin Hay, 'Labour's Thatcherite Revisionism: Playing the politics of catch-up', *Political Studies*, 42 (1994), pp. 700–7.

30 Martin J. Smith, 'Understanding the "politics of catch-up": the modernization of the Labour Party', *Political Studies*, 43,4 (1994), pp. 711, 714. Similar points are made by Raymond Plant in defence of the Policy Review in 'The case for the defence', *Contemporary Record*, 3,2 (November 1989), pp. 7–8. Elsewhere Martin Smith writes: 'With the policy review the Labour leadership made a complete break with reformist socialism . . . Labour's ideology became a commitment to maintaining welfare capitalism within the context of the European Community', p. 559: 'Neil Kinnock and the modernization of the Labour Party', *Contemporary Record* 8,3 (Winter 1994), pp. 555–66.

31 Mark Wickham-Jones, 'Recasting social democracy: a comment on Hay and Smith', *Political Studies*, 43,4 (December 1995), pp. 698–702.

32 Tudor Jones, 'The case against Labour's rethink', *Contemporary Record*, 3,2 (November 1989), p. 6.

33 See David Miller, *Market, State and Community: Theoretical Foundations of Market Socialism* (Clarendon Press, Oxford, 1990).

34 Jones, 'The case against Labour's rethink', p. 7; Plant, 'The case for the defence'.

35 Jones, *Remaking the Labour Party*, pp. 149, 155.

36 Donald Sassoon, *One Hundred Years of Socialism: The Western European Left in the Twentieth Century* (I. B. Tauris, London, 1996), p. 706.

37 Sassoon, *One Hundred Years of Socialism*, p. 648.

38 Padgett, 'Social democracy in power', p. 119. For details of Left winners and losers, see Sassoon, *One Hundred Years of Socialism*, tables 16.3 and 16.4 for summaries, and chapters 16–24.

39 Sassoon, *One Hundred Years of Socialism*, p. 735.

40 See, in particular, Colin Crouch and David Marquand, *Ethics and Markets* (Political Quarterly/Blackwell, Oxford, 1993).

41 David Willetts, *Why Vote Conservative?* (Penguin, Harmondsworth, 1997). See also Willetts's *Blair's Gurus* (Centre for Policy Studies, London, 1996); and review by Peter Riddell, 'I'm a guru; are you one too?', *The Times* (8 July 1996), who argues that: 'Insofar as Mr Blair has gurus, they are from across the Atlantic.'

42 See Graeme Duncan, *The Australian Labor Party: A Model for Others?* (Fabian Society, London, 1989); Francis Castles and Christopher Pierson, 'A new convergence? Recent policy developments in the United Kingdom, Australia and New Zealand', *Policy and Politics*, 24,3 (1996), pp. 233–45.

43 See John Rentoul, *Tony Blair* (Little, Brown, London, 1995), pp. 271–81.

44 A. Heath, R. Jowell and J. Curtice (eds), *Labour's Last Chance? The 1992 Election and Beyond* (Dartmouth, Aldershot, 1994).

45 Radice and Pollard, *Any Southern Comfort?*, p. 16.

46 Speech by Tony Blair to Labour Party conference, Blackpool, 4 October 1994.

47 *London Evening Standard* (23 May 1996).

48 Tony Wright, *Why Vote Labour?* (Penguin, Harmondsworth, 1997), p. 26.

49 Stuart Hall and Martin Jacques (eds), *New Times: The Changing Face of Politics in the 1990s* (Lawrence & Wishart, London, 1989), pp. 11, 15.

50 Rentoul, *Tony Blair*.

51 Tony Blair, 'Faith in the City – Ten Years On', 29 January 1996 (The Labour Party); See Rentoul, *Tony Blair*, pp. 38–47. As a number of writers have pointed out since Blair became leader of the Labour Party, Macmurray

was much more radical than Blair – more a young Hegelian Marx than a New Labour modernizer. See, for example, Bruce Anderson, 'Warm fuzzies for everyone', *The Spectator* (20 January 1996).

52 Blair, 'Faith in the City – Ten Years On'.

53 In academic literature communitarianism is principally a philosophical critique of liberalism. Communitarian political philosophers such as Alistair MacIntyre, Michael Sandel, Charles Taylor and Michael Walzer attack the liberal conception of the person, its asocial individualism and its universalistic claims. See Stephen Mulhall and Adam Swift, *Liberals and Communitarians* (Blackwell, Oxford, 1992) and Shlomo Avineri and Avner de-Shalit (eds), *Communitarianism and Individualism* (Oxford University Press, Oxford, 1992) for good summaries and readings. See also Amitai Etzioni, *The Spirit of Community: Rights, Responsibilities and the Communitarian Agenda* (Fontana, London, 1995). For discussion of New Labour's communitarianisms, see Stephen Driver and Luke Martell, 'New Labour's communitarianisms', *Critical Social Policy*, 17,3 (August 1997), pp. 27–46.

54 Blair, 'The Rights We Enjoy Reflect the Duties We Owe', *The Spectator* Lecture, 22 March 1995; and Blair in Giles Radice (ed.), *What Needs to Change: New Visions for Britain* (HarperCollins, London, 1996), p. 8.

Chapter 2   The New Economics

1 Michael White, 'IMF praises Brown but urges curbs on spending', *The Guardian* (22 July 1997); Alex Brummer, 'Britain awarded IMF's seal of merit', *The Guardian* (17 September 1997).

2 See Eric Shaw, *The Labour Party since 1945* (Blackwell, Oxford, 1996) for a history of postwar Labour which gives good attention to economic and industrial policy. See also Noel Thompson, *Political Economy and the Labour Party: The Economics of Democratic Socialism 1884–1995* (University College London Press, London, 1996).

3 Tony Crosland, *The Future of Socialism* (Jonathan Cape, London, 1964) [first pubd 1956].

4 Stuart Holland, *The Socialist Challenge* (Quartet, London, 1975).

5 Key party documents setting out the background to New Labour's economic policy and the policies themselves include *Vision for Growth: A New Industrial Strategy for Britain* (Labour Party, London, 1996) and *A New Economic Future for Britain* (Labour Party, London, 1995). Also, of course, the 1997 manifesto, *New Labour: Because Britain Deserves Better* (Labour Party, London, 1997). Speeches and pamphlets by Tony Blair and Gordon Brown referred to below are also important sources on New Labour's economic rethinking. This rethinking is also reflected in other publications such

as Commission on Public Policy and British Business, *Promoting Prosperity: A Business Agenda for Britain* (Vintage, London, 1997), a report linked to the Centre Left think-tank the Institute for Public Policy Research; Peter Mandelson and Roger Liddle, *The Blair Revolution* (Faber & Faber, London, 1996); and Richard Layard, *What Labour Can Do* (Warner, London, 1997).

6 Tony Blair, speech to the Party of European Socialists' Congress, Malmö, 6 June 1997.

7 These themes on globalization and economic policy are set out, among other places, in Tony Blair, 'The Global Economy', speech to the Keidanren, Tokyo, 5 January 1996, in *New Britain: My Vision for a Young Country* (Fourth Estate, London, 1996) and Gordon Brown, *Fair is Efficient* (Fabian Pamphlet 563, Fabian Society, London, 1994).

8 Daniel Bell, *The Coming of Post-Industrial Society* (Heinemann, London, 1974); Alain Touraine, *The Post-Industrial Society* (Random House, New York, 1971).

9 Early interest on the Left in post-Fordism can be found in Robin Murray's 'Fordism and Post-Fordism' and 'Benetton Britain', in Stuart Hall and Martin Jacques (eds), *New Times* (Lawrence & Wishart, London, 1989). Many theories of post-Fordism are influenced by the analysis of flexible specialization in M. Piore and C. Sabel, *The Second Industrial Divide* (Basic Books, New York, 1984).

10 Anthony Giddens, *The Consequences of Modernity* (Polity Press, Cambridge, 1990).

11 Anthony Giddens, *Beyond Left and Right* (Polity Press, Cambridge, 1994); 'Unstuck in Middle England', *The Guardian* (27 February 1995); 'Dare to care, conserve and repair', *New Statesman and Society* (29 October 1993); 'Brave New World: the new context of politics', in David Miliband (ed.), *Reinventing the Left* (Polity Press, Cambridge, 1994). This view of the role of Right and Left is echoed also in the writings of John Gray.

12 See, for example, Barry Jones, *Sleepers, Wake!* (Oxford University Press, Oxford, 1982).

13 Gordon Brown, 'The politics of potential: a new agenda for Labour', in D. Miliband (ed.), *Reinventing the Left*; Tony Blair, 'The Global Economy'.

14 See *Vision for Growth* and *New Opportunities for Business* (Labour Party, London, 1996); Tony Blair, 'New industrial world', in *New Britain*, 'The Global Economy', 'Britain can remake it', *Guardian* (22 July 1997), speech to the 1995 Labour Party conference, Brighton, 3 October 1995; Lina Saigol, 'Chancellor of youth culture', *Guardian* (4 July 1997). See also Dick Sorabji, 'Rules of the information age', *Renewal*, 4,1, (1996) pp. 7–14, an enthusiast for the information age as the best big idea for New Labour.

15 For the policy proposals discussed in this section, see: Tony Blair, 'Britain can remake it'; Labour Party, *New Opportunities for Business, Vision for Growth* and *A New Economic Future for Britain*.

16 Krishan Kumar, *Prophecy and Progress: The Sociology of Industrial and Post-Industrial Society* (Penguin, Harmondsworth, 1978) is an early doubter about post-industrialism. Paul Hirst and Jonathan Zeitlin, *Flexible Specialisation Versus Post-Fordism: Theory, Evidence and Policy Implications* (Birkbeck Public Policy Centre Working Paper, London, 1990) provide a critique of theories of post-Fordism. Paul Hirst and Graeme Thompson, *Globalization in Question* (Polity Press, Cambridge, 1996), criticize globalization theories. Frank Webster, 'The information age: What's the big idea', *Renewal*, 4,1 (1996) expresses concern about the information age as the big idea for New Labour.

17 Michel Albert, *Capitalism against Capitalism* (Whurr, London, 1993); Will Hutton, *The State We're In* (Jonathan Cape, London, 1995). See also C. Crouch and D. Marquand (eds), *Ethics and Markets: Cooperation and Competition within Capitalist Market Economies* (Blackwell, Oxford, 1993).

18 Will Hutton, *The State We're In*, ch. 10.

19 Ibid.

20 Ibid.

21 David Willetts, for example, is one right-wing critic of the Centre Left evaluation of global models of capitalism as put forward by figures such as Will Hutton: see Willetts, 'The poverty of stakeholding', in Gavin Kelly et al. (eds), *Stakeholder Capitalism* (Macmillan, London, 1997).

22 Compare Blair's Singapore speech, discussed below, and the 1995 document *A New Economic Future for Britain* with the 1997 manifesto.

23 Mark Atkinson, 'Stop boasting EU tells Blair and Clinton', *The Observer* (22 June 1997). Although some argue that, as Labour learns some lessons from the European model and European social democrats beyond Britain are forced to more prudent economics by EU convergence, the differences are not so great as party leaders' statements sometimes make them appear to be. See, for instance, Donald Sassoon, 'Don't misread Jospin', *New Statesman* (25 April 1997).

24 In, for example, Tony Blair, speech to the Singapore business community, 8 January 1996.

25 Tony Blair, 'The Mais Lecture', City University, 22 May 1995. See also Alistair Darling, 'A political perspective' in Gavin Kelly et al. (eds), *Stakeholder Capitalism*; Labour Party, *A New Economic Future for Britain*; John Gray, 'Revival of reforms', *The Guardian* (8 July 1996); John Gray, *After Social Democracy* (Demos, London, 1996) and other of his writings where, for reasons similar to Blair's, he doubts the usefulness of foreign models to British

circumstances. Similar scepticism about the appropriateness of foreign models to Britain are expressed by C. Leadbeater and G. Mulgan, 'Stakeholding: Nice idea, shame about the reality', *The Observer* (6 October 1996) and Demos, *Mistakeholding* (Demos, London, 1996).

26 See, for example, Tony Blair, speech to the 1997 Labour Party conference, 30 September 1997.

27 Tony Blair, speech to the Singapore business community; 'Faith in the City – Ten Years On', speech at Southwark Cathedral, London, 29 January 1996; 'The John Smith Memorial Lecture', Queen Elizabeth II Conference Centre, London, 7 February 1996.

28 Tony Blair, speech to the Singapore business community.

29 Michael White, 'Tories mix it in battle of slogans', *Guardian* (11 January 1997). 'Who is raising the stakes?', *Guardian* (17 January 1996).

30 This is to list just some of the alleged originators of stakeholding. J. K. Galbraith, *The New Industrial State* (Hamish Hamilton, London, 1967); John Kay, *The Foundations of Corporate Success* (Oxford University Press, Oxford, 1993); R. Dahrendorf et al., *The Report on Wealth Creation and Social Cohesion in a Free Society* (Commission on Wealth Creation and Social Cohesion, London, 1995); Royal Society for the Arts Inquiry, *Tomorrow's Company* (RSA, London, 1995).

31 Andrew Gamble and his colleagues make a similar distinction. See Kelly et al., 'Conclusion: stakeholder capitalism', in Kelly et al. (eds), *Stakeholder Capitalism*; Andrew Gamble and Gavin Kelly, 'Stakeholder capitalism and one nation socialism', *Renewal*, 4,1 (1996).

32 John Kay, *The Foundations of Corporate Success*; Hutton, *The State We're In*.

33 Hutton, *The State We're In*; David Marquand, 'Elusive visions', *The Guardian* (24 June 1996).

34 Hutton, *The State We're In*, chs. 11 and 12.

35 John Kay, 'The stakeholder corporation', in Gavin Kelly et al. (eds), *Stakeholder Capitalism*.

36 Blair, speech to the Singapore business community.

37 Blair, 'Mais Lecture'; Darling, 'A political perspective'; Labour Party, *Vision for Growth*; Some New Labour sympathizers argue that, because of this inappropriateness to the UK, New Labour should concentrate on individual stakeholding, education and training rather than company stakeholding. See C. Leadbeater and G. Mulgan, 'Stakeholding: nice idea, shame about the reality'; Demos, *Mistakeholding*.

38 The Labour policies discussed in this section are outlined in *New Opportunities for Business* and *Vision for Growth*. Many of the proposals discussed in this section, it should be noted, were in 1995 or 1996 policy documents. Not all of them, especially not the more interventionist ideas, made it to the

1997 manifesto, or into the first Queen's speech or budget.

39 Tony Blair, speech to the Party of European Socialists' Congress.

40 Balancing these contrary tendencies, flexibility and security, autonomy and community, Anthony Giddens and John Gray argue, is Labour's big challenge, one on which the Tories failed. See Anthony Giddens, 'Unstuck in middle England', *The Guardian* (27 February 1995), and John Gray, *After Social Democracy* (Demos, London, 1996). The attempt to balance such tendencies, Gray argues, is what concerned the New Liberalism of J. A. Hobson and L. T. Hobhouse. Blair, skipping postwar social democracy in his appeal for roots, also appeals to the New Liberal tradition: see his *Let Us Face the Future*.

41 As in Gordon Brown's speech to the 1997 Labour Party conference.

42 Tony Blair, speech to the Singapore business community; Gordon Brown, 'Why Labour is still loyal to the poor', *The Guardian* (2 August 1997).

43 As well as references already given, see also Tony Blair, 'Labour and the Unions', speech to the Unions '94 conference, London, 19 November 1994, in *New Britain*, and Commission on Social Justice, *Social Justice: Strategies for National Renewal*, Vintage (London, 1994). We shall return to many of these issues in the next chapter. The minimum wage should also prevent the necessity for payments in benefits to the low-paid which subsidize low-paying employers at the expense of the tax-payer. The social chapter of the Maastricht Treaty also leaves open the possibility of Britain joining in further social protection for workers (when Labour signed up in 1997 it included only provision for works councils for some larger companies – already implemented by some – and provision for unpaid parental leave).

44 Tony Blair, speech to the 1995 Labour Party conference.

45 Gordon Brown, *Fair is Efficient*.

46 Robert Reich, *The Work of Nations: Preparing Ourselves for 21st Century Capitalism* (Simon & Schuster, London, 1991); and 'New Deal and fair deal', *Guardian* (14 July 1997). Patrick Wintour, 'Labour looks abroad for ideas', *Guardian* (6 October 1995); Patrick Wintour and Will Hutton, 'How Brown borrowed to give Britain a New Deal', *The Observer* (6 July 1997).

47 John Gray, *After Social Democracy*, p. 26.

48 For the New Labour view on the egalitarianism in its stakeholding, see Gordon Brown, 'The Anthony Crosland Memorial Lecture', 13 February 1997, and 'Why Labour is still loyal to the poor'.

49 'Who is raising the stakes?' *The Guardian* (17 January 1996); Melanie Phillips, 'Just another soundbite, or a policy with teeth?', *The Observer* (14 January 1997); William Keegan, 'Blair's bland "stakeholder" blend must mean justice for all', *The Observer* (14 January 1996).

50 Roy Hattersley, 'Why I'm no longer loyal to Labour', *The Guardian* (26 July

1997). Hattersley does not use the word stakeholding but his critique is of the policies of stakeholding. See Ruth Levitas, 'The concept of social exclusion and the new Durkheimian hegemony', *Critical Social Policy*, 16,1 (1996) for a critique of proposals such as those of the EU, the Commission on Social Justice and Will Hutton for being too focused on employment as the route for inclusion. Ruth Lister, 'Social inclusion and exclusion', in Kelly et al. (eds), *Stakeholder Capitalism*, endorses Levitas's point.

51 Helen Rainbird, 'Training is not enough', *Renewal*, 3,1 (1995); Robert Kuttner, 'Don't forget the demand side', in David Miliband (ed.), *Reinventing the Left*; Will Hutton, 'Keynes still has the answers', *The Guardian* (1 April 1996). These three argue that training on the supply side can provide better trained job applicants, but this is not enough without macro-economic-demand management to actually create jobs. See also John Grieve Smith, 'Jobs plan could lead nowhere', *The Guardian* (14 July 1997). Former EU president Jacques Delors is perhaps one of the most prominent campaigners for Euro-Keynesianism. See Paul Anderson and Kevin Davey, 'A farewell to Keynes?', *New Statesman and Society* (23 February 1996), on the complex and changing role and meaning of Keynesianism among recent Centre Left thinkers.

52 David Willetts, 'The poverty of stakeholding', in Kelly et al. (eds), *Stakeholder Capitalism*, proposes a number of these right-wing criticisms. Other commentators who are more sympathetic to New Labour but echo some of these criticisms of stakeholding include John Lloyd, 'Stakeholding: the great debate', *New Statesman* (12 July 1996), pp. 27–9, and David Soskice, 'Stakeholding yes; the German model no', in Kelly et al. (eds), *Stakeholder Capitalism*; Leadbeater and Mulgan, 'Stakeholding: nice idea shame about the reality'.

53 Tony Blair, 'New Labour, New Economy', speech to the annual conference of the Confederation of British Industry, 13 November 1995, reprinted in Tony Blair, *New Britain*.

54 Tony Blair, 'The Mais Lecture', City University, London, 22 May 1995. This section and some of the policy outlines in the next are based on Blair's discussion in this lecture.

55 Tony Blair, 'The Mais Lecture', where Blair sets out his view of Keynesian and Thatcherite economics and his proposals for Labour's macro- and micro-economic policy discussed in this section. See also his 'New Labour, New Economy' and 'The Global Economy'. John Gray, *After Social Democracy*, also sets out the case for the death of New Right and old social democratic economics and for an alternative along lines very similar to Blair's. Labour's policies discussed in this section and the next are also set out in Labour Party *Vision for Growth* and *A New Economic Future for Britain*.

56 Tony Blair, 'The Global Economy'.

57 Philip Webster, 'Chancellor goes to Europe with plan to create more jobs', *The Times* (5 June 1997). Tony Blair, speech to the European Socialists' Congress.

58 Patrick Wintour, 'Labour looks abroad for ideas'; Patrick Wintour and Will Hutton, 'How Brown borrowed to give Britain a New Deal'.

59 William Keegan, 'Labour's terror of old mistakes', *The Observer* (6 July 1997); Larry Elliott, 'As ever, we must fight and fight again', *The Guardian* (12 May 1997); Roy Hattersley, 'Just one per cent on top tax wouldn't hurt', *The Guardian* (24 June 1997).

60 Michael White and Seamus Milne, 'A new credo for new Labour', *The Guardian* (14 March 1995). The 349-word clause also makes commitments about matters such as democracy, the environment, Britain's international role and its relations with the unions and other groups.

61 Ted Benton, 'Clause 4', *Radical Philosophy*, 72 (July/August 1995), pp.2–4.

62 Alistair Darling, 'A political perspective', p. 13.

63 Francis McGowan, 'Labour's new competition policy: market forces and the public interest', *Renewal*, 3,4 (1995).

64 Tony Blair, 'New Labour and the unions'.

65 Andy McSmith, *Faces of Labour* (Verso, London, 1996), p. 340. A critique of neo-classical theories for treating factors such as technology and individual tastes as exogenous to the economic system is given by the institutional economist Geoff Hodgson in his book *Economics and Institutions* (Polity Press, Cambridge, 1988), pp. 13–19. Such factors, he argues, are endogenous to growth, not outside it.

66 On Labour's transport and environment policies, see: Labour Party, *New Labour: Because Britain Deserves Better*, 1997 general election manifesto; Paul Brown, 'Prescott targets two-car culture', *The Guardian* (22 August 1997); *Consensus for Change* (Labour Party, London, 1996); *Leading the Future* (Labour Party, London, 1994).

67 As well as the policy documents referred to above, see also Tony Blair's speech to the Royal Society, 27 February 1996, reported by Paul Brown, 'Blair puts environment centre stage', *The Guardian* (28 February 1996) and Robin Cook, 'Less must be more', *The Guardian* (24 June 1997).

68 Ian Willmore, 'Sun sets on a greener future', *Guardian* (23 July 1997); Larry Elliott, 'Going from red to green with a pollution solution', *Guardian* (19 May 1997); Paul Brown, 'Blair's fine words ignored', *Guardian* (3 July 1997).

195

Chapter 3   Welfare and Social Policy

1 Tony Blair, *Let Us Face the Future: The 1945 Anniversary Lecture* (Fabian Society, London, 1995), pp. 2, 14. See also Brown, *Fair is Efficient* (Fabian Pamphlet 563, Fabian Society, London, 1994). For an influential elaboration of the 'new times' theme in social policy, see Gosta Esping-Anderson, 'Equality and work in the post-industrial life-cycle', in David Miliband (ed.), *Reinventing the Left* (Polity Press, Cambridge, 1994); and *The Three Worlds of Welfare Capitalism* (Polity Press, Cambridge, 1990).

2 First used on Radio 4's 'The World this Weekend', 10 January 1993. See John Rentoul, *Tony Blair* (Little, Brown, London, 1995), pp. 283–7.

3 'Labour examines plans to privatise the welfare state', *The Times* (5 January 1996).

4 Chris Smith, 'When the music stops', *The Guardian* (7 May 1996).

5 Eric Shaw, *The Labour Party since 1945* (Blackwell, Oxford, 1996), p. 37.

6 Pete Alcock, *Social Policy in Britain* (Macmillan, London, 1996), p. 48.

7 Tony Crosland, *The Future of Socialism* (Jonathan Cape, 1964), pp. 165, 169.

8 Ibid., pp. 224–5.

9 Ibid., pp. 148–9.

10 Although, as Raymond Plant stresses, Crosland took a Rawlsian position on the egalitarian effects of public services in that they allowed 'the absolute position of the better off to be sustained while incrementally improving the position of the worst off'. In David Marquand and Anthony Seldon, *The Ideas that Shaped Post-War Britain* (Fontana, London, 1996), p. 175.

11 David Marquand, 'Moralists and hedonists', in Marquand and Seldon, *The Ideas that Changed Post-War Britain*, p. 23.

12 Shaw, *The Labour Party since 1945*, p. 93.

13 See John Hills, *The Future of Welfare: A Guide to the Debate* (Joseph Rowntree Foundation, York, 1993), esp. figure 2.

14 See Hills, *The Future of Welfare*, figures 2 and 3, p. 9.

15 Nicholas Timmins, *The Five Giants: A Biography of the Welfare State* (HarperCollins, London, 1995), pp. 315–16.

16 Ibid., p. 368.

17 See Peter Taylor-Gooby, *Public Opinion, Ideology and State Welfare* (Routledge & Kegan Paul, London, 1985).

18 See, for example, Peter Townsend, *Poverty in the United Kingdom: A Survey of Household Resources and Standards of Living* (Penguin, Harmondsworth, 1979).

19 See Julian Le Grand, *The Strategy of Equality* (Allen & Unwin, London, 1982).

20 Hills, *The Future of Welfare*, figures 9 and 10, pp. 16–17.

21 Ibid., p. 19 and figure 12, p. 20.

22 *The Times* (8 December 1997).

23 Frank Field, *Making Welfare Work: Reconstructing Welfare for the Millennium* (Institute of Community Studies, London, 1995), pp. 1–2.

24 Field, *Making Welfare Work*, p. 122. See Field's *Inequality in Britain: Freedom, Welfare and the State* (Fontana, London, 1981) for an earlier statement of his views on welfare reform.

25 Gordon Brown, 'The Anthony Crosland Memorial Lecture' (Labour Party, 13 February 1997). Brown said in this speech: 'We reject equality of outcome not because it is too radical but because it is neither desirable nor feasible.'

26 Gordon Brown, Second John Smith Memorial Lecture, reproduced in *Fabian Review*, 108,3 (1996), pp. 1–2.

27 Geoff Mulgan, 'Think well-being, not welfare', *New Statesman* (17 January 1997). See also John Lloyd, 'A plan to abolish the underclass', *New Statesman* (29 August 1997), which is partly based on an interview with Mulgan.

28 *The Times* (7 August 1997). Frank Field, 'Give them the tools', *The Guardian* (12 August 1997).

29 See *Getting Welfare to Work* (Labour Party, London, 1996).

30 Peter Mandelson, *Labour's Next Steps: Tackling Social Exclusion* (Fabian Society, London, 1997), p. 6.

31 Roy Hattersley, 'Just one per cent on top tax wouldn't hurt', *Guardian* (24 June 1997); 'Why I'm no longer loyal to Labour', *Guardian* (26 July 1997)

32 Tony Wright, *Why Vote Labour?* (Penguin, Harmondsworth, 1997), p. 49.

33 Le Grand himself offers what he calls a 'robust' welfare strategy: 'strategies or institutions that are robust to whatever assumption is made about human motivation'. Julian Le Grand, 'Knights, knaves or pawns? Human behaviour and social policy', *Journal of Social Policy*, 26,2 (1997), pp. 149–69.

34 Field, *Making Welfare Work*, pp. 2–3.

35 *The Future of Welfare*, p. 57.

36 *The Times* (17 July 1997).

37 'Safe in Labour's hands?', *The Times* (8 January 1997).

38 For an evaluation of NHS reforms, see Ray Robinson and Julian Le Grand, *Evaluating the NHS Reforms* (Kings Fund Institute/Policy Journals, Hermitage, 1993); Howard Glennerster, *Implementing GP Fundholding: Wild Card or Winning Hand* (Open University Press, Buckingham, 1994). For support for a non-competitive purchaser/provider NHS, see Chris Ham, *Public, Private or Community: What Next for the NHS?* (Demos, London, 1996).

39 See Nicholas Deakin and Anthony Wright (eds), *Consuming Public Services* (Routledge, London, 1990).

40 Albert O. Hirschman, *Exit, Voice, and Loyalty: Responses to Decline in Firms,*

Organizations and States (Harvard University Press, Cambridge, MA, 1970).

41 See Julian Le Grand and Will Bartlett, *Quasi-Markets and Social Policy* (Macmillan, London, 1993).

42 See, for example, 'Brave New World: the new context of politics', in Miliband, *Reinventing the Left; Beyond Left and Right: The Future of Radical Politics* (Polity Press, Cambridge, 1994).

43 See his *Legislators and Interpreters: On Modernity, Post-Modernity and Intellectuals* (Polity Press, Cambridge, 1987).

44 In Ulrich Beck, Anthony Giddens and Scott Lash, *Reflexive Modernization: Politics, Tradition and Aesthetics in the Modern Social Order* (Polity Press, Cambridge, 1994), p. 13.

45 For the influence of postmodern ideas on social policy, see Tony Fitzpatrick, 'Postmodernism, welfare and radical policies', *Journal of Social Policy*, 25,3 (1996), pp. 303–20; Paddy Hillyard and Sophie Watson, 'Postmodern social policy', *Journal of Social Policy*, 25,3 (1996), pp. 321–46. On education, see David Hargreaves, *The Mosaic of Learning* (Macmillan, London, 1994). See also Will Hutton, *The State We're In* (Jonathan Cape, London 1995); John Gray, *After Social Democracy* (Demos, London, 1996).

46 'The global economy', in Tony Blair, *New Britain: My Vision for a Young Country* (Fourth Estate/New Statesman, London, 1996), p. 125.

47 Although many of the ideas can be found in James Callaghan's 'Great Debate' speech on education in 1976. See James Callaghan, 'The Ruskin College speech', in John Ahier, Ben Cosin and Margaret Hales, *Diversity and Change: Education, Policy and Selection* (Routledge, London, 1996).

48 *Diversity and Excellence* and *Excellence for Everyone* (both Labour Party, London, 1995).

49 Tony Blair, 'Why schools must do better', *The Times* (7 July 1997).

50 'The tough truths of Dearing', *The Times* (24 July 1997).

51 Howard Glennerster and Julian Le Grand, 'Tickets please, children', *The Guardian* (5 April 1995).

52 Geoff Mulgan, *The Other Hand: Remaking Charity for the 21st Century* (Demos, London, 1995); Charles Leadbeater, *The Rise of the Social Entrepreneur* (Demos, London, 1997); David Green, *Reinventing Civil Society: The Rediscovery of Welfare Without Politics* (Institute of Economic Affairs, London, 1993).

53 See Field, *Making Welfare Work*, esp. ch. 7; Field, *How to Pay for the Future: Building a Stakeholders' Welfare* (Institute of Community Studies, London, 1996); and Labour Party, *Getting Welfare to Work*, pp. 11–19.

54 'Rebates plan for top-up pensions', *The Times* (17 July 1997).

55 *The Times* (13 August 1997).

56 Report of the Commission on Social Justice, *Social Justice: Strategies for Na-*

tional Renewal (Vintage, London, 1994), pp. 84–5.

57 *Social Justice*, p. 97. See also Brown, *Fair is Efficient*.

58 *Social Justice*, p. 113; see also Gosta Esping-Andersen, 'Equality and work in the post-industrial life-cycle', in Miliband (ed.), *Reinventing the Left*; and his *The Three Worlds of Welfare Capitalism* (Polity Press, Cambridge, 1990).

59 See Chris Pierson, 'From words to deeds: Labour and the just society', *Renewal*, 3,1 (1995), pp. 45–55; Stuart White, 'Rethinking the strategy of equality: an assessment of the report of the Commission on Social Justice', *Political Quarterly*, 66,3 (1995), pp. 205–10.

60 Gordon Brown, *Fair is Efficient*, p. 22.

61 Tony Blair, 'Why schools must do better', *The Times* (7 July 1997).

62 In terms of employer contributions, these would be voluntary in nature: the 1995 policy proposal to charge a training levy on employers has disappeared from Labour policy. See *A New Economic Future for Britain* (Labour Party, London, 1995), p. 20. In October 1997 there were suggestions that the forthcoming White Paper on Lifelong Learning would extend individual learning accounts to all students. See *Times Higher Education Supplement* (10 October 1997).

63 *A New Economic Future for Britain*; *Getting Welfare to Work*.

64 'Workshy young face huge cut in benefits', *The Times* (4 July 1997).

65 See *Getting Welfare to Work*, pp. 3, 9–10.

66 For early Clinton reforms, see Simon Crine, *Reforming Welfare: American Lessons* (Fabian Society, London, 1994).

67 *Getting Welfare to Work*, p. 9.

68 'Beckett seeks minimum wage exemption for young people', *The Times* (25 September 1997).

69 See *A New Economic Future for Britain*; *Getting Welfare to Work*.

70 See Crine, *Reforming Welfare*.

71 Quoted in *The Observer* (6 July 1997).

72 See 'Making it work', *The Economist* (28 June 1997), pp. 28–33.

73 See Dennis Snower, 'Three diseases that could kill the welfare to work initiative', *The Guardian* (11 August 1997). See also Richard Thomas, 'Strong welfare and flexible labour? Why Kenneth Clarke is wrong', *Renewal*, 3,1 (1995), pp. 37–44; and 'Cost worry over New Deal jobs', *The Guardian* (19 September 1997).

74 Thomas, 'Strong welfare and flexible labour?', p. 43.

75 Esping-Andersen, 'Equality and work in the post-industrial life-cycle', p. 182.

76 Although not by everyone. See Anatole Kaletsky of *The Times* and William Keegan of *The Observer*, as well as economists such as the late J. E. Meade, *Full Employment Regained?* (Cambridge University Press, Cambridge, 1995).

77 Robert Reich, 'New deal and fair deal', *The Guardian* (14 July 1997).
78 'Labour unveils New Deal for the young unemployed', *The Guardian* (10 November 1995).
79 Budget speech, full text, *The Times* (3 July 1997), p. 17.
80 *Social Justice*, p. 183.
81 This section draws on David Downes and Rod Morgan, 'Dumping the "hostages to fortune"? The politics of law and order in post-war Britain', in Mike Maguire, Rod Morgan and Robert Reiner, *The Oxford Handbook of Criminology*, 2nd edn (Clarendon Press, Oxford, 1997). Thanks to Karim Murji for this reference.
82 *Tackling the Causes of Crime* (Labour Party, London, 1996), p. 6.
83 See *Protecting our Communities: Labour's Plans for Tackling Criminal, Anti-Social Behaviour in Neighbourhoods* (Labour Party, London, 1996).
84 Downes and Morgan, 'Dumping the "hostages to fortune"?', p. 105.
85 *Tackling the Causes of Crime*, p. 4.
86 *The Economist* (15 February 1997)
87 *The Times* (4 December 1997).
88 Hugo Young, 'Police march over the Straw barricade', *The Guardian* (14 October 1997).
89 See Stephen Driver and Luke Martell, 'New Labour's communitarianisms', *Critical Social Policy*, 17,3, (1997), pp. 27–46.
90 Tony Blair, in Giles Radice (ed.), *What Needs to Change: New Visions for Britain* (HarperCollins, London, 1996), p. 8.
91 Wright, *Why vote Labour?*, pp. 78–9.

Chapter 4   Government and the Constitution

1 'Blair on the constitution', *The Economist* (14 September 1996), pp. 33–5.
2 Vernon Bogdanor, *Power and the People: A Guide to Constitutional Reform* (Victor Gollancz, London, 1997), p. 15.
3 David Marquand, 'Reaching for the levers', *Times Literary Supplement* (11 April 1997), pp. 3–4.
4 See Tony Benn, *Arguments for Democracy* (Penguin, Harmondsworth, 1982); and *Parliament, People and Power* (Verso, London, 1982).
5 See David Marquand, *The Unprincipled Society: New Demands and Old Politics* (Fontana, London, 1988).
6 Will Hutton, *The State We're In* (Jonathan Cape, London, 1995), pp. xi–xii.
7 In David Miliband (ed.), *Reinventing the Left* (Polity Press, Cambridge, 1994), pp. 27–8.
8 See Colin Crouch and David Marquand (eds), *Ethics and Markets: Cooperation and Competition within Capitalist Economies* (Blackwell/Political Quar-

terly, Oxford, 1993); Miliband (ed.), *Reinventing the Left*; Colin Crouch and David Marquand (eds), *Reinventing Collective Action: From the Global to the Local* (Blackwell/Political Quarterly, Oxford, 1995).

9 Marquand, 'After socialism', *Political Studies*, 41 (1993), pp. 43–56.

10 Tony Wright and David Marquand, 'Come the revolution', *The Guardian* (23 October 1995). See also Marquand, 'Vision wanted', *The Guardian* (18 September 1995).

11 Paul Hirst, 'From the economic to the political', in Gavin Kelly et al., *Stakeholder Capitalism* (Macmillan, London, 1997), p. 64.

12 'Blair on the constitution'.

13 Gillian Peele, 'The constitution', in Patrick Dunleavy, Andrew Gamble, Ian Holliday and Gillian Peele, *Developments in British Politics*, 4 (Macmillan, London, 1993), p. 30.

14 See Geoff Andrews (ed.), *Citizenship* (Lawrence & Wishart, London, 1991).

15 Interview with Lord Irvine of Lairg, *New Statesman and Society* (6 December 1996), pp. 18–20; and interview with Irvine, *The Observer* (27 July 1997).

16 'Blair on the constitution'.

17 See in particular Blair, 'The Rights We Enjoy Reflect the Duties We Owe', *The Spectator* Lecture, 22 March 1995.

18 From a vast literature, see Carole Pateman, *Participation and Democratic Theory* (Cambridge University Press, Cambridge, 1970) and C. B. Macpherson, *The Life and Times of Liberal Democracy* (Oxford University Press, Oxford, 1977). For a good collection of essays, see David Held (ed.), *Prospects for Democracy* (Polity Press, Cambridge, 1993) and Held, *Models of Democracy* (Polity Press, Cambridge, 1987); Anthony Arblaster, *Democracy* (Open University Press, Buckingham, 1987); Sheila Rowbotham, *Beyond the Fragments: Feminism and the Making of Socialism* (Merlin, London, 1980). For contemporary advocates of more direct forms of democracy, see Andrew Adonis and Geoff Mulgan, 'Back to Greece', and Charles Leadbeater and Geoff Mulgan, 'Lean democracy and the leadership vacuum', in Mulgan (ed.), *Life After Politics: New Thinking for the Twenty-First Century* (Fontana, London, 1997).

19 Tony Blair, *Let Us Face the Future: The 1945 Anniversary Lecture* (Fabian Society, London, 1995), p. 5.

20 Tony Blair, 'The John Smith Memorial Lecture', Queen Elizabeth II Conference Centre, London, 7 February 1996.

21 See David Osborne and Ted Gaebler, *Reinventing Government* (Addison Wesley, Reading, MA, 1992).

22 Robin Butler, 'Reinventing government', *Public Administration*, 72 (summer 1994), pp. 263–70, p. 266, emphasis in original.

23 Mulgan, in Crouch and Marquand, *Ethics and Markets*, p. 47.

24 Bogdanor, *Power and the People*, pp. 29–30.

25 Ibid., p. 22.
26 On a turnout of 60.3 per cent, 74.3 per cent of Scottish voters supported Labour's devolution plans. The referendum on Welsh devolution the following week was won by the 'yes' campaign by 6721 votes – a 0.6 per cent majority.
27 Patrick Wintour, *The Observer* (30 June 1996).
28 See Bogdanor, *Power and the People*, p. 36.
29 Tam Dalyell, 'Why I despair at my party's fatal blindness', *The Observer* (24 August 1997).
30 Bogdanor, *Power and the People*, p. 38.
31 John Lloyd, 'Does Blair know how to save the union?', *The Times* (22 August 1997).
32 *A Choice for England: A Consultation Paper on Labour's Plans for English Regional Government* (Labour Party, London, 1995).
33 *New Politics, New Britain* (Labour Party, London, 1996).
34 Desmond King, 'Government beyond Whitehall: local government and urban politics', in P. Dunleavy et al., *Developments in British Politics 4* (Macmillan, London, 1993).
35 *Renewing Democracy, Rebuilding Communities* (Labour Party, London, 1995), pp. 3–4, 13–14.
36 See Margaret Hodge and Wendy Thompson, *Beyond the Town Hall – Reinventing Local Government* (Fabian Society, London, 1994); Robert Hill, 'Mission impossible: a new role for the local state', *Renewal*, 4,2 (1996), pp. 21–7; Paul Corrigan, *No More Big Brother* (Fabian Pamphlet 578, Fabian Society, London, n.d.).
37 See Simon Jenkins, 'Blair's cap doesn't fit', *The Times* (24 July 1996).
38 For a good discussion of New Labour's approach to local government post-election, see *New Statesman*, local government special (25 July 1997).
39 Steve Richards, 'A question of trust', *New Statesman* (25 July 1997). [Blair quoted by Richards.]
40 'Put the local back into government', *The Times* (3 December 1997).
41 See *The Future of the European Union: Report on Labour's Position in Preparation for the Intergovernmental Conference, 1996* (Labour Party, London, 1995).
42 See Giles Radice, *Offshore: Britain and the European Idea* (Tauris, London, 1992); Stephen Tindale, 'A people's Europe', in Radice (ed.), *What Needs to Change: New Visions for Britain* (HarperCollins, London, 1996); Liz Kendall, *Wherever Next? The Future of Europe* (Fabian Society, London, 1996).
43 See Peter Hennessy, *The Hidden Wiring: Unearthing the British Constitution* (Indigo, London, 1996), pp. 30–7.
44 *The Guardian* (12 July 1997).
45 'Blair on the constitution'.

46 'Mandelson argues for strong centre', *The Independent* (17 September 1997). See also Mandelson, *Labour's Next Steps: Tackling Social Exclusion* (Fabian Pamphlet 581, Fabian Society, London, 1997).
47 Peter Riddell, *The Times* (8 May 1997 and 1 August 1997).
48 Simon Jenkins, 'Blair's major-generals', *The Times* (7 May 1997).
49 *The Economist* (7 June 1997), p. 38.
50 Bogdanor, *Power and the People*, p. 97.
51 'Blair on the constitution'; see also 'The John Smith Memorial Lecture'.
52 *The Times* (25 July 1997).
53 Quoted in *The Times* (December 1997).
54 'A winning formula for Labour', *The Independent* (16 August 1995).
55 'Blair on the constitution'.

Chapter 5 Post-Thatcherism

1 On the use of the media in the 1997 general election, see Nicholas Jones, *Campaign 1997: How the General Election Was Won and Lost* (Indigo, London, 1997). Martin Rosenbaum, *From Soapbox to Soundbite: Party Political Campaigning in Britain since 1945* (Macmillan, London, 1997), traces the changing marketing techniques used by political parties.
2 See David Willetts, *Why Vote Conservative?* (Penguin, Harmondsworth, 1997).
3 See G. A. Cohen, 'Back to socialist basics', *New Left Review*, 201 (September/October 1994).
4 See Stuart Hall, 'Son of Margaret', *New Statesman* (6 October 1994); Stuart Hall and Martin Jacques, 'Blair: is he the greatest Tory since Thatcher?', *The Observer* (13 April 1997); Eric Shaw, *The Labour Party since 1945* (Blackwell, Oxford, 1996); Cohen, 'Back to socialist basics'. On these and other interpretations of New Labour, see Michael Kenny and Martin J. Smith '(Mis)understanding Blair', *Political Quarterly*, 68,3 (1997), pp. 220–30.
5 Gordon Brown, 'The Anthony Crosland Memorial Lecture', 13 February 1997; and 'The politics of potential: a new agenda for Labour' in David Miliband (ed.), *Reinventing the Left* (Polity Press, Cambridge, 1994).
6 Michael Barber, talk to *Guardian*/Nexus Conference, LSE, London, 1 March 1997.
7 For a fuller discussion of our argument on Labour's communitarianism, see Stephen Driver and Luke Martell, 'New Labour's communitarianisms', *Critical Social Policy*, 17,3 (1997), pp. 27–46.
8 See also Stephen Driver and Luke Martell, 'Beyond equality and liberty: Labour's liberal-conservatism', *Renewal*, 4,3 (1996), pp. 8–16; and 'New Labour's communitarianisms'.

9 Hall, 'Son of Margaret'.
10 Ross McKibbin, 'Very Old Labour', *London Review of Books* (3 April 1997).
11 Eric Shaw, *The Labour Party since 1945*, pp. 217–18.
12 John Gray, *After Social Democracy* (Demos, London, 1996), p. 10.
13 See Blair's attacks on the New Right in, for example, 'Power for a purpose', *Renewal*, 3,4 (1995) and 'The Rights We Enjoy Reflect the Duties We Owe', *The Spectator* Lecture, 22 March 1995.
14 Roger Scruton, *The Conservative Idea of Community* (Conservative 2000 Foundation, London, 1996), p. 11.
15 See Willetts, *Why Vote Conservative?*; 'The free market and civic conservatism', in Kenneth Minogue (ed.), *Conservative Realism: New Essays in Conservatism* (HarperCollins, London, 1996); and *Modern Conservatism* (Penguin, Harmondsworth, 1992). For Gray's break with the Conservatives, see two collections of his essays: *Beyond the New Right: Markets, Government and the Common Environment* (Routledge, London, 1993); and *Enlightenment's Wake: Politics and Culture at the Close of the Modern Age* (Routledge, London, 1995). See also Gray and Willetts, *Is Conservatism Dead?* (Profile Books, London, 1997), which reprints two earlier essays by the authors.
16 Martin Kettle, 'Labour's bright new dawn ends at Dover', *The Guardian* (21 June 1997). Also 'Jospin's pole position: France could have a lesson for New Labour', leader article, *The Guardian* (27 May 1997).
17 Tony Blair, speech to the Party of European Socialists' Congress, Malmö, Sweden, 6 June 1997.
18 'Chancellor goes to Europe with plan to create more jobs', *The Times* (5 June 1997).
19 Hugo Young, 'Change of watch on the Rhine snubs Bonn', *The Guardian* (15 July 1997).
20 Jonathan Steele, 'End to "social dumping" unites the European quest for new ideals', *The Guardian* (3 June 1997).
21 Indeed the American path is one recommended for further development in Britain by some on the Centre Left: see Charles Leadbeater, *Britain: The California of Europe?* (Demos, London, 1997).
22 Denis Staunton, 'German left put hope in lessons from Blair', *The Guardian* (16 September 1997).
23 Blair, speech to the Party of European Socialists' Congress.
24 'Jospin's pole position'.
25 Jospin has also expressed this view: see Jonathan Steele, 'End to "social dumping" unites the European quest for new ideals'.
26 Blair himself has suggested that Germany and Japan may have distinctive structures which cannot simply be transposed to British circumstances: see his 'Mais Lecture', City University, London, 22 May 1995.

Chapter 6 Beyond Left and Right?

1 Geoff Mulgan (ed.), *Life After Politics: New Thinking for the Twenty-First Century* (Fontana, London, 1997), p. xviii.

2 Blair has put this point of view in many places, for example: his speech to the *Guardian*/Nexus conference 'Passing the Torch', 1 March 1997; *Let Us Face the Future: The 1945 Anniversary Lecture* (Fabian Society, London, 1995); speech to the Labour Party conference, 4 October 1994; 'Power for a purpose', *Renewal*, 3,4 (1995), pp. 11–16; *New Labour: Because Britain Deserves Better*, Labour Party manifesto 1997.

3 Anthony Giddens, *Beyond Left and Right* (Polity Press, Cambridge, 1994) and 'Brave New World: the new context of politics', in David Miliband (ed.), *Reinventing the Left* (Polity Press, Cambridge, 1994). See also Vincent Cable, 'Identity politics', in Geoff Mulgan (ed.), *Life After Politics: New Thinking for the Twenty-First Century* (Fontana, London, 1997).

4 In speeches by both to *Guardian*/Nexus conference. See also Julian Le Grand, 'the third way begins with cora', *New Statesman* (6 March 1998).

5 John Gray, speech to *Guardian*/Nexus conference. See also Gray, *Enlightenment's Wake: Politics and Culture at the Close of the Modern Age* (Routledge, London, 1995).

6 See Stephen Driver and Luke Martell, 'Beyond equality and liberty: Labour's liberal-conservatism', *Renewal*, 4,3 (1996), pp. 8–16.

7 See, for example, Blair's speech to the special conference of the Labour Party, 29 April 1995.

8 'Clinton and Blair hail new partnership', *The Times* (30 May 1997). Interestingly Clinton responded to Blair's description with a slightly less radical interpretation: 'I don't think it is the end of ideology, but I think it is the end of yesterday's ideology.' See also Blair, 'Power for a purpose'; speech to the *Guardian*/Nexus conference.

9 *New Labour: Because Britain Deserves Better* (Labour Party, London, 1997).

10 See Roy Hattersley, 'Pragmatism must not still conscience', *The Guardian* (14 May 1997).

11 Notably the advocates of the Thatcherism Mark II model of New Labour discussed in the last chapter.

12 This is a view outlined in his book *The State We're In* and in his weekly columns in *The Observer* in 1997, such as 'Blair is forcing us to make the hardest choice', *The Observer* (5 October 1997). See also: Simon Buckby and Neal Lawson, 'Third way? No way, Tony', *New Statesman* (13 March 1998), self-styled 'New social democrats'; and in response, Philip Collins and Ian Corfield, 'The wrong set of trousers', *New Statesman* (20 March 1998), who argue that the 'New social democrats' are just as wedded to the state as the old ones were. The debate continues.

Index